THE IDEA OF PURITY
IN
ANCIENT JUDAISM

STUDIES IN JUDAISM IN LATE ANTIQUITY

FROM THE FIRST TO THE SEVENTH CENTURY

EDITED BY

JACOB NEUSNER

VOLUME ONE

THE IDEA OF PURITY IN ANCIENT JUDAISM

THE IDEA OF PURITY IN ANCIENT JUDAISM

THE HASKELL LECTURES, 1972-1973

BY

JACOB NEUSNER
Professor of Religious Studies
Brown University

WITH A CRITIQUE AND A COMMENTARY BY

MARY DOUGLAS
Professor of Social Anthropology
University College, London

Wipf & Stock
PUBLISHERS
Eugene, Oregon

Wipf and Stock Publishers
199 W 8th Ave, Suite 3
Eugene, OR 97401

The Idea of Purity In Ancient Judaism
The Haskell Lectures, 1972-1973
By Neusner, Jacob

ISBN: 1-59752-584-7
Previously published by E. J. Brill, 1973

For

Jonathan Z., Elaine,

Siobhan, and Jason Smith

CONTENTS

Preface IX
Abbreviations XIV

Foreword 1

I. The Biblical Legacy 7
II. Ideas of Purity in the Literature of the Period of the Second Temple 32
III. Purity in Talmudic Judaism 72
IV. The Idea of Purity in Ancient Judaism 108

Bibliography 131

Critique and Commentary . . . .
Mary Douglas, University College, London 137

Index of Scriptures and Talmudic Passages 143
General Index 149

PREFACE

This book contains the text of the Haskell Lectures for 1972-1973, delivered at Oberlin College, April 3 through April 6, 1973, the assignment being four lectures on a topic in post-biblical Judaism. The form of the book is shaped by its origin in a series of lectures. The lectures have been expanded only by footnotes and bibliography.

I chose to make use of the opportunity afforded by the invitation of the Haskell Lectures Committee to explore not solely a given topic, but also the methodological issues pertinent to the study of any problem in the history of ideas in ancient Talmudic Judaism. These issues are addressed in the foreword. This has entailed explaining my conception of how Talmudic Judaism as a structure of religious ideas is to be historically investigated. By doing things the way I think they should be done, I am spared the necessity of criticizing former efforts. In further work on the laws of purity, I hope to do the same for the far more difficult problem of the history of Talmudic law. Detailed comparative studies of Jewish and Hellenistic-Roman, or Iranian religion and law fall outside my competence. The "comparative study of religions" here is undertaken through the comparison of stages and groups within the history of Judaism alone.

It is not inappropriate to include an autobiographical note, for scholarship does not proceed in a vacuum, but in response to issues and ideas which are "in the air." That must account for the fashions and fads—the "sociology"—of learning. When I began my studies of Talmudic Judaism, time and again I came up against laws of impurity, the details of which mystified me even more than did their frequency and evident importance in the rabbinic system of theology and law. I began to realize, in studies on the *History of the Jews in Babylonia*, and in particular, on the Talmudic rabbis as holy men, that purity and impurity were immensely important to the law as a whole. When, in work on *The Rabbinic Traditions about the Pharisees before 70*, I observed that the larger part of the laws attributed by the post-70 rabbis to the pre-70 Pharisees concerned these same matters, and that the external evidence—for instance Mark 7, Matthew 15 and 23—supported the same observation, I could no longer ignore the larger issue. Imbedded within Talmudic Judaism, important within its laws, therefore expressive of its underlying construction and interpretation of reality, lay a pre-Talmudic body of laws about purity. Study of the idea of purity in Talmudic Judaism rose to the top of the agenda for my studies.

At nearly that same time, in May, 1971, I had occasion to lecture at various European universities, and, to my surprise, found that various friends, working in historically cognate, but quite unrelated fields, had come to the realization of the importance of purity in the study of religions. Conversations with Professors Carsten Colpé and R. Macuch in Berlin, Geo Widengren in Uppsala, Mary Boyce in London, and Peter Brown in Oxford, revealed that historians of religion in quite autonomous fields of study—Mandaeism, Manichaeism, Zoroastrianism, Late Antique Christianity—all were tending to focus upon the same issue. It goes without saying that scholars in fields more closely related to my own, for instance Professors Johann Meyer, Cologne, Geza Vermes, Oxford, and Wayne A. Meeks, Yale University, working on the Jewish sects of Second Temple times and early Christianity, shared this interest. Not only so, but friends in the quite separate fields of philosophy of religion and anthropology were studying with great care the—to them—important books of Paul Ricoeur, *The Symbolism of Evil* (Boston, 1967), and Mary Douglas, *Purity and Danger* (London, 1966), not to mention the *Proceedings of the XIth International Congress of the International Association for the History of Religions. II. Guilt or Pollution and Rites of Purification* (Leiden, 1968). In all, it seemed that everyone I knew was talking about purity.

Yet when I examined accounts of Talmudic Judaism, I found barely a word on the subject. The monumental studies of George F. Moore, Jean Bonsirven, S. J., and, most recently, Professor E. E. Urbach, Hebrew University, treat the subject casually, if at all. Of these, only Urbach pays any attention to purity, and then primarily in the context of the Pharisaic *ḥavurah*. One has to go back to the work of A. Büchler to find serious and sustained attention to the role of purity in ancient Judaism. (Perhaps the most valuable service of Büchler was to provoke G. Allon to his brilliant, if methodologically very primitive, critique). And, of course, Büchler's interest in purity began as a response to the ignorant accounts of New Testament scholars of his day, accounts which he rightly saw as prejudiced and bigoted against rabbinic Judaism. So for perhaps fifty years there has been a hiatus in the consideration of the question. And now it seems to be of interest everywhere, in a wide variety of disciplines, as well as in the narrower field of the study of ancient Judaism. Indeed, even the students of Talmudic texts have returned to those tractates which center upon purity. Saul Lieberman's *Tosefet Rishonim*, parts III and IV (Jerusalem, 1939)—half of that monumental work—are on purity-laws. I draw attention also to the compendious Talmudic dissertation of Jacob Zussman, *Sugyiot bavliot lisedarim zera'im vetohorot* [Babylonian Pericopae for Orders Seeds and Purities] soon to be published by the Israel Academy of Sciences.

To be sure, I cannot account for this interesting turn in scholarly interests. But I have to stress that what seemed to me my own quite private and capricious notion that purity constituted a more important theme in Talmudic Judaism than had been appreciated now turns out to be nothing more than an expression of a common concern.

It is my pleasant duty to thank the generous friends and colleagues who read and carefully criticized the manuscript. Since I have to refer to matters in which I am in no way expert, I am especially grateful for having been saved from blundering into areas under dispute among specialists in the biblical and Second Temple periods as though controverted matters were clear. In general I have tried so to phrase matters as to avoid moot interpretations and to take account of, and avoid, scholarly disputes not pertinent to my main inquiry. In this regard, the helpful correction of the following proved exceedingly valuable: Chapter One, Professors Nahum Sarna, Brandeis University, and Brevard S. Childs, Yale University; Chapter Two, Professors John Strugnell, Harvard University, Wayne A. Meeks, Yale University, Horst R. Moehring, Brown University, and Wendell S. Dietrich, Brown University; Chapter Three, Professor Baruch A. Levine, New York University. The following read the entire manuscript: my teacher Professor Morton Smith, Columbia University, who annotated the whole second draft; and Professors Hans H. Penner, Dartmouth College, Jonathan Z. Smith, University of Chicago, Ernest S. Frerichs and David Goodblatt, Brown University, as well as Professors Levine, Meeks, and Strugnell. Professors Levine and Meeks also read the third draft in its entirety. My graduate students at Brown University also commented on the early drafts: William Scott Green, Gary G. Porton, Baruch M. Bokser, Joel Gereboff, Jack Lightstone, and Charles Primus. I enjoyed the counsel of Professor Frank M. Cross, Jr., former Haskell Lecturer, in preparing my lectures. None of these friends is to be blamed for the writer's deficiencies.

The book is dedicated to Professor Jonathan Z. Smith and his family. It was he who originally made me aware of the fruitful approaches to the study of religions made available by historians of religions and who raised for me questions which continue to prove provocative and illuminating. I cannot claim to have much transcended my origins as a historian of a decidedly positivist orientation, less interested in general concepts than in historical- and literary-critical modes of establishing facts, and more involved in inferring rather small ideas out of the accumulation of still smaller details, than in large conceptions. But Jonathan Smith for fifteen years has shown me not to find entire satisfaction in those earliest and enduring commitments. His own scholarly achievements, which are formidable, instruct me. But letters and conversations even more teach me what is to be hoped from the history of religions and its methods. The friendship I and my family enjoy with him and his family brighten our lives.

It remains to observe that the publication of the pertinent sources on the Dead Sea community is not complete, and therefore my account of ideas and laws associated with purity in the *yaḥad* is necessarily partial. My friend and sometime colleague, Professor Yigael Yadin, is in the last stages of publishing the Temple scroll, which contains important materials on the subject. Professor Strugnell kindly showed me unpublished fragments from Qumran on purity-laws. These too will appear in the near future. It did not seem to me appropriate to refer to the findings of my colleagues before these have appeared, properly analyzed, in their own names.

The honor of the invitation extended by the Haskell Lectures Committee at Oberlin College and the hospitality shown me during my visit are gratefully acknowledged.

I cannot close without a word of thanks to my friend, Dr. Frits Wieder, Jr., and his firm, E. J. Brill of Leiden. Many authors of scholarly works are in the debt of that excellent firm, for, without it, publishing the results of scholarship for the attention and criticism of colleagues would be exceedingly difficult, and, for many, not possible at all. My personal indebtedness to Brill is a matter of public record. I am deeply and happily grateful.

J. N.

Providence, Rhode Island

5 Sivan 5733
Erev Shavu'ot
5 June 1973

ABBREVIATIONS

b.	Babylonian Talmud
CD	Covenant of Damascus. Damascus Document
Chron.	Chronicles
Cor.	Corinthians
Deut.	Deuteronomy
Ex.	Exodus
Ezek.	Ezekiel
Gal.	Galatians
Gen.	Genesis
Hos.	Hosea
Is.	Isaiah
Jer.	Jeremiah
Jn.	John
Lev.	Leviticus
Lk.	Luke
M.	Mishnah
Mal.	Malachi
Mk.	Mark
Mt.	Matthew
Neg.	Nega'im
Neh.	Nehemiah
Num.	Numbers
1 QH	Hymns of Thanksgiving
1 QM	War of the Sons of Light with the Sons of Darkness
1 QS	Manual of Discipline
Prov.	Proverbs
Ps.	Psalms
R.	Rabbah
R.	Rabbi
RQ	*Revue de Qumran*
Sam.	Samuel
T.	Testament
Thes.	Thessalonians
Tos.	Tosefta
y.	Yerushalmi, Palestinian Talmud
Zech.	Zechariah

FOREWORD

Purity and impurity—ṬHR and ṬM'—are not hygienic categories and do not refer to observable cleanliness or dirtiness. The words refer to a status in respect to contact with a source of impurity and the completion of acts of purification from that impurity. If you touch a reptile, you may not be dirty, but you are unclean. If you undergo a ritual immersion, you may not be free of dirt, but you are clean. A corpse can make you unclean, though it may not make you dirty. A rite of purification involving the sprinkling of water mixed with the ashes of a red heifer probably will not remove a great deal of dirt, but it will remove the impurity.

An inductive inquiry into the uses of the words unclean and clean in biblical literature will show that they occur chiefly with reference to the cultic acts. If you are impure, you cannot enter the Temple or participate in certain cultic acts. If you are pure, you may do so. But limiting purity to cultic actions is itself an *interpretation* of the matter —a priestly viewpoint. So we are left with definitions which do not greatly transcend the thing to be defined. The words ṬM' and ṬHR are here translated with various English equivalents: clean and cleanness, unclean and uncleanness, pure and impure, polluted, defiled, contaminated. All go back to the same Hebrew words and refer to the same status or situation.

The one translation here avoided is "*ritual* purity" and "*ritual* impurity," for attaching the adjective "ritual" raises two problems. It first requires the definition of "ritual" and implies a distinction between "ritual" and something-other-than-ritual—"substantive", "real," or "moral," for example. So that distinction in our culture will carry in its wake the assertion that "ritual" stands against "real" or "substantive," "meaningful" or "actual," as though for the ancient Israelite "ritual impurity" were somehow not real or substantive or actual, as if it bore no material meaning. But if impurity has concrete and important effects in practical, everyday affairs, and if a concrete act ("ritual") of purification has to be undertaken to remove those effects, then it hardly constitutes something not real, substantive, or actual.

Second, for the present-day ear, "ritual" provokes as its antonym "moral." From the prophetic polemic, carried on in Western civilization in countless ways, people are used to posit a tension between "empty," "formalistic" or even "childish" rituals, on the one side, and "ethics" or "the heart" or "inwardness", on the other. The antonymic relationship between ritual and morality obscures the absence of such distinctions in biblical Israel and within Talmudic Judaism as well. Bibilical Hebrew only infrequently employed a substantive concept for ritual, i.e. *'abodah*, but most often spoke of the acts, or praxis, involved, and expressed such acts in verbal or participial forms of the root *'abodah* ('BD). This is pointed out to me by Professor Baruch A. Levine, who adds that these specific actions constituted the ingredients of rituals. He refers to Isaiah 1:11-15 for a catalogue of ritual forms. Strikingly, this passage ends with the counsel to "wash yourselves, make yourselves clean." It would be accurate to speak of cultic purity and impurity, but even that adjective will obscure the range and role of purity within non-cultic life and the religious imagination. And it would beg the question, what ideas were associated with purity and impurity at various stages in ancient Judaism?

Here I propose to set forth the interpretations associated with the states of uncleanness and cleanness in the successive forms of ancient Judaism known to us from the surviving literature.

The first evidence, that of the Hebrew Scriptures, *Tanakh*, is treated as a unity, though it is anything but that in origin. But in the history of post-biblical Judaism with which I am concerned, the *Tanakh* was perceived as a whole and single document, whose history was part of the history it purported to narrate.

Second come the ideas about purity and impurity in the extant post-biblical literature produced before the destruction of the Second Temple in 70 A. D. These evidences are of various sorts, derive from varying circles, and are differentiated from one another.

Third are the interpretations of purity and impurity in Talmudic and cognate literature, that is, those characteristic of earlier rabbinic Judaism.

To a considerable degree I have taken as my primary task the arranging of a repertoire of pertinent sources, without claiming greatly to contribute to the understanding of any particular one of them. While this work in some, though not entire, measure is that of collection and arrangement, not novel interpretation of all that is collected, I hope that what is arranged may add up to more than the sum of the parts. For when we see laid out before us the range of ideas historically associated with purity for nearly a millenium, we are able to perceive both continuities and development, enduring viewpoints and novel interpretations and applications, which are not apparent in a piecemeal examination of ideas about purity and impurity in a single stage of their unfolding. We are able, moreover, to perceive that the ideas associated with purity and impurity at particular stages in the history of Judaism or by specific groups within Jewry, are suggestive, far beyond their specificities, of the larger conceptions held in such ages or by such groups. For instance that the Pharisees required an act of purification of the hands before eating suggests that Pharisaism saw the act of eating as a cultic rite and further implies that Pharisaism compared the table to the altar, the home to the Temple, and the private person to the priest.

But my real interest and area of competence (if any) are solely in Talmudic Judaism. My primary agendum is the examination of the ideas and laws of the rabbis. Past efforts at the study of Talmudic religion, in particular theology, have characteristically committed one of three errors which are avoided here. Either Talmudic ideas are examined entirely by themselves, not in historical context or by their strata, and without reference to the ideas put forth in other forms of Judaism of the same or an earlier age. Or all the ideas associated with any group in Judaism and found in any sort of literature have been combined with those found within the Talmud as though these all together added to a single and undifferentiated religious system—"Judaism." Let me cite illustrations of these first two erroneous approaches before alluding to the third.

George Foot Moore's *Judaism* (Cambridge, 1927) tends to treat the Tannaitic sources without much attention to other, earlier Jewish sources, thus in a social and cultural vacuum. On the other hand, G. Allon, for instance in "The Limits of Purity" (*Meḥqarim* I [Tel Aviv, 1957], pp. 148-176), is apt to employ evidence deriving from a wide range of sources, over a long period of time, even from several different geographical settings, to describe a given law and its application and interpretation. He conceives of a single "law"—the *halakhah*—attested by any Jewish source as much as by any other, without regard to the party it may represent. For instance, the Sibylline Oracles and the story of Judith and Holofernes, which long antedate rabbinic Judaism, are equally able to testify to the requirement of washing hands before prayer which, in rabbinic Judaism, is first found much later on in Amoraic sources. Philo "proves" that *the law* required purity under normal circumstances.

The third source of error in former accounts of Talmudic Judaism has been the assumption that all things attributed to all authorities were actually said by those authorities and therefore supply evidence as to what was believed and actually done at this time. This conception characterizes even the most sophisticated accounts of Talmudic theology. For example, Ephraim E. Urbach, *Ḥazal* ([English title: *The Sages. Their Concepts and Beliefs*] Jerusalem, 1969), will routinely cite as evidence for the opinions of Hillel or ʿAqiba sayings attributed to them in documents redacted long after their times. He may then demonstrate how ʿAqiba's saying "reflects" or "develops" the "earlier" opinion of Hillel. But the assumption that the Talmudic sayings were actually said by those to whom they are attributed is fraught with difficulties. No responsible account of Talmudic ideas may ignore those difficulties or take for granted that what has not yet been demonstrated is in fact the case.

I here seek to confront these three problems and so to suggest and, for this small specimen, to vindicate a better way of studying the history of Talmudic thought.

First, I approach Talmudic thought on a given problem in the context of ancient Judaism as a whole. This makes possible the examination of Talmudic ideas as part of a much longer development of Judaic thought.

Second, at the same time I treat Talmudic sayings separate from those deriving from sources representative of other groups and earlier forms of ancient Judaism. We therefore are able to see in what ways Talmudic sayings continue earlier themes and in what ways they present entirely new ideas and even distinctly different modes of thought.

Third, I take into account the problem of the reliability of attributions. This is done by paying close attention to the notions clearly characteristic of a single given stratum of Talmudic literature, without supposing that all attributions to specific authorities contained within that stratum are sound. I think we may reliably claim Mishnah-Tosefta, coming in the early third century, will testify to the state of mind of the second century authorities. When we locate within that stratum of the literature a well-defined and pronouncedly integrated set of ideas, and when, as it happens, these ideas are consistently attributed to a single group of authorities in a single rabbinical circle of that time, then we are secure in supposing such ideas do represent the mind of a given generation of authorities. We then are justified, furthermore, in interpreting those ideas, when, as here, they are without precedent, as pertinent to the problems and issues of a specific period and place.

Then, too, we are able to show how an interpretation offered at one point will later on generate elaboration and further development and application, long after the time that this interpretation represented a response to a particular religious concern. The conservative tendency of later rabbinic thought thus finds illustration, but only when the stages in the development of that thought are clearly established and reliably delineated.

This is a very long way indeed from the prevalent notions, both that every saying attributed to someone was actually said by him, no matter the age of the document in which the attribution occurs, and that every deed attributed to a Talmudic authority was actually done by him, at the time and in the place in which he lived. But it also is a long way from the utter exclusion of all Talmudic evidences on the grounds of their "lateness" or of that of the redaction of the documents in which they occur. In both cases I think matters are considerably more complicated. I claim much less than is normally claimed in behalf of Talmudic sayings. But the questions I propose to answer are formulated differently, and the answers consistently take account of the point at which documents are generally believed to have reached their final stages of redaction. Indeed, that matter becomes central to my account of the last stages in the Talmudic interpretation of the idea of purity.

The only innovation herein attempted is the application to the study of Talmudic Judaism of approaches commonplace in other areas of learning.

Two closely-related disciplines, specifically, are not present in this work. These are comparative religions and history of religions. No effort is made to relate the ideas of purity in ancient Judaism to those of neighboring religions. Before the work had proceeded very far, I realized that the ideas before me were so much part of a larger system that without considerable knowledge of the system as a whole, the small segment of it represented by ideas of purity would easily lead to misinterpretation. If that was so for purity in ancient Judaism, then it probably would be so for purity in other religious systems. Simply pointing to similarities or differences between Judaic and Mazdean concepts or laws of purity, which do have interesting traits in common, or between purity laws in the Israelite shrine at Jerusalem and in contemporary shrines of the Greco-Roman cults, would produce an appearance of significant knowledge where none was present. Comparisons are not to be drawn without attention to their larger settings, which alone impart to them meaning and importance. Indeed, even among the varieties of Judaism itself, we are engaged in a comparative task, for we have to deal with forms of Judaism spread over a long period of time, each of them subject to specialized inquiry. But this cannot be offered as a legitimate form of the comparative study of religion or use of the comparative method.

A fortiori, it follows that no effort is made to point to similarities between ideas and laws of purity in ancient Judaism and similar phenomena in entirely unrelated cultural settings. Everyone knows that the uncleanness of the corpse is taken for granted not only in Mazdaism and Mandaeism, contemporaries to Talmudic Judaism, but in many communities, primitive and otherwise. Each community is apt to explain in terms of its own larger perception of the world the "fact" of the corpse's impurity. I readily concede the correctness of Angelo Brelich, who insists:

> Nello studio di un particolare rito di purificazione appartenente a una particolare religione, lo storico delle religioni dovrà cercare di capire perché in quella particolare religione quel tip di rito, conosciuto anche da altre religioni, ha assunto quelle determinate forme e non altre.[1]

Accordingly, I do not offer this work as a study within the history of religions, for I cannot even begin to undertake the search Brelich correctly requires. I hope those who do so will not be ungrateful for the materials assembled here. But at the outset they are warned that neither the study of comparative religions nor that of the history of religions supplies the methodological framework for the present inquiry.

---

[1] Angelo Brelich, "Thargelia," *Proceedings of the XIth International Congress of the International Association for the History of Religions. II. Guilt or Pollution and Rites of Purification* (Leiden, 1968), p. 64.

CHAPTER ONE

THE BIBLICAL LEGACY

What is the relationship between ritual and the religious imagination in ancient Judaism? To answer that question, I have chosen to analyze the laws of purity and impurity: What interpretations were developed to make sense of the primitive nonsense represented by the biblical purity-laws? Obviously, the interpretations are secondary to, and originate much later than, the laws themselves. The laws constitute the given. The interpretations take the laws for granted and assume them to be normative, therefore to require "reasons." First comes the practice of not stepping on the cracks in the cement. Then comes the story about bad luck. Our problem is not the origins of impurity-phobia or their place in the psychic history of mankind. We want to know only how those groups in Judaism from the third century B. C. to the seventh century A. D. whose writings have been preserved understood the biblical and traditional laws on this subject.

At the outset we had best consider the despairing judgment of Maimonides, who, having completed his monumental account of the Talmudic laws of cleanness, concluded, "It is plain and manifest that the laws about uncleanness and cleanness are decrees laid down by Scripture and not matters about which human understanding is capable of forming a judgment; for behold, they are included among the arbitrary decrees."[1] That is to say, these particular laws are not susceptible of rational explanation; the arbitrary divine decrees are simply to be accepted and obeyed. But, having said that, Maimonides attempts to exploit the symbolism of impurity: "Nevertheless, we may find some indication (for the moral basis) of this: just as one who sets his heart on becoming clean becomes clean as soon as he has immersed himself, though nothing new has befallen his body, so, too, one who sets his heart on cleansing himself from the uncleannesses that beset men's souls...becomes clean as soon as he consents in his heart to shun those counsels and brings his soul into the waters of pure reason..."[2] As an aftermath of literally thousands of legal rulings, that is not much of

---

[1] Maimonides, *Mishnah Torah. The Book of Cleanness.* viii. *Immersion Pools* 11:12. Trans. Herbert Danby, *The Code of Maimonides, Book Ten. The Book of Cleanness* (New Haven, 1954: Yale University Press), p. 535.

[2] *Ibid.*

an intellectual and rational interpretation. Though obvious and feeble, it is the best he was able to do.

To begin with, I exclude the words "myth" or "theology." The former is inapplicable simply because, however the word is defined, myth simply is not articulated in the literary evidence before us. Nor shall we see much that can be called theology, either systematic or otherwise. Yet purity was not left without interpretation in terms of ethics or some other comparatively rational set of values and meanings. When the interpretation is more than episodic and exhibits the traits of sustained thought, we are justified in calling it an ideology—a system of ideas. We shall examine a range of ideologies. But not all ideas concerned with religious issues are to be called theological; the cultically- and ethically-oriented ideas before us hardly qualify.

We shall first review the state of affairs at about 300-200 B.C., that is to say, the Scriptural situation before the time of the Maccabees. Our discussion will then proceed through the several bodies of evidence contained in the Apocryphal and Pseudepigraphic literature, Philo, the Dead Sea Scrolls, Josephus, the Gospels and the letters of Paul. All of these materials will be dealt with in brief. But we are justified in our limited inquiry, for the data on, and interest in, ritual purity and the ideas connected to it are in all this literature extremely sparse in proportion to the whole. In rabbinic literature, by contrast, purity is a central theme of law—nearly 25% of Mishnaic law in quantity concerns purity—and, consequently, of Talmudic religious thought. In quantity and in significance, the largest body of law and ideology of purity is contained in that literature.

Two distinct and entirely contradictory views of the meaning of purity in Israelite religion have been put forth. The first is best expressed in the writings of W. Robertson Smith and is central to Yehezqel Kaufmann's theory of Israelite monotheism; we shall consider it in the formulation of Smith. It regards impurity as a status, and not as expressive of the presence of demonic forces operating independently of the will of one, omnipotent God. The second view has most recently been formulated by Baruch A. Levine. It holds that impurity results from the working of destructive or demonic forces which may operate independently of the will of God and may threaten the deity in the same way as man. Impurity is not merely a status and is not limited to the cult, though it is most dangerous there, because in the cult the domicile of the deity is affected. We shall now state these two contradictory interpretations.

Smith stresses the fact that in Israelite religion the concept of purity is explained—treated ideologically. This according to Smith constitutes the fundamental neutralization and rationalization of impurity, its sources, dangers, and taboos. We find the purity-taboo everywhere interpreted, chiefly in terms of the cult, and never allowed to stand in terms of its obvious meaning as an omnipresent danger. It is not treated as an autonomous force, an evil spirit, able to operate against the divinity. Taboos about purity are reduced to an aspect of the will of the divinity. The rules are not represented as precautions against malignant enemies, operating independent of the divine will. Supernatural dangers deriving from formidable evil spirits provoked by birth, blood, or death do not enter the biblical framework of interpretation. Levitical legislation reduces the fear of unknown or hostile unclean powers to a matter of God's law: uncleanness is hateful to God and must be avoided by all who have to do with the divinity.[1] W. Robertson Smith claims even to discern "a great moral difference between precautions against the invasion of mysterious hostile powers and precautions founded on respect for the prerogative of a friendly god. The former belong to magical superstition... But the restrictions on individual license which are due to respect for a known and friendly power allied to man ... contain ... germinant principles of social progress and moral order."[2] This seems to me to claim far too much. The important point, however, is that all of the biblical views of purity and impurity, whether in the Levitical or the prophetic or the wisdom traditions, represent a neutralization of taboos by the attribution of such matters to the divine will. The taboo of the woman in her menses, for instance, is understood as founded on the will of the divinity, not because it involves autonomous action of superhuman agencies of a dangerous kind.[3]

The contrary view is stated by Baruch A. Levine (*In the Presence of the Lord. Aspects of Ritual in Ancient Israel*, in the press for 1974), as follows:

> Underlying the priestly regulations relevant to the purity of the sanctuary was a demonic conception of sin, offense, and transgression. This demonic conception is epitomized in the dispatching of the sin-laden scapegoat into the wilderness ... The magical character of that act is blatant, whereas the equally magical quality of expiation is more

[1] W. Robertson Smith, *The Religion of the Semites* (1889, Repr. N.Y., 1956), p. 152f.

[2] *Ibid.*, p. 154.

[3] *Ibid.*, p. 446f.

> subtle. Contamination is the effect of infractions against the purity of the sanctuary. This is caused either by the improper ministrations of the priests and other cultic servitors ... or by the sinful acts of members of the Israelite community, not directly perpetrated in the sanctuary itself, but resulting, nevertheless, in its contamination. Such sinful acts give open access to the demonic forces of impurity which, once they gain a foothold in the human community, can rarely be contained.
>
> Impurity, in the form of sins ... was viewed as an external force which entered the person or attached itself to him. The primary purpose of expiation was, therefore, to rid one's self of this foreign force ...
>
> Our theory [is] of expiation as a process involving a complex of rites possessed of an essentially magical character ... The prevailing view understands expiation in a different way. According to that view, expiatory activity was necessitated by the fact that, by their offences against the deity, individuals and groups had threatened the whole relationship between the deity and the Israelite community ... Such offenders either had to be banished from the community permanently, or had to be reinstated after their sins were expiated in the proper way.
>
> In our view, expiation addressed itself to the presence of impurity, *the actualized form of demonic forces operative in the human environment*. The process of expiation bore a practical relationship to the covenant. It was to assure the continued residence of Yahweh in the Israelite community by enforcing the basic precondition for such residence, that is, the purity of Yahweh's surroundings. It is not so much that Yahweh had to be appeased for the offenses committed. To the extent that this was the case, such mollification took the form of the actual sacrifice ... The accompanying blood became necessary simply because Yahweh insisted that the forces of impurity unleashed by offenses committed be kept away from his immediate environment. There is thus a good reason for Yahweh's wrath. It is not mere displeasure at being disobeyed. His wrath results from a vital concern for his own protection ...

Levine thus conceives that priestly literature takes for granted the independent, active existence of demonic forces. Impurity is not a state of being, but an active force. Impurity is demonic, and demonic forces of impurity endanger men and deities, just as in other ancient Near Eastern religions. Levine also states:

> The objectives of magic and of the cult converged toward the common end of eliminating destructive or demonic forces identified as the sources of impurity and viewed as the matrix of sinfulness and offense to the deity. Apotropaic and prophylactic magic thus figures in the enterprise of cleansing or purifying cultic persons, objects, buildings, sacred cites, and sacrificial materials, so as to render them fit for cultic use, and so as to protect their state of purity, once attained, from contamination.

Levine develops these theses through careful studies of important cultic terminology, e.g., KPR, and of sacrificial rites and distinctions among them, in particular, the ḤṬ'T and the 'ŠM. It will not be necessary for our purposes to follow these studies in detail. It suffices to present his perspective on purity and, especially, impurity as a destructive force, not merely as a matter of status relative to the cult alone.

The difference between the two views just now summarized is important as to the origins and understanding of impurity. For Robertson Smith and especially for Kaufmann, "monotheism" effects so complete a revolution in the antecedent Israelite cult that all traces of a polytheist conception of impurity as a source of independent demonic power are wiped out. For Levine the Israelite cult is perceived in the context of the other cults of the same time and place.

Let us examine the biblical writings as they would have been known in the third century B.C., that is, at the threshold of the two and three quarters centuries in which flourished the Dead Sea community, Philo, the writers of the Apocryphal and Pseudepigraphic books, Josephus, the Pharisees, and the early Christians. What does the Hebrew Bible tell about purity to those various individuals and groups whose writings are in our hands? The biblical corpus of ideas about purity may be divided into two distinct parts, the interpretation of purity and impurity as a metaphor of morality, on the one hand, and the specific laws about purity and impurity in connection with the Temple cult, on the other.

The passages taking purity as symbolic are diverse. They exhibit in common the use of the idea of purity or impurity to express approval or disapproval, in fairly strong terms, for something about which there is nothing intrinsically or cultically pure or impure. Not infrequently, purity is treated as an ethical category; one who does the right thing is pure, the wrong thing, impure. What makes this usage interesting is the fact that the terms "pure" and "impure" originally had no ethical value. That is to say, a woman in her menses or a man suffering a flux in the law is not, as we shall see, held in the priestly law-code to be ethically or morally impure. That a man is impure means only that there are certain things he must not do, others he must do in order to return to a state of purity. One has to destroy a house on the walls of which certain growths appear. But the house is not regarded as evil or as a place where evil things have taken place. (The rabbis later on would claim exactly that.) Yet the employment of purity and impurity as value-judgments asserts that the one represents the equivalent of the good or morally right, the other, of the evil or of immorality. This obviously results from the fact that impurity was in its origin connected with loathing—reptiles, dead bodies, menses and other excretions, birds of prey that eat dead bodies, eels, octopus, insects and the like. These are primary sources of impurity and the concept was extended to other objects by analogy and pseudosystematic reasoning.

To be sure, entirely neutral things, for instance, in reference to gold or silver, could be called pure or impure.[1] Similarly, when Job says, "Who can bring a clean thing out of an unclean?", or when Ezekiel says the priests will teach the people how to distinguish between unclean and clean, each takes for granted the existence of the categories of clean and unclean, without thereby assigning moral or religious value to either of them.

That makes all the more striking the tendency of biblical literature to regard purity as other than a neutral trait and to transform the concept into a metaphor or simile for the good, right, or, even, holy. The simplest instance of the symbolic use of purity is in a simile, as in Is. 66:20: "The nations will bring your brethren from all nations as an offering to the Lord just as Israelites bring cereal-offering in a clean vessel to the House of the Lord." But one cannot claim this simple simile represents a considerable development of the idea of purity. What does indicate such a development occurs in the same passage, Is. 66:17, where it is taken for granted that there is a contrast between purifying oneself and committing a sin. Possible allusion to the equation of purity with a pure heart is found in II Chron. 30:18-19, which refers to Hezekiah's praying for those unclean people who ate the Passover while yet unclean, seeking pardon for "everyone who sets his heart to seek God ... even though not according to the sanctuary's rules of cleanness." Here we find the tendency to downgrade the importance of the purity-rules. They are important, but are less important than the effort to purify one's heart.[2]

[1] Ex. 25:11, 17, 24, 29, 31, 36, 38, 39 (pure gold); 27:20 (pure olive oil); 28:36, 30:3, 37:2, 6, 11, 16, 22, 23, 24, 26 (pure gold); 31:8, 37:17, 39:37 (pure lampstand); 39:15, 30 (pure gold); I Chron. 28:17 (pure gold); II Chron 3:4, 8, 13:11 (pure gold); Job 28:19 (pure gold); Ps. 12:6 (refined silver); Ps. 19:10 (fine gold).

[2] Job. 14:4, Ezekiel 44:23. Job 4:17 (Can a man be pure before his Maker?); Job 17:9 (He that has clean hands grows stronger and stronger); Ps. 12:6 (Promises of the Lord are pure); Prov. 22:11 (He who loves purity of heart and whose speech is gracious will have the king as his friend); Prov. 30:12 (There are those

Cleanness is equated with doing good, without explicit reference to the cultic terms, ṬM' and ṬHR, purity and impurity, in Is. 1:16, "Wash you, make yourselves clean ... cease to do evil, learn to do good" (note also Ps. 18:21, 25, 24:3-5). Here we have an explicit effort to compare being washed and clean to doing good, being unclean to doing evil. Isaiah's vision in the Temple (Is. 6:5) represents a still more striking revision of the concept of purity into a symbol of sinlessness. His being a "man of unclean lips" is forthwith interpreted in ethical terms: "Behold, this has touched your lips, your *guilt* is taken away." Third Isaiah (64:5) speaks of becoming "like one who is unclean, and all our righteous deeds are like a polluted garment"—again an allusion to the incongruity of one who, while ritually pure, does impure deeds. This interpretation is not unique to prophetic literature. Ps. 51:9 refers to a "clean heart", compared to a new and right spirit; Prov. 20:9 refers to "purity from sin"; Ecclesiastes 9:2 equates the righteous and wicked with the clean and unclean.

What are the specific and concrete meanings assigned to the metaphors of purity and impurity? First, impurity is seen as a sign of rejection of God or by God. Thus Is. 35:8 refers to a holy highway, over which God will not permit the unclean or the fools to pass. Jer. 33:8 has God say he will clean Israel of the guilt of their sin and will forgive their rebellion. Ezek. 14:11 equates going astray from God with defiling oneself by transgression, and, concommitantly, God refers to rejecting Israel: "And I defiled them through their gifts" (Ezek. 20:26). That Israel is unclean is taken as a sign of rejection in Lam. 4:15. Haggai (2:11-14) expresses the divine rejection of the people by the image of uncleanness; that the people and their sacrifices are unclean is taken as the sign that the people are themselves rejected. By contrast, Zech. 3:5 makes pure garments the sign of divine acceptance.[1]

Closely related to the use of purity as an indication of divine acceptance, second, is the very frequent allusion to idolatry as unclean. Just as impurity signifies the rejection of God, so the greatest rejection of all, represented by idolatry, will be understood as a principal source of

---

who are pure in their own eyes but are not cleansed of their filth); Is. 6:5ff. (I am a man of unclean lips...Behold this has touched your lips, your *guilt* is taken away); Ezek. 36:33 (I will cleanse you from all your iniquities); Zech. 3:5.

[1] Note also Hos. 9:1-4 (You played the harlot, forsook God...they shall eat unclean food in Assyria...all who eat of their [sacrificial] bread shall be defiled); Mal. 3:3 (He will purify the sons of Levi and refine them...until they present right offerings to the Lord).

impurity. Foreign gods defile, so Gen. 35:2. One must defile foreign gods and prohibited forms of worship, as in the case of Josiah, who burned corpses' bones on the high places to defile them (II Kings 23:8-16 = II Chron. 34:3-8). Jeremiah regards as equivalent both going after Baals and being unclean (Jer. 2:23). Therefore the houses of Jerusalem, where other gods were served, will be defiled like the place of Topheth (19:13). Ezek. 23:30 states the matter clearly: Idols have polluted the land, and again in 36:25 he equates uncleanness with idolatry: "You shall be clean from all your uncleannesses, and from all your idols I will cleanse you." Numerous other passages, chiefly in prophetic literature, treat idolatry as a source of uncleanness.[1]

The third application of purity as a sign of moral blamelessness and of impurity as a sign of moral evil comes in reference to sexual relations. This closely relates to the foregoing, for, particularly in prophetic literature, loyalty to God is compared to marital fidelity. In some passages to be made impure means to have illicit sexual relations, as in Gen. 34:5-13, where Shechem defiles Dinah, or Ezek. 24:11, where Ezekiel refers to intercourse with one's daughter-in-law as unclean lewdness. Here, however, matters are not entirely clear, since sexual intercourse produced legal impurity. To say "he defiled her" may have been a euphemism for sexual relations, nothing more. But very commonly the metaphor of sexual disloyalty is applied to Israel's relationship to God, therefore uncleanness metaphorically here represents both rejection of God and sexual defilement.[2]

---

[1] Ps. 106:38-9 (They sacrificed to the idols of Canaan; and the land was polluted with blood); Is. 30:22 (Then you will defile your...images); Jer. 7:30 (For the sons of Judah have done evil in my sight...they have set their abomination in the house which is called by my name to defile it); Jer. 32:34 = Jer. 7:30; Ezek. 22:4 (Defiled by the idols you have made); Ezek. 23:30 (You polluted yourself with their idols); Ezek. 37:23 (They shall not defile themselves any more with their idols...but I will cleanse them...); Zech. 13:2 (I will cut off the names of the idols...and also I will remove from the land the prophets and the unclean spirit). Mishnaic law (M. Avodah Zarah 3:8) declares one unclean who sits in the shade of an *asherah*.

[2] Deut. 24:4: Divorcee may not remarry first husband, having been defiled by her second; Joshua 22:17 (We have not yet cleansed ourselves from the sin at Peor); Ezra 9:11-12 (Peoples have made the land unclean, therefore do not intermarry with them); Ps. 106:39 (They became unclean by their acts and played the harlot in their doings); Jer. 13:27 (I have seen...your adulteries...How long will it be before you [Jerusalem] are clean?); Ezek. 23:17 (Babylonians defiled her with their lust); Ezek. 24:13 (filthy lewdness); Ezek. 33:26 (You defile neighbor's wives); Ezek. 43:7 (The house of Israel shall no more defile my holy name...by their harlotry); Hos. 5:3 = 6:10 (Ephraim played the harlot, Israel is defiled).

Fourth, the land may be made unclean by evil doings, very frequently having to do with idolatry; thus, as we saw, Ezek. 36:18 says idols polluted the land. The rejection of Israel is symbolized by the pollution of the land, and the exile from the land is taken to have been caused by the uncleanness produced by iniquity; therefore the resettlement of the land will mark the purification of Israel, as in Ezek. 36:33, "I will cleanse you from iniquities, I will cause the cities to be inhabited."[1] Rabbinic exegetes would return to this theme.

The several metaphorical usages of pure and impure have in common an indifference to the actual, material details of the laws of ritual purity and impurity. Slight effort is made to refer to, or make use of, the concrete laws. The symbol of purity or impurity as used above is left without further specification. Purity simply is the given. Indeed, one may characterize as superficial and homiletical the various usages we have just reviewed. The prophetic and sapiential contrast between the ritually pure and the ethically impure requires little imagination, but only a preacher's sense of the homiletical potentialities of ambiguous words. The Temple supplied to purity its importance in the religious life. As the Temple signified divine favor, and as the cult supplied the nexus between Israel and God, so purity, associated so closely with both, could readily serve as an image either of divine favor or of man's loyalty to God. From that fact followed the assignment of impurity to all that stood against the Temple, the cult, and God: idolatry first of all. As to the use of purity in connection with sexual relations, that was, as we shall now see, a usage of the law itself. In all, one would not have to exhibit considerable powers of imagination to create the metaphorical interpretations of purity and impurity we have rapidly surveyed.

The priestly law-code utilizes purity and impurity primarily with reference to the cult. The practical consequence of being impure, according to the priestly code, is that one may not participate in the cult. This applies, first of all, to the priests themselves, which may account for the importance accorded to the symbol of purity by both

---

[1] Note also Deut. 21:23 (Corpse defiles the land if hung overnight); Deut. 24:4 (defiled woman brings guilt upon the land); Joshua 22:19 ("If your land is unclean"); Ezra 9:11 (Peoples of the land have made the land unclean, therefore do not intermarry with them); Ps. 106:38 (The land was polluted with blood); Jer. 2:7 (You defiled my land); Ezek. 22:24 (You are a land that is not cleansed); Ezek. 39:12, 16 (They will bury corpses of God in order to cleanse the land); Amos 7:17 (You shall die in an unclean land); Micah 2:10 (Arise and go, for this is no place to rest, because of uncleanness that destroys...).

Jeremiah and Ezekiel, the one a priest, the other an exponent of the official priesthood.

If purity and impurity are made relative to the cult, Robertson Smith will hold they are emptied of intrinsic power. One who is impure is not a bearer of a malevolent, autonomous, and independent force. The menstruating woman or the leper is not dangerous; the house afflicted with a growth is not "haunted." The unclean person merely cannot come to the Temple—until he is purified. But for Levine, the cultic focus in no way neutralizes impurity, it demonstrates its material, demonic reality. It is difficult to regard the position of Robertson Smith in this regard as founded on decisive arguments. For limiting impurity to the cult is not necessarily the same as neutralizing it. Impurity within the cult may remain a powerful force, dangerous precisely because it affects the divinity as much as the man, and therefore is to be excluded for the protection of the God in his abode. To claim that the interpretation of impurity as a status rather than as an autonomous force is implied by its limitation to the cult is a non-sequitur. To treat purity as a matter of relationship to the cult does not remove from impurity any sort of material, non-relative significance. Later on, at the very end of our period, the full implications of the neutralization of impurity by Talmudic law indeed would be drawn out: the corpse does not really render unclean, the rite of purification does not really render clean, but these rites represent the will of God and that alone. But the biblical writers never say so.

We may briefly digress to expand this point. In Talmudic law purity indeed is made relative. The Talmudic purity laws comprise and create a wholly abstract set of relationships, a kind of non-Euclidean geometry of the cultic realm. There is nothing material about purity or impurity. We here are no longer dealing with a belief that something evil really enters into the person or food or a utensil. If purity and impurity constitute a set of highly complex relationships, in Talmudic law these have nothing to do with the physical world. A great deal depends upon intention and purpose, circumstance and time, as Maimonides asserts. For instance, a vessel which is not completed may touch a corpse and yet remain clean, for it is not susceptible to uncleanness until it has been entirely finished, *and* its owner regards it as finished. So corpse-uncleanness in itself is not effective *ex opere operato*. A common person is normally regarded as unclean. But during a religious festival in Jerusalem he is regarded as clean. If the outer side of a vessel becomes unclean through contact with an unclean liquid, and food touches the outer side, it remains clean. A vessel whose outer side alone is unclean does not render ordinary food unclean. But if the food is connected with the cult (as in II Chron. 30:18-19, cited above), then it is a Holy Thing, and if so, it *is* made unclean by touching the outer side of the vessel. So you might have two identical substances in different categories. One may be ordinary food; the other a Holy Thing. Both touch the same outer side of the same vessel. The one is clean, the other unclean.

Clearly, in Talmudic purity law everything is relative to everything else. So the saying appearing in a late compilation of rabbinic exegeses, though attributed to Yoḥanan ben Zakkai, that the corpse is not intrinsically unclean, and the rite is not effective *ex opere operato*, may be prefigured in the Talmudic law itself. This is what I mean by the effective neutralization of the force of impurity (therefore of purity as well). The actual process of contamination or purification is made entirely relative. The focus of purity in the cult, as much as its transformation into a moral symbol, may be seen as parts of the same process of neutralization. But it remains to be demonstrated that this is the meaning or implication of the priestly code's concentration on questions of purity in matters affecting the Temple.

In the priestly laws a great many diverse matters are reduced to the single consequence: impurity. The predicate of many subjects is made the same: the leper is—"impure"; so too, a house with a growth on its walls; so too a menstrual woman; so too one who touches a creeping thing; so too a woman in child-birth; so too a whole variety of growths—boils, swelling, raw flesh—on one's body; so too one who has a discharge from his body; so too a corpse; so too a spot on a piece of linen or wool. These may seem to bear some slight relationship to one another. But the same word, *unclean*, is applied to illicit sexual relations. A Nazir is supposed to avoid becoming "unclean." A woman suspected of having committed adultery is regarded as having become "unclean." And there are no distinctions among these various applications of the word "unclean." Thus we have once again little more than the reduction of diverse conditions to one metaphor. But a little more there is, and it must not be overlooked. In the cases of "leprosy," for instance, the absence in the priestly code of a negative moral evaluation of the condition of uncleanness makes it difficult to regard uncleanness as a metaphor for immorality. Furthermore, the provision of a practical ritual of purification precludes its being wholly a metaphor.

Let us now examine the priestly code of purity, both to survey the laws which would have been known to the Israelites from the beginning of the third century B.C., and to set into mind the major details of the laws which later on would stimulate and generate ideas about purity.

The priestly laws make tediously explicit the connection between purity and the cult.[1] Lev. 7:19-21 states that meat from the sacrificial meal must not come into contact with impurity; if it does, it must be burned. An unclean person must not eat of the sacrifice. The Temple is presumed to be clean; therefore the reference to uncleanness and the unclean person suggests the sanctuary is not the location of the meal. The bulk of the purity regulations occurs in Lev. 11-15. Uncleanness, first, pertains to animals. One must not eat unclean animals, birds, creeping things, and must not touch their carcasses (Lev. 11:1-47). (Lev. 17:15-6 extends this rule to what dies of itself.) The violator is unclean until the evening, must wash, and then wait for sunset. A reason follows (Lev. 11:44): "For I am the Lord your God. Sanctify yourselves and be holy, for I am holy. You will not defile yourselves with any swarming thing ... for I am the Lord, who brought you up out of the land of Egypt to be your God. You shall be holy for I am holy." What is new here is the equation of purity with holiness, a theme virtually absent in the narrative, prophetic, and sapiential materials we have just examined. But what we are not told is why these particular animals are unclean and lead to unholiness; the pre-history of the forbidden creatures is not recorded. All living creatures are simply divided into clean and unclean, without explanation.[2]

The second source of uncleanness is childbirth (Lev. 12:1-8). A

---

[1] On the priestly code and narratives, I consulted the following: Martin Noth, *Leviticus* (Philadelphia, 1965); *idem., Numbers* (Philadelphia, 1968); N. H. Snaith, *Leviticus and Numbers* (London, 1967); James L. Mays, *The Book of Leviticus. The Book of Numbers* (Richmond, 1963); Klaus Koch, *Die Priesterschrift von Exodus 25 bis Leviticus 16. Eine überlieferungsgeschichtliche und literarkritische Untersuchung* (Göttingen, 1959), pp. 74-95; Rolf Rendtorff, *Die Gesetze in der Priesterschrift* (Göttingen, 1954), pp. 38-65; Karl Elliger, *Leviticus* (Tübingen, 1966), pp. 140-199; and David Hoffmann, *Sefer Vayiqra* (Jerusalem, 1953, I-II, trans. of *Das Buch Leviticus. Übersetzt und erklärt von Dr. D. Hoffmann* [1904]). Of greatest value was Wilfried Paschen, *Rein und Unrein. Untersuchung zur biblischen Wortgeschichte* (Munich, 1970).

[2] Unclean animals and food: Gen. 7:2, 8 (Noah's ark); Deut. 14:3-20 (birds); Judges 13:4, 7, 14 ("Eat nothing unclean"); Ezek. 4:14 (I have never defiled myself...foul flesh has not come into my mouth). Unclean people and food: Deut. 12:15, 22 (Clean and unclean may eat flesh); I Sam. 20:26 (David did not join Saul at a meal. Saul: "Something has befallen him; he is not clean"); II Chron. 30:18-19 (Unclean people ate the Passover offering).

woman who has given birth is ruled unclean, just as at the time of her menstruation, for seven plus thirty-three days for a male child, and fourteen plus sixty-six for a female. She then has to bring a burnt-offering and a sin-offering; "and the priest shall make atonement for her and she shall be clean." We are not told the nature of her "sin."

The third source of uncleanness (Lev. 13:1-14:57) is swellings, eruptions, or spots on the skin, generally mistranslated as "leprosy," though that cannot have been the correct diagnosis of these curious conditions. The same word is applied to "leprous diseases"—mildew—in a garment or in a house, and these are not susceptible to what we know as leprosy. When such skin-ailments appear, the priest is to examine the person and, under certain conditions, pronounce the person unclean as a "leper." The leper must announce his condition and remain outside the "camp." Once the disease is healed, the leper is subject to a rite of purification. The priest takes two living, clean birds, cedar wood, scarlet stuff, and hyssop. One of the birds is killed in an earthen vessel over running water; the living bird is dipped into the blood of the dead one. The priest sprinkles the blood seven times over the one to be cleansed of leprosy, who then is pronounced clean. The living bird is let go. The man then washes his clothes, shaves all his hair, bathes himself, and repeats the process seven days later. On the eighth day full-scale offerings—two male lambs, a ewe-lamb, a cereal offering with oil, and an oil offering—are to be brought. A *ḥaṭ'at*, generally translated guilt-offering, is made of one of the lambs with the oil. But an element of guilt is not necessarily implied; *ḥaṭ'at* here means in effect purification; the rite surely is magical. A bit of the blood of the offering is put on the tip of the right ear of the one to be cleansed, also on the thumb of the right hand and on the big toe of the right foot: "Thus the priest shall make atonement for him, and he shall be clean." If the leper is a poor man, appropriate revisions are made in the sacrificial requirements.

The fourth source of uncleanness is a "disease" or mildew on the walls of a house. The house is shut up and resurveyed after seven days. If the disease is still on the stones, the stones are removed. If the disease breaks out again, then the house has to be broken down. If the disease does not recur, the house is cleansed as is the leper: "So he shall make atonement for the house and it shall be clean." Now what is striking throughout is the requirement to "make atonement"; no sin has been specified. The cultic usage, however, will generate in rabbinic Judaism a search for exactly the sin presumed to have been committed, since the text said "atonement" must be made. It is difficult, however, to maintain that the issues of sin and guilt have predominated in P's exposition. The viewpoint of the priestly code has been imposed upon the laws; the concern of all the laws is, primarily, cultic acceptability, secondarily, holiness. The cultic community is kept free of those who have skin-diseases. As we have already observed, uncleanness is discussed with reference to a single consequence, participation in the cult. But here that consequence is not explicitly indicated (as in Lev. 11:44), but only by the redactional context in which the law is given and by the repeated allusion to the priest's supervision of the rites. That the leper has to sit apart is assigned no pejorative significance. That would come later. Similarly, although the cleansing rite is full of magical overtones, these are passed over silently—or taken for granted! The priest does everything according to God's instructions, and the only result of his action is that the subjects "become clean," i.e., become once more acceptable in the cultic community.

The fifth source of uncleanness is bodily discharges (Lev. 15:1-33).[1] The text lists persons made unclean by these. The first is a man who suffers a discharge. The man's capacity for rendering other objects unclean is spelled out in detail. Whatever he sits on, whatever touches what he has sat on, whoever touches him, anyone on whom he spits, any saddle on which he rides, whoever carries such a thing—all are unclean. When the discharge stops, the man counts seven clean days and washes, bathes, and is clean. The eighth day sets the occasion for an offering. The second of these people made unclean by a discharge is the man who has an emission of semen. The third is a woman who discharges blood during her regular period. The fourth is a woman who has a discharge of blood not during her period. At the end comes a general explanation for the foregoing (Lev. 15:31): "You shall keep the people of Israel separate from their uncleanness, lest they die in their uncleanness by defiling my tabernacle that is in their midst." Here in a single sentence is the complete priestly ideology of purity. All matters of purity attain importance because of the cult. No other occasion for attaining or preserving purity is considered. The same idea recurs in Lev. 16:16, "Thus he [the priest] shall make atonement for the holy place, because of the uncleanness of the people of Israel, and because of their transgressions, all their sins." Here we again

[1] See also Deut. 23:10 (Uncleanness through nocturnal admission); II Sam. 11:4 (Bathsheba was purifying herself from her [menstrual] uncleanness); II Kings 5:10-14 (Naaman was unclean with leprosy and bathed in the Jordan).

discern the priestly ideology, that uncleanness affects the cult; but now comes the equation of uncleanness with transgression and sin. The priest therefore has to atone for the holy place on account of the uncleannesses of the people (Lev. 16:19) and then offer sin-offering. So uncleanness is like sin. But here uncleanness is separate from sin, and not another way of referring to iniquity. While the priestly code approaches the notion of uncleanness as a metaphor for sin, it holds back from finally coming to that conclusion.

The sixth source of uncleanness is sexual misdeeds: "You will not lie carnally with your neighbor's wife and defile yourself with her." The same applies to bestiality. Then "Do not defile yourselves by any of these [aforementioned illicit sexual relationships], for by all these the nations I am casting out before you defiled themselves, and the land became defiled, so that I punished its iniquity, and the land vomited out its inhabitants" (Lev. 18:24). Here (as in 20:21) are combined two already familiar themes: uncleanness through sexuality, uncleanness of the land. The striking omission is the cult, which now does not enter the matter. So the land, like the cult, must be kept clean. The land may be made unclean by the sexual misdeeds which occur upon it. Num. 35:34 adds that murder pollutes the land. Lev. 21:25 then ties up the several themes—the uncleanness of animals, the possession of a holy land, the sexual misdeeds of the former inhabitants: "You shall therefore make a distinction between the clean beast and the unclean ... you shall not make yourselves abominable by beast or by bird or by anything with which the ground teems, which I have set apart for you to hold unclean. You shall be holy to me, for I the Lord am holy, and have separated you from the peoples, that you should be mine." Here we come upon the last important motif of the priestly cleanness-ideology: the equation of cleanness with sanctity, along with the imputation of cleanness and sanctity to Israel, uncleanness and profanity to the nations.[1] The cult and the land are now joined to the people: all three must be kept free of impurity. The purity of cult, land, and people signifies God's favor; the divine favor is joined to the specific rules concerning purity in food and sex.

The seventh source of uncleanness is the corpse, presented specific-

---

[1] Note also Neh. 12:30, 45 (Priests and Levites purified themselves, the people, and the gates and wall; priests and Levites performed the service of purification); Neh. 13:30 (Nehemiah cleansed the priesthood of everything foreign); Is. 52:11 (Touch no unclean thing...purify yourselves, you who bear the vessels of the Lord).

ally as the concern of the priesthood (Lev. 21:1-24; but Num. 31:19-20 involves laymen). The priest is not to defile himself with the dead, except for his nearest of kin. The uncleanness of the corpse is not explained, but taken for granted. That uncleanness will prevent the priest from going into the sanctuary or participating in the cult (Lev. 21:10ff.), but so too the priest is profaned (not "polluted" here) by sexual misdeeds—marriage to an inappropriate woman. "Cleanness" is applied to the prohibition against contact with the corpse. "Holiness" pertains to marriage. The one then is equated with the other. Not only the priesthood but also the holy things of the cult are to be kept pure or holy. A person who approaches the holy things while unclean "will be cut off from my presence" (Lev. 22:1-9). A priest who is a leper or suffers a discharge, whoever touches something unclean through contact with the dead or with a man who has had an emission of semen, whoever touches a creeping thing or an unclean man—all are unclean and may not eat the holy food. What dies of itself or is torn by beasts may not be eaten by the priest, for it will make the priest unclean. Lev. 22:1-9 offers the fullest claim that the whole range of purity laws pertains primarily to the priest and to the cult. The pericope ends (Lev. 22:31-3) with an allusion to God's holiness: "I will be hallowed among the people of Israel, I am the Lord who sanctify you." Rules of different origin thus are put together and linked to a single outcome: the purity of the cult.[1]

The priestly laws of Numbers do not materially change the picture. Num. 5:1-4 repeats the rule that lepers, people with discharges, and people unclean through contact with the dead have to be put outside the camp; they may not defile the camp, where God dwells. Cultic uncleanness thus must be kept from the presence of God. Noth comments, "A material understanding of cultic 'cleanness' lies at the basis of this." The "camp" is to be kept clean on account of the divine presence. This "camp" may be the Temple's cult, the holy land, or the holy people. An already familiar concept of purity recurs in Num.

[1] Note also I Chron. 23:28 (Sons of Aaron clean the holy); II Chron. 29:15 (Levites cleaned the Temple); II Chron. 23:19 (Jehoiada stationed gatekeepers at the Temple so that no one should enter who was in any way unclean); II Chron. 36:14 (Priests under Zedekiah made Temple unclean); Ezra 6:20 (Priests and Levites purified selves, so killed the Passover lamb for themselves and all the returned exiles); Neh. 13:9 (Nehemiah cleansed the chambers); Ps. 79:1 (The heathens have defiled the Temple and ruined Jerusalem); Ezek. 9:7 (Defile the house); Ezek. 23:38 (They have defiled my sanctuary [parallel to adultery, idolatry, murder]); Ezek. 43:26 (Seven days they shall purify the altar).

5:11-31, defilement through sexual misdeed. In this instance uncleanness is imputed to a woman who has supposedly committed adultery.

Num. 6:1-21 introduces a new setting for cleanness, the Nazir. He is to keep clean, which means separate, and is instructed not to become unclean, in particular through contact with a corpse. Judges 13:4, 7 has the Nazir keep away from unclean food as well. The Nazir may be compared to the priest; both are consecrated to God, serving as mediators of divine grace. But here, the primary matter of uncleanness is that of a corpse. The later law would take for granted that all other uncleannesses are equally at issue; the word "unclean" will draw in its wake a whole range of matters intrinsically not interrelated.

Num. 8:5-22 conceives of the Levites as an offering to God; they therefore are to be cleansed prior to being offered. The idea is already familiar: purity is to characterize all aspects of the cult.[1]

Num. 9:1-14 takes account of uncleanness in connection with offering the Passover. Moses was informed that some people had become unclean by contact with a corpse, so could not offer the Passover with the community. God then told Moses that in such an event, those unclean should still keep the Passover, but a month later. The requirement of purity for the cultic act of slaughtering the Passover is taken for granted. Finally, Num. 19:1-22 specifies the means by which a person may be purified from corpse-uncleanness. He who touches a corpse will be unclean for seven days. He will be sprinkled on the third and seventh days with water prepared with the ashes of the red heifer. This rite has to do with the tabernacle: "Whoever touches a dead person ... and does not cleanse himself defiles the tabernacle of the Lord, and that person shall be cut off from Israel, because the water for impurity has not been thrown upon him, he shall be unclean, his uncleanness is still on him" (Num. 19:13). It is further ruled that if a man dies in a tent, the tent will convey uncleanness to whoever enters and to open vessels in the tent. The same explanation is added: one must return to a condition of cleanness before entering the tabernacle. What is striking is that the sole explanation for all this hocus-pocus is that this is the way one becomes clean before entering the tabernacle. The actual rites—which cannot be other than magical—are left without explanation; no theory of purification is offered. The source of impurity and the means of purity are treated as neutral, given and of self-evident effect.

---

[1] Note also Deut. 26:14 ("I have not removed any of it while I was unclean").

One ethical motif in the priestly narratives was discerned by the later rabbis. When Miriam and Aaron speak against Moses for marrying a Cushite woman (Num. 12:1-16), Miriam becomes leprous, "as white as snow." Moses prays that Miriam may be healed, and after seven days she is cured. So the advent of leprosy is regarded as punishment for a specific sin: speaking ill against Moses. The rabbis, as we shall see, later on take this sequence of events as a sign that one who speaks ill of his fellow or gossips is smitten by leprosy. Turned around, this thought will produce the view that one who is leprous has been guilty of gossiping. A few other forms of uncleanness likewise will be attached to ethical or moral failures. But the narrator of Num. 12:1-16 does not hint he conceives leprosy to result from gossip. The attack of leprosy is represented merely as divine punishment; only later on would the exact sin for which Miriam was culpable be specified, and then associated with the "punishment" of leprosy, along with many other sins.

The priestly laws and narratives thus remain strikingly reticent about what lies behind the specific rules of cleanness. In other religions certain animals were sacred or served as totems for shrines or were associated with demons and evil powers. The separation of sex from the cult, making it defiling because of its use in other cults, is taken for granted. But why sex must be divorced from the sanctuary is not explained. Perhaps the motive here was reaction against the Canaanite cults, in which sexual acts were prominent. Making the dead unclean likewise removes the cult of the dead from the holy place. Primitive taboos of all sorts are before us. But behind all of them the primary ideological motif is cultic purity. Almost all specific uncleannesses are to be avoided on that account, either explicitly or implicitly. The holiness of the cult may then be extended to the priesthood, the land, the people. But these represent merely further developments of what is, to begin with, a concern for cultic and priestly purity.

When we compare the references to purity in prophetic, sapiential, and historical literature with those presented in the priestly code of laws, we find a remarkable correspondence. Indeed, the interpretation of the purity-laws contains virtually all of the motifs important in the use of purity as a moral or other sort of metaphor. One therefore cannot distinguish legal from non-legal views of the matter; the one represents in the context of concrete cultic ritual what the other describes in the setting of ethics, morality, or theology.

Let us review the main results of our rapid survey of both types of literature. Treatment of purity as symbol, metaphor, or allegory involves the assignment to purity of a value extrinsic to the cult. To be impure is to be guilty of something, normally, though not always, having to do with ethics. A woman impure on account of birth, however, also has to bring a guilt-offering. A leper brings a "sin-offering." The water that purifies one who has touched a dead body is known as "sin-water." It is possible that the notion of "an ethical offense, a sin" evolved from the general class of "acts that make you unfit for the holy community." So these traces of "ethical" terminology in purity law may be not late contaminations, but fossils from an earlier time when all offenses produced impurity, and all impurities were offenses. Uncleanness means "guilt" for Isaiah—but in the cult the unclean person likewise is regarded as guilty. Purity is the prerequisite of the grace of God; the rejection by God, or of God, is the concommitant of impurity. But the cultic laws interpret matters in an identical way; what is impure is rejected for the cult, what is pure is accepted. Idolatry is the exact opposite of the cult of the Lord; it is impure, as the Lord's cult is pure. Purity and impurity are applied to sexual relationships in the priestly law-code itself; the usage in other Scriptures hardly marks a development of the association, in the law, between impurity and illicit sexual relations. That the land may be polluted by idolatry or illicit sexuality clearly is the view of the law as much as of the non-legal literature.

The sole significant difference between legal and other types of literature is concern for the details of purity and the specific things to be done, in each case, to restore purity. But this is natural, for the task of legislation is to supply specific instruction, while interpretive literature is going to use the general categories established and given material weight by the law. A contrast between cultic purity and ethical impurity will not be made explicit in the priestly code. But the priestly code takes for granted that impurity is like sin; purification frees one from sin. The implication that purity is to be contrasted with sinfulness, as with impurity, is not left without articulation. For the priestly code equates purity with holiness, and the details of holiness concern as much ethical as ritual matters (as in Lev. 19 or Is. 5:16). Purity concerns cult, land, food, sex, the divinity, the relations between individuals. In varying ways and degrees both legal and non-legal writings reveal a common priestly ideology and employ a common hermeneutical corpus of symbols and metaphors based upon the holiness of the cult.

That the common ideology is cultic, and is characteristic chiefly of the priests, may now be shown statistically. Pure and impure (ṬM'/-ṬHR) in their various forms are primarily found in priestly literature, and, within that corpus, chiefly in Leviticus and Numbers. As to unclean (ṬM'), the root occurs approximately 283 times, as follows:

	Number	*Percentage*
Leviticus and Numbers:	182	64.3%
Ezekiel	44	15.5%
Other	57	20.0%
	283	

Micah	2
Haggai	4
Jeremiah	5
Psalms	2
Genesis	3
II Kings	4
Isaiah	7
Chronicles	3
Hosea	4
Judges	3
Lamentations	2
Deuteronomy	11
Rest	7

As to clean (ṬHR), the root occurs approximately 212 times, and the majority of occurrences come either in the priestly literature or in reference to the cult:

	Number	*Percentage*
Leviticus and Numbers	93	43.7%
Ezekiel (16) + Chronicles (15)	31	14.2%
Exodus (pure gold for cult)	33	15.6%
Other	55	25.9%
	212	

Proverbs	4
Kings	4
Psalms	7
Job	5
Malachi	3
Jeremiah	2
Nehemiah	6
Ezra	2
Isaiah	3
Genesis	7
Deuteronomy	7
Zechariah	2
Rest	3

If we add to the occurrences in Leviticus and Numbers, those in Exodus, Ezekiel and Chronicles, we find that 157 of 212—74.0%—belong in priestly literature; to these further are to be added the seven occurrences in Genesis, which are within P, as is to be expected. As we have already observed, the use of "pure" in Exodus differs from the sense assigned to the word in priestly documents.

The significance of this fact in the period of the Second Temple has been made clear by Morton Smith.[1] It would in time to come lay the foundations for the formation of sects in ancient Judaism, from the fifth century B.C. (Nehemiah) onward:

> Differences as to the interpretation of the purity laws and especially as to the consequent question of table fellowship were among the principle causes of the separation of Christianity from the rest of Judaism and the early fragmentation of Christianity itself. The same thing holds for the Qumran community and, within Pharisaic tradition, the *haburah*. They are essentially groups whose members observe the same interpretation of the purity rules and therefore can have table fellowship with each other.

A second important observation by Smith is that a characteristic charge of a sect against its opponents is that of polluting the Temple:

> ... and here too we encounter what is most characteristic of Israelite sectarianism, the claim that laymen can be better informed as to the purity laws than the Temple priesthood. This is a noteworthy thing. Customarily the priesthood had been the religious authority, and so especially on questions of purity. But now a layman, relying on his own knowledge and interpretation of the sacred law, purifies the temple from pollutions for which the priests have been responsible. Christian story will make Jesus do the same; Pharisaic story represented the Pharisees as supervising the Temple ritual and forcing the priests to follow Pharisaic regulations ...

Smith points out that the same also is so for the Qumran community.

Ideas associated with purity and impurity therefore would be formed chiefly within the priestly caste until the development of special legal traditions by dissident parties in the exilic period. From then on even lay party members would, on the basis of their sectarian legal training, challenge priestly authorities. In Second Temple times these sectarian laws about purity would serve to differentiate from those who accept the predominant cult both priests and laymen who rejected the regnant priesthood or its conduct of the cult or its view of purity, and

[1] Morton Smith, "The Dead Sea Sect in Relation to Ancient Judaism," *New Testament Studies* 7, 1960, pp. 347-360.

who therefore coalesced to form a sect. The larger history of Judaic sectarianism in the period of the Second Temple therefore is centered in the microcosm of ideas associated with purity. That history is the story of dissenters, of new efforts to interpret the cult and to reinterpret the foci of cultic sanctity, thus of a reinterpretation of one of the basic symbolic systems of the country's cultural-religious life. Since the period indeed concludes with the destruction of the Temple itself, the several sectarian efforts at the reinterpretation of the meaning of its cult, of the community it symbolizes, and of the purity-rules which serve to distinguish and to sanctify the place and cultic community—these assume an importance wholly incommensurate with their trivial nature. And the ideas laid out in elaboration of the several types of reinterpretation of purity would continue for many centuries to form the focus of the Judaic and, in lesser measure, the Christian religious imagination.

My contention in the following survey is that purity is an essential element in the interpretation of Israel's total religious system over sixteen centuries. The ideas we are about to review reflect a much larger perspective upon reality than is contained within their specific explanations of purity and impurity. They give us a brief glimpse into the 'sacred canopy' beneath which ancient Judaism, from the tenth century B.C. to the destruction of the Second Temple and beyond, down to the advent of Islam, organized and interpreted existence.

In the sources before us, as in the Hebrew Scriptures, that glimpse focuses upon the Temple itself, its priesthood, cult, rites, and their larger meanings. Extant ideas, centered on the Temple, about purity and impurity in microcosm reveal a conception far greater than themselves. They show how the day-to-day issues of community and common life were understood in terms of the cult. In this regard Mary Douglas, in *Purity and Danger. An Analysis of Concepts of Pollution and Taboo* (London, 1966), states, "... Pollution is a type of danger which is not likely to occur except where the lines of structure, cosmic or social, are clearly defined." The data before us on the surface will support this contention, for they consistently seem to center upon the Temple. When ideas of purity are removed from the physical Temple itself, they continue to testify to the importance of the Temple, for they serve to define communities which compare themselves to the Jerusalem Temple, claiming to constitute a surrogate or to replace it. Or they provide metaphors for social virtues or vices which attain transcendent importance because they can be referred back to the cult. The Temple in retrospect therefore would evidently turn out to be the one point in Israelite life upon which the lines of structure —both cosmic and social—converge. Therefore social values are going in some measure to depend for both vividness and moral authority upon their capacity to find a place within the Temple symbolism. Religious sins will in like manner be made to fit within, or to form an analogy to, the Temple's imagery. The Temple's centrality in the Israelite conception of the cosmos therefore will seem to account for the centralization of impurity within the cultic framework, then its generation of evocative metaphors for the secular world outside. When impurity is seen to be entirely divorced from the Temple, and purity is filled with meanings entirely without pertinence to the cult—philosophical, social, or ethical virtues, for instance—then we stand in a world to which the Temple as a physical reality and a unifying, organizing force in the perception of the world, has ceased to impart meaning. When, as in the last stratum of rabbinic literature, leprosy comes to allude to the conquerors of Israel—Babylon, Media, Greece, and Rome—and it no longer attempts to link the Temple to the concrete historical or social reality outside, then we know the Temple has lost all significance in the religious imagination of Israel. But that was a long time in coming.

In so stating matters, I accurately report what, as we have seen, the sources consistently allege. Yet I must now take account of an important fact, the bias of our sources.

First of all, the vastly larger number of biblical sources derives from priestly writers. The biblical usages of purity and impurity occur chiefly in priestly documents—law-codes, histories, and prophecies. In the sectarian writings in post-biblical literature the Temple and priesthood remain important issues. So in claiming that the Temple is central for the interpretation of purity, I merely repeat what the sources themselves allege. The priestly authorities clearly have taken over for the Temple, and for that alone, nearly the whole corpus of laws and symbols associated with purity.

The substance of those laws and symbols, however, is strikingly pertinent to ordinary, non-cultic affairs. Impurity is imparted by all sorts of loathsome things—bodily discharges, reptiles, lepers, mysterious growths on stone walls. These have no intrinsic relationship to the cult. They will have been loathsome anywhere. Later interpretations of purity depend upon biblical literature. Yet unclean animals in period of the Second Temple were prohibited to all Israelites, not only to priests, and were avoided throughout the land of Israel and the diaspora, not merely in the Temple. The avoidance of the prohibited animals is certainly well attested in every piece of evidence pertinent to Judaism, deriving from Greek, Latin, pagan, Christian, and Jewish sources alike. The menstrual taboos were observed by people who had no intention whatever of entering the Temple. We certainly cannot maintain, therefore, that purity was primarily a cultic concern, or important only when a non-priest intended to go to the Temple. The contrary was in fact the case.

The contention that pollution occurs "where the lines of structure, cosmic or social, are clearly defined" therefore accords with the perspective of the priestly writers, but seems not to conform to the entire range of applications of purity and impurity. Animals were unclean; the menstrual woman was unclean; reptiles and corpses were sources of impurity. One cannot easily subsume these several sorts of uncleanness within a single institution, nor, so far as I can see, do they serve to define other social structures. (I cannot say anything about cosmic ones.) For example, it may be alleged that impurity served to remove from the community at large people who were considered dangerous, such as the leper. But impurity applied not only to people, but also to inanimate objects as well as to animals. And it was not always a societal concern. A husband and wife observed the purity rules in the privacy of the home; no one would know if they violated them. We therefore cannot regard impurity as important primarily in connection with rites of passage (birth) or with dangerous individuals (lepers, people with a flux). It is claimed that unclean animals are differentiated from clean ones according to a particular, rational pattern. That may be so. Yet such a pattern is not then applied to the differentiation between other aspects of cleanness and uncleanness; it is a pattern which organizes and explains only what it to begin with contains.

As we examine the references to purity in post-biblical literature, we therefore need to keep in mind several facts. First of all, all authorities regarded Scriptures as authoritative, and biblical ideas therefore predominated even among non-priests. Second, purity was one of the givens of the world; where it is not mentioned, it is still a consideration. Third, we cannot be certain that the entire range of interpretation is before us. This makes exceedingly difficult the task of interpreting the meaning of purity to the individuals and sects whose literature we have. The Temple will bulk larger in references to purity than it did in practical applications of purity to the common life, in part on account of the established tendency of Scriptures, in part because of the character of the limited sample of literature in our hands. We must keep in mind the deliberate bias introduced by the biblical priests and the accidental distortion resulting from the limited sample of evidence. While purity is essential to the religious system of Israel, its larger implications are exceedingly difficult to determine. But we must not be confused or taken in by the priestly lawyers, historians, and prophets.

The mode of our interpretation of later views of purity now is clear: to what degree and in what way do the important personalities and communities in Judaism make use of the biblical legacy of ideologies of purity? To what extent is the rich and varied set of metaphors exploited? How are the details of the laws made the vehicle for conveying important ideas? To suggest in advance the result of the following inquiry, I may say that the ideas of neither significant individuals, such as Philo and Josephus, nor important first-century communities, the Qumran *yaḥad*, the Pharisaic *ḥavurah*, and the Christian Church, include much attention to the *details* of the laws as a source of idology or even of evocative metaphors. All treated purity as one-dimensional, viewing it as important in the cult, sometimes adding to it fairly obvious homilies. They used the purity-laws, at most, for some extrinsic purposes or arguments, as do Philo and Josephus. Or they alluded to the concept of purity without any considerable articulation (in the preserved literature) of its detailed requirements, its meaning for moral life, or its larger implications for ethics, as do the *yaḥad*, the *ḥavurah*, and Christian community. The *yaḥad* and the *ḥavurah* take for granted the importance of purity, but add nothing new to its ideology, in general or in detail. The Christians (to the end of New Testament times) reverted to the prophetic and sapiential contrast between ethical and cultic purity, but developed nothing in the already-available interpretive legacy. Only with rabbinic Judaism do we see a sustained and original effort to renew the inquiry into the meaning and potentialities of the details of purity both as law and as metaphor.

CHAPTER TWO

IDEAS OF PURITY IN THE LITERATURE OF THE PERIOD OF THE SECOND TEMPLE

The post-biblical history of the concept of purity and impurity is divided by the destruction of the Temple in A.D. 70. Before that time the practical application of the purity-laws in the cult preserved their immediacy and social relevance. Afterward the law remained significant, since the menstrual and food rules bore important consequences for everyday life. But going to the Temple no longer was important among the reasons for keeping the laws. Evidence on the interpretation of purity before 70 derives from the writings, originating in widely divergent periods and circles, collected in the Apocrypha and Pseudepigrapha, from the Dead Sea Scrolls, from Philo, and from Paul. Three other important sources, completed after 70, contain information on the period during which the Temple stood as well as on the decades immediately thereafter, when the Temple's influence on the Judaic religious imagination remained formative. These are, first, the writings of Josephus, second, the New Testament Gospels, and third, the rabbinic traditions about the Pharisees before 70.

These several sources are not wholly comparable to one another. Three tell us about the conceptions of purity held by individuals, Paul, Josephus, a priest in Jerusalem, and Philo, a philosopher in Alexandria. Josephus thought of purity primarily in connection with the Temple and the cult. For Philo the Temple was remote, and the purity laws were matters for private practice and figurative interpretation. The Dead Sea writings, by contrast, are not to be assigned to an identifiable author; they represent, and were preserved by, a community which saw itself as the holy sanctuary. The rabbinic traditions about the Pharisees and the New Testament Gospels have in common a considerable history of formulation and transmission by people themselves not witnesses to the events they relate and to the opinions they attribute to their predecessors. But the traditions provide a fairly reliable account of the varieties of interpretation of purity in the respective communities which formulated and preserved them.

Specific references to the biblical laws and metaphors of purity in the three centuries before the destruction of the Second Temple were for the most part routine. Among individual writers, only Philo and (after 70) the author of Hebrews creatively used and developed the concept—for their own purposes to be sure. But purity and impurity played a more central role in the Judaic religious imagination, both at home and in the diaspora, than the references in the preserved remains suggest, for many groups within Judaism had to come to grips with the issues raised by the Temple. In a practical way the resolution of these issues in part was expressed by the treatment of the purity-laws. Every important sect had to define its relationship to the Temple, and one predominant question concerned actually keeping or not keeping the purity laws, making them into a metaphor for the ethical life, or otherwise reinterpreting them. The only thing no one could do was ignore them. A group claiming to constitute a holy community and comparing itself to the Temple would have to interpret in terms of its sectarian life the Temple's chief characteristics, including purity rules, cult, and priesthood. Much that is not explicitly said about purity, therefore, is going to reveal conceptions directly pertinent to it. Much that is said, furthermore, will adumbrate a broader polemic, comprehending purity, against the Jerusalem Temple itself; or, as in the case of Josephus, against people who (in his opinion falsely) claim to defend the Temple's purity; or, as in the case of the Christian community, against the common, literalist conception of the concrete meaning of the laws.

We shall first survey the allusions to purity in the miscellaneous writings collected under the name of Apocrypha and Pseudepigrapha, even though these documents have little in common. The justification for treating them as a group is that, except in Jubilees, purity and impurity occur in routine ways and entirely within the interpretive framework set forth in the Hebrew Scriptures. Jubilees, which we shall examine in connection with the Dead Sea community, is exceptional for its sustained interest in, and use of, the symbols of purity. We shall see unimportant uses of impurity to refer to pollution through, first, idolatry, second, moral transgression, and third, sexual misconduct. In none of the Apocryphal and Pseudepigraphic writings, deriving from various periods and differing social settings, is purity a major concern. Only when we turn to the writings of Philo and Josephus, on the one side, and to the literature of the sects—the nascent Christian community, the *yaḥad*, and the *ḥavurah*—on the other, do we find that pollution and purification become central concerns. Reviewing the commonplace references to purity in a considerable and varied body of writings serves simply to underline the unusual and distinctive importance of purity in these latter, chiefly sectarian settings.

The first important theme is the pollution of the cult by idolatry, a question made prominent by the actions of Antiochus and the consequent purification of the cult by the Maccabees. The decisive, even traumatic, importance of those events will be seen again when we consider the Jewish sects. Just as the Greeks were said to have polluted the cult by putting an idol in the Temple, so the Maccabees later on would be accused of making it unclean by installing "false priests," among other iniquities. The biblical narrative provided further instances of cultic impurity, for reference is made to the Babylonians' "removing" the Temple's purity, as in I Esdras,[1] which merely translates II Chronicles, in this case 36:14, and alludes in passing (1:49) to the defilement of the Jerusalem Temple in the time of King Nabuchodonosor. The pollution of the land by its former inhabitants and their filling it with uncleanness is also mentioned as the reason not to intermarry with them (8:83-4). I Maccabees, written in Hebrew about 100 B.C. by a Palestinian Jew,[2] frequently alludes to the pollution of the sanctuary caused by the edict of Antiochus. Judah Maccabee cleanses the Temple and rededicates it. The primary source of uncleanness here is idolatry; uncleanness is concrete and this-worldly, not a metaphor for some "higher" meaning. While the interpretation of impurity as caused by idolatry is commonplace, its importance cannot be overstated. The purification of the Temple was a primary concern of the Maccabees; its pollution was seen as a horror. In the background of the entire history therefore is concern for purity.

The author of II Maccabees, believed to have lived in the second century B.C.,[3] likewise focuses upon the Temple, for history is written in terms of the freedom of the Temple. Menelaus "laid polluted hands on the sacred vessels"; the pagans had sexual intercourse in the Temple

---

[1] Bruce M. Metzger, *An Introduction to the Apocrypha* (N. Y., 1957), p. 12; texts: S. A. Cook in R. H. Charles, ed., *Apocrypha and Pseudepigrapha of the Old Testament* (Oxford, 1913), I, pp. 24, 53.

[2] Metzger, *op. cit.*, pp. 130-1; also *The First Book of Maccabees*, trans. Sidney Tedesche; Introduction and Commentary by Solomon Zeitlin (N.Y., 1950); texts: 1:44-5 (pollution of sanctuary); 4:36ff. (purification of Temple from idolatrous things); 13:47 (purification of houses in which idols had been located); 13:50 (cleaning the citadel from pollutions). Note also 14:36. Texts: W. O. E. Oesterley in R. H. Charles, ed., *op. cit.*, II, pp. 70-1, 81-2, 116-7, 119.

[3] Metzger, *op. cit.*, pp. 139-141; also *The Second Book of Maccabees*, trans. Sidney Tedesche, Introduction and Commentary by Solomon Zeitlin (N.Y., 1954); texts: 5:16, 27; 6:3-4; trans. James Moffatt, in R. H. Charles, ed., *op. cit.*, I, p. 139.

itself. This last point is not unique to Jason; sex was common ancient Temples, and Jason's noting that fact does not materially add to the interpretation of sexual impurity.

The Psalms of Solomon, written in the middle of the first century B.C. in Hebrew,[1] refer to "utterly polluting the holy things of the Lord" (1:8). Here the source of pollution is moral transgression. The sons of Jerusalem "defiled the holy things of the Lord, profaned with iniquities the offerings of God" (2:3). The daughters of Jerusalem were defiled through unnatural intercourse (2:13). Similarly, "They [the priests] trode the altar of the Lord (coming straight) from all manner of uncleanness; and with menstrual blood they defiled the sacrifices, as though these were common flesh" (8:13). "They defiled Jerusalem and the things that had been hallowed to the name of God," "doing according to their uncleanness just as had their fathers" (8:25-26). Finally, the author prays for deliverance "from the uncleanness of unholy enemies" (17:51); "May God cleanse Israel against the day of mercy" (18:6). Here we find a somewhat broader spectrum of applications of purity, for the "holy things" will be polluted by sexual transgression and other sins; in the Dead Sea writings we shall again find numerous references to pollution of the sacrifices through the defilement imparted by menstrual blood. But for the Psalms of Solomon, the focus of impurity remains the cult, despite the variety of the sources of uncleanness.

IV Maccabees refers to defiling oneself with unclean things; in context these are things offered to idols. Unclean meat is referred to in the same setting; it is rejected because it is bad for one's soul (5:2ff; 8:1,12). The book, written in Greek, probably comes at ca. 50 A.D.[2] Here the cult is figurative, not actual, and, in the Alexandrian mode, reasons are found for the ritual laws.

The Assumption of Moses, originally written in Hasmonean times, about 160 B.C.,[3] refers to the pollution of idolatry: "They shall defile with pollutions the house of their worship" by following strange gods (5:3). A new theme is the contrast between purity and arrogance: "Though with their hands and minds they touch unclean things, yet

---

[1] G. B. Gray, in R. H. Charles, ed., *op. cit.*, II, p. 625; texts: pp. 631-2, 640-1, 651; Albert-Marie Denis, *Introduction aux Pseudépigraphes grecs d'Ancien Testament* (Leiden, 1970), pp. 60-9.

[2] R. B. Townshend in R. H. Charles, ed., *op. cit.*, II, pp. 654, 656; Moses Hadas, *The Third and Fourth Books of Maccabees* (N.Y., 1953) places it in 40 A.D. Texts: pp. 670-675, pass.

[3] R. H. Charles, in R. H. Charles, ed., *op. cit.*, II, p. 407, 411; texts: pp. 418-420.

their mouth shall speak great things, and they shall say furthermore, 'Do not touch me, lest though shouldst pollute me in the place' [where I stand]" (7:9-10). But this theme is not much of a development of the biblical contrast between moral impurity and ritual purity. It will recur in the Synoptic Gospels.

The Letter of Jeremiah, written in Hebrew or Aramaic some time after 300 B.C.,[1] warns against idolatry, pointing out that sacrifices to idols may be touched by women in menstruation or at childbirth (vs. 29), therefore are unclean. Here, therefore, purity serves as a reason for separation from gentile offerings, but the concrete reason—they are unclean—is unexpected. The biblical view that idolatry in itself is unclean is a metaphor and ignores the uncleanness imparted by failure of idolators to observe biblical purity laws.

The Book of Tobit,[2] composed about 190-170 B.C., represents its hero as a Galilean Jew of the eighth century B.C. The author makes use of uncleanness as a simple metaphor in reference to illicit sexual behavior: "I am pure from all uncleanness with man, and I never polluted my name" (3:15).

The author of the book of Judith, probably a Palestinian Jew of the middle second century B.C.,[3] has the heroine scrupulously obey the law of Moses. The gentiles are going to defile the tabernacle and profane the sanctuary (9:8). The reference to Judith's washing herself and "entering in clean" (12:7-9) may allude to a ceremonial washing. While it is insisted that Judith ate only her own food in the camp of Holofernes, curiously, the matter of the impurity of gentiles' food is not made explicit; their food is not called unclean. But that surely is the point of the story, and, once again, absence of concrete allusions to purity is not significant.

The use of impurity as a metaphor for moral defilement, as much as for sexual sin, recurs in the Testaments of the Twelve Patriarchs, probably a Palestinian work of about the first century B.C.[4] Here, however, the practical effects of impurity remain linked to the cult; the priest should refrain from sexual misdeeds so as not to pollute the cult. The idea of purity is extended to general moral, chiefly sexual,

---

[1] Bruce Metzger, *op. cit.*, p. 99; C. J. Ball, in R. H. Charles, ed., *op. cit.*, I, p. 604.

[2] Bruce Metzger, *op. cit.*, p. 31; Frank Zimmerman, *The Book of Tobit* (N.Y., 1958); text: D. C. Simpson, in R. H. Charles, ed., *op. cit.*, I. p. 209.

[3] Bruce Metzger, *op. cit.*, pp. 43ff.; texts: A. E. Cowley, in R. H. Charles, ed., *op. cit.*, I, pp. 258-261-2.

[4] R. H. Charles, in R. H. Charles, ed. ,*op. cit.*, II, p. 282; texts: pp. 208-212, 326, 344, 347, 358, 364-5; Denis, *op. cit.*, pp. 49-59.

conduct. The Testaments refer to Shechem's defiling Dinah (T. Levi 7:4). Levi is anointed as a priest (8:5) with pure water. The priesthood is warned against fornication, which will pollute the holy place: "Take therefore a wife without blemish or pollution" (T. Levi 9:10). Before entering the holy place, the priest is to bathe, also when offering a sacrifice and after the sacrifice. In the earliest stratum, Levi is to keep away from all defilement and all sin (Aramaic fragment, 1. 13). Defiling is further used with reference to illicit sexual relations (14:6-7). When the priesthood is profaned, and the sacrifices polluted, the holy places will be laid waste, "and you shall have no place that is clean" (T. Levi 16:1-5). The Testament of Issachar advises the reader not to look on the beauty of women, "lest he should pollute his mind with corruption" (T. Issachar 4:4). Those who walk in zeal for the Lord are altogether clean; they are compared to stags and hinds, because they seem to be unclean but are altogether clean (T. Asher 4:5). Adultery is called uncleanness in the Testament of Joseph (4:6-7). One should have a pure heart and undefiled lips. The same view of uncleanness occurs in T. Benjamin 8:1-2. "The pure mind, though encompassed by the defilements of earth, rather cleanseth them and is not itself defiled" (8:3). The Greek fragment of T. Levi states, "And always wash thy hands and feet when thou goest to the altar and when thou goest forth from the sanctuary let no blood touch thy garments. And thy hands and thy feet wash continually from all flesh" (1s. 53-5), also familiar in Jubilees. In the Testaments, therefore, the established set of interpretations is reviewed, with emphasis on the concept of purity as a metaphor for the moral life.

For Ben Sira purity provides a source of routine homiletic dicta on the moral life. Writing in Hebrew in about 180 B.C.,[1] Ben Sira refers explicitly to corpse-uncleanness: "He who washes after contact with a dead body and touches it again—what has he gained by his bathing? So a man fasting for his sins and again doing the same—who will listen to his prayer? And what hath he gained by his humiliation?" (34:25). Just as it is futile to become clean and immediately thereafter to contract uncleanness, so it is futile to seek forgiveness without repentence.

We conclude this rapid survey with a few miscellaneous references. Book III of the Sybelline Oracles, commonly assigned to an Egyptian

[1] Bruce Metzger, *op. cit.*, p. 78; text: G. H. Box and W. O. E. Oesterly, in R. H. Charles, ed., *op. cit.*, I, p. 436.

Jew about 140 B.C.,[1] refers to the race of Phoenicians, who live a lawless and unclean life and open their mouth for uncleanness (III:496-8). They open their filthy mouth with falsehood (500). This commonplace use of purity seems wholly unrelated to the cult.

The author of the Wisdom of Solomon, probably writing in Greek in the first century B.C.,[2] refers in passing to the fact that the righteous man abstains from the ways of the wicked as from uncleannesses (2:16). To him, therefore, the good man will be morally pure.

The collection of apocalyptic literature assembled in the Book of Enoch contains only routine allusions to purity, so we need not be detained by the complex problems of its sources, divisions, authorship, and dating.[3] The first occurs in 5:4, which refers to "impure mouths" speaking against God's greatness. The Noah-book includes a reference to angels' taking wives "to defile themselves with them" (7:1). The same source refers to "cleansing the earth from all oppression, unrighteousness, sin, godlessness, and all the uncleanness that is wrought upon the earth." The earth shall be cleansed by the flood from all defilement, sin, punishment, and torment (10:18-22).

Josephus, the Jewish general and historian who in 75 wrote the history of the war of 66-73 and about twenty years later published a history of the Jews, interprets or explains the purity laws primarily in relationship to the Temple cult. He rarely treats purity in other than a cultic setting. This viewpoint was natural to him, for he was a priest and took for granted that the Mosaic legislation about purity applied primarily to the Temple. In his writings on the Temple, purity and impurity seldom occur in a metaphorical sense. Josephus's view that the purity-laws are for the Temple's protection is stated as follows: "In view of the sacrifices the Law has prescribed purifications for various occasions, after a funeral, after child-birth, after conjugal union, and many others" (Against Apion 2:198).

In his account of the Maccabean wars, he refers to Judah Maccabee's cleaning the Temple area and replacing the polluted vessels (War 1:39). He moreover alludes to the burning of the red heifer and the use of its ashes in the rite of purification from corpse-uncleanness. The ashes

---

[1] H. M. Lanchester, in R. H. Charles, ed., *op. cit.*, II, p. 372. Text: pp. 387-8.

[2] Bruce Metzger, *op. cit.*, p. 67; Joseph Reider, ed. and trans., *The Book of Wisdom* (N.Y., 1957); text: Samuel Holmes, in R. H. Charles, ed., *op. cit.*, I, p. 538.

[3] R. H. Charles, in R. H. Charles, ed., *op. cit.*, II, pp. 170-1; texts: pp. 190, 192, 194-5; Denis, *op. cit.*, pp. 15-30.

were collected by a man who was ceremonially clean; he deposited them in a place of spotless purity (Antiquities 4:80). When someone was polluted by contact with a corpse, the ashes were put in water drawn from a well or spring, and the polluted man was sprinkled on the third and seventh days, a sprig of hyssop being used to dip out the water. After telling of a slaughter of Jews in the Temple, he does not claim the cultic area was purified with the water of purification. For instance, he notes that when Pompey took the Temple, many priests were butchered at the altar; the necessarily consequent corpse-uncleanness is not even alluded to. Pompey thereafter enters the Temple and looks at its treasures: "However, he touched neither these nor any other of the sacred treasures, and the very day after the capture of the Temple, gave orders to the custodians to cleanse it and to resume the customary sacrifices" (War 1:148-153). The cleansing of the Temple from corpse-uncleanness—a more severe source of uncleanness does not exist—is not described. It would have been a considerable operation. Josephus's persistent silence on how the Temple was purified is curious. Perhaps such technical details would have delayed the story and bored the gentiles and probably many of the diaspora Jews for whom he was writing.

That the purity-laws practically governed the Temple, moreover, is everywhere taken for granted, Hyrcanus tried to keep Herod out of Jerusalem by posting orders that aliens could not come into Jerusalem during the festival, a period of purification. Herod come anyhow (War. 1:229-30).

Since the purity-laws did apply, the defilement of the Temple becomes one of the chief accusations against the Zealots, whom Josephus despised. Zealot blood defiled the sanctuary (War 4:202). In the civil war between the Zealots and Ananus, Ananus refrained from assaulting the Temple portals, for, if he were victorious, he would thereby "introduce those crowds without previous purifications" (War 4:205). So the opponents of the Zealots protected the Temple. Josephus cites his own speech to the Zealots. He says that when Titus learned the continual sacrifice had ended in the Temple, he sent Josephus to talk to John of Gischala, the Zealot chief, asking him to leave the city and fight outside of it: "Without involving the city and the sanctuary in his own ruin... He should no longer pollute the Holy Place nor sin against God." Josephus accuses John of not having kept the Temple pure for God, of having defiled the holy place. God has been deprived of his daily food, and the Romans are not at fault. John himself caused the interruption of the sacrifices. The city certainly will fall, for "God himself with the Romans is bringing the fire to purge his Temple and exterminate a city laden with pollutions" (War 6:93-111). John of Gischala not only ate unlawful food, but "abandoned the established rules of purity of our forefathers; so that it could no longer excite surprise that one guilty of such made impiety towards God failed to observe towards men the offices of gentleness and charity" (War. 7:264). Keeping the purity-laws, seen as an act of piety, is equivalent to deeds of charity; he who does not do the one is unlikely to do the other. Josephus is particularly eager to emphasize the Zealots' indifference to the Temple's purity, because they themselves probably stressed their hope to purify the Temple, as had the Maccabees before them.[1] The Maccabees had purified the land of all pollution (Antiquities 12:285-6). But God himself turned away from the Temple "because he deemed the Temple to be no longer a clean dwelling place for Him, [he] brought the Romans upon us and purification by fire upon the city ... With such pollution did the deeds of the brigands infect the city" (Antiquties 20:166-7).

The Zealots therefore are shown to have been indifferent to the sanctity of the Temple, while their moderate opponents were scrupulous to preserve its purity. Josephus makes the same point time and again. Ananus and his party "were anxious on their side to preserve the Temple from pollution and that none of their countrymen should fall within its walls" (War 4:215). "These frenzied men," that is, the Zealots, "stopped short of no impiety." They admitted those who wished to offer sacrifices, carefully searching them, but then many were killed, priests and worshippers alike, by the missiles of war: "The dead bodies of natives and aliens, of priests and laity, were mingled in a mass, and the blood of all manner of corpses formed pools in the courts of God" (War 5:15-19). What rite of purification follows? Josephus says the Romans entered to purge with fire Jerusalem's internal pollutions (War 5:19)—a rite of purification no where alluded to in Scripture. So the Zealot's concern for purity, perhaps in the model of the Maccabees, produced the defilement of Temple, part of Josephus' broad indictment of Zealotry.

[1] Martin Hengel, *Die Zeloten. Untersuchungen zur jüdischen Freiheitsbewegung in der Zeit von Herodes I bis 70 N. Chr.* (Leiden, 1961), pp. 188-234, in particular, pp. 211-226. On the Zealot's view of the Maccabees, William Reuben Farmer, *Maccabees, Zealots and Josephus* (N.Y., 1956). On Hengel's larger view of the Zealots, see Morton Smith, "Zealots and Sicarii, their Origins and Relation," *Harvard Theological Review* 64, I, 1971, pp. 1-19.

Describing the Temple's purity, Josephus stresses three things. First, the "law of purification" was that no foreigner could enter the holy place (War 5:194). Second, people afflicted with gonorrhoea or leprosy could not enter the city. Women during their menstruation could not come to the Temple, and "even when free of impurity" had to stay within their boundary. Third, men not thoroughly clean could not enter the inner court, and even priests could not go there when undergoing purification (War 5:227, 6:426-7; Apion 2:103-4). In Antiquities 9:260ff., he has Hezekiah tell the priests to put impiety out of their minds and to purify themselves from their former pollutions and to purify the cult "and restore it to the ancient service of our country, for in this way we might make God put aside his anger and become gracious." Josiah purified the entire country of idolatry (Antiquities 10:70). In the history (Antiquities 3:261-4), he says Moses banished from the city those with leprosy and contageous disease (gonorrhoea), as well as women during their menstrual period. Those who have paid the last rites to the dead—therefore unclean with corpse-uncleanness—likewise are kept out. One who has an issue in his sleep will "cleanse himself" by a cold bath. Women after child-birth cannot enter the Temple or touch the sacrifices (Antiquities 3:269).

The law against lepers forms part of a considerable polemic, this time against Manetho, an Egyptian anti-Semite. In Antiquities 3:265, Josephus refers to the "absurd charge" of those who assert Moses was forced to flee Egypt on account of his being a leper, and was placed in command of all others who had been expelled from the country on the same pretext. In refutation Josephus cites the Mosaic legislation requiring lepers to stay outside of the city and to be treated like corpses. "Moses would never have issued to his own humiliation statutes such as these." Among many nations lepers are honored, not exiled; they may enter sacred courts and Temples (II Kings 5:1, 18). So Moses and his host could have laid down concerning lepers laws of the most favorable character, instead of imposing any penalty on them (Antiquities 3:266-8). People who say Moses was a leper are jealous; he acted only for God's honor. In his later treatise, Against Apion ("Or, On the Antiquity of the Jews"), Josephus returns to this theme. The enemies of the Jews assert the libel, motivated by hatred and envy, that the Jews were expelled from Egypt because they were lepers or otherwise polluted. Manetho, to whom this accusation is attributed, says all the maimed people were first segregated, then expelled (Against Apion, 233-236; also, Lysimachus, 1:304-9). But these accusations are ridiculous. Among the many reasons adduced against Manetho's claim is the evidence of the Mosaic laws (Against Apion 1:279-286). Moses forbids lepers to reside in towns, they have to be solitary vagrants, and whoever touches them or lives under the same roof with them is unclean. If the malady passes, the leper has to be purified and offer numerous sacrifices. Would people brought together because they were lepers have enacted laws to their own disgrace and injury?

Josephus refers to purity outside the Temple cult in two contexts. With reference to the building of Tiberius by Herod Antipas (Antiquities 18:36-8) he says that people had to be forced to live there, "For he knew that this settlement was contrary to the law and tradition of the Jews because Tiberias was built on the site of tombs that had been obliterated, of which there were many there. And our law declares that such settlers are unclean for seven days." In point of fact, that uncleanness should have been important only if the settlers later on planned to visit the Temple, in which case they could purify themselves, or if they proposed to preserve purity under ordinary circumstances. The second, and more important context, is the purity-rites of the Essenes. They regard oil as defiling and do not use it; they keep skin dry and always dress in white (War 2:123). "At the fifth hour they gather in one place, gird their loins with linen cloths, bathe their bodies in cold water, then the initiated, now pure, go to the refectory and eat their meal, as in a sacred shrine" (War 2:129-131). Supper is eaten in the same way. A candidate for admission is kept as a probationer for a year; then he is allowed "to share the purer kind of holy water" (War 2:138). But before he may touch the common food, he is made to swear oaths regarding piety, justice and obedience, and so forth. If one is expelled from the group, he still is bound by "their oaths and usages," so he cannot eat other men's food and dies of starvation (War 2:143-4). The order is divided into four grades; if a junior member touches a senior one, the latter must take a bath, as after contact with an outsider (War 2:150). Purity does not enter Josephus's description of the Pharisees (War 2:164ff.). In the later description of the sects (Antiquities 18:12ff.). Josephus says the Essenes send offerings to the Temple, but employ "a different ritual of purification" (Antiquities 18:19). They therefore are barred from the inner precincts of the Temple frequented by all the people, and perform their rites by themselves. The text here is unclear, and its sense therefore in doubt. Otherwise, Antiquities 18:18-22 omits reference to purity-laws. Josephus does not supply the theory according to which the Essenes kept ritually clean outside of the Temple, nor does he remark on the peculiarity of their concern for extracultic purity. In his account of history from the beginnings to the present, Josephus further alludes to purity.[1]

Josephus occasionally suggests there are "higher reasons" behind the purity laws, or that uncleanness testifies to some other sin. For example he explains the requirement for purification after sexual relations (Lev. 15:18) between husband and wife: "For the Law regards this act as involving a partition of the soul [part of it going] into another place [There is transference of part of the soul or life-principle from the father]; for it suffers both when being implanted in bodies and when severed from them by birth. That is why the Law has enjoined purifications in all such cases" (Against Apion 2:203). This explanation does not occur in any other Jewish source, nor does Josephus elaborate it. Clearly, Josephus regards the uncleanness imputed to leprosy as a penalty imposed upon the leper: "It was in God's honor that he [Moses] thus acted" in prohibiting lepers to enter the Temple and declaring them sources of impurity. But Josephus does not explain why God was honored in this way, or what is dishonorable about the favorable treatment of lepers in other cultures (Antiquities 3:266-8). In his account of John the Baptist, Josephus says John had exhorted the Jews to lead righteous lives as a preliminary to baptism: "They must not employ it to gain pardon for whatever sins they

[1] He explains that Moses segregated the Levites, made them a holy tribe, and purified them with the waters of perennial springs and with sacrifices (Antiquities 3:258). The impurity deriving from sexual intercourse is alluded to in connection with the story of David and Saul. When David was absent from a meal, it is assumed "that he had been delayed by not having finished his purification after sexual intercourse" (Antiquities 6:238). Solomon set up a pool in the Temple for the use of the priests, to wash their hands and feet when they entered the Temple (Antiquities 8:87). He marked off the sacred precinct, so that only those people "distinguished by purity and by their observance of the laws might enter" (Antiquities 8:96).

Josephus praises Agrippas for residing in Jerusalem and scrupulously observing the traditions of his people: "He neglected no rite of purification and no day passed for him without the prescribed sacrifice" (Antiquities 19:331). When he was accused of "unholiness" which would have excluded him from the Temple, "since the right of entrance was restricted to those who were ritually clean" (Antiquities 19:333), Agrippas asked what is contrary to the law, and, hearing no answer, dismissed the accuser. But the MSS evidence here is unclear; the allusion may have been to the exclusion of those who were not natives, not to those who were unclean. See Louis H. Feldman, *Josephus*. IX. *Jewish Antiquities, Books XVIII-XX* (Cambridge, 1965), pp. 370-1, ns. b-c. "The only reason for claiming that Agrippas ought to have been excluded is that he was impure." I do not follow Feldman's reasoning.

committed, but as a consecration of the body implying that the soul was already cleansed by right behavior" (Antiquities 18:117-8). But, overall, Josephus stands a long way from the position of Philo, for whom the purity-laws are wholly figurative.

The tendency of Egyptian Jews allegorically to explain purity and impurity in terms of something other than the cult and its requirements begins long before Philo. We have already observed a few 'reasons' for specific laws supplied by Egyptian Jews. The first substantial effort occurs in the Letter of Aristeas, which purports to explain the translation of the Torah into Greek, dramatically set in Alexandria in 278-270 B.C.[1] The letter itself dates from the second or first century B.C.; an Alexandrian Jew wrote it. He states, "Therefore, lest we should be corrupted by any abomination or our lives be perverted by evil communications, he [Moses] hedged us round on all sides by rules of purity, affecting alike what we eat or drink or touch or hear or see" (142). Thus, for example, Moses prohibited mice and weasels, not out of regard to them, "but for the sake of righteousness, to aid the quest for virtue..." The birds Jews do use are "tame and distinguished by their cleanliness" (145). The contrary is the case for the birds not to be eaten. It is considered unseemly "even to touch such unclean animals" (149). Most other men defile themselves by promiscuous intercourse (152), but Israelites are kept separate from such sins. Mice "defile and destroy" (164), weasels defile because they "conceive through the ears and bring forth through the mouth. And it is for this reason that a like practice is declared unclean in men. For by embodying in speech all that they receive through the ears, they involve others in evils and work no ordinary impurity, being themselves altogether defiled by the pollution of impiety" (166). This brings us close to the later rabbinic notion that gossiping causes the uncleanness of leprosy. "And so concerning meats and things unclean, creeping things and wild beasts, the whole system aims at righteousness and righteous relationships between man and man" (169). Before the Jews pray, they wash their hands, "a token that they have done no evil" (306). One cannot suppose the purity-laws here have been thoroughly allegorized, that is, explained in terms of some other, wholly separate set of ideas. The rules of purity here are rationally explained chiefly as a discipline. They are for the sake of virtue, frequently symbolizing,

---

[1] Herbert T. Andrews, in R. H. Charles, ed., *op. cit.*, II, pp. 85-7; also Moses Hadas, *Aristeas to Philocrates (Letter of Aristeas)*, (N.Y., 1951); texts: Andrews, pp. 103, 108-110, 120-1.

in one detail or another, a higher value. For a systematic effort at extreme allegorization one rather has to turn to Philo. That Philo will allegorize the purity-laws may be taken for granted. The interesting question is, Which laws does he choose, and in terms of what other issues or ideas does he attempt to interpret them?

Philo takes into account a wide range of biblical purity-laws and pays close attention to their details. He contributes far more than generalized homilies about ethical purity or sexual impurity. To be sure, he makes use of uncleanness in terms entirely divorced from the Scriptural sense. For example he says that all genuine votaries of philosophy discern truths which none of the unclean may touch: "By unclean I mean all those who, without ever tasting education at all ... have changed the stamp of wisdom's beauty into the ugliness of sophistry" (Every Good Man Is Free 4). The use of "uncleanness" here bears no resemblance to any hitherto examined. But more commonly Philo will resort to Scriptural concepts, even for his more allegorical interpretations of purity. In the prophetic and sapiential tradition, he contrasts purity and wickedness. Wickedness makes purity impure, as it makes truth into falsehood: "Furthermore, they cleanse their bodies with lustrations and purifications, but they neither wish nor practise to wash off from their souls the passions by which life is defiled" (On the Cherubim, 94-5). Here is a second-level metaphor. First, purity is treated as a metaphor for moral cleanness, as in Scripture. But second, it further serves as a metaphor for self-control, since the self-controlled are not 'defiled' by the passions. Without self-control, "A man may submit to sprinklings with holy water and to purifications, befouling his understanding while cleasing his body" (The Worse Attacks the Better 20), a commonplace contrast between cultic purity and a "spiritual" impurity.

One may, moreover, become figuratively clean by cultivating the practice of rendering thanks and honor to God: "We shall be pure from wrongdoing and wash away the filthiness which defiles our lives in thought and word and deed. For it is absurd that a man should be forbidden to enter the temples save after bathing and cleansing his body, and yet should attempt to pray and sacrifice with a heart still soiled and spotted" (The Unchangeableness of God 7-8). One must resolve not to commit further sin, and to wash away the past (*ibid.*, 9). Likewise the tabernacle's being "set up in the midst of our uncleanness" (Lev. 16:16) means that we have through the tabernacle, which is wisdom, "wherewith to scour and wash away all that defiles our life" (Who Is the Heir 113). The contrast between impurity and vice, purity and virtue, has been supplied by Scripture; what is new is Philo's extension of the process of allegorization to what has *already* been treated as a metaphor, so a second-level metaphor.

The interpretation of cultic and priestly purity emphasizes the spiritual or philosophical virtue symbolized by purity. The priests have to wash their hands and feet, which symbolizes a blameless life: "years of cleanliness employed in laudable actions" (Moses 2:138). The priests must not be blemished; if they suffer leprosy or a seminal emission, they must not touch the holy table; if they touch an impure object, they must not partake of consecrated food. Philo cites these rules (Lev. 22:4-7; The Special Laws 1:118) without comment. But in discussing the regulations for those who offer the sacrifices (Special Laws 1:257), he offers the general rule: "The law should have such a person pure in body and soul, the soul purged of its passions ... the body of the defilements which commonly beset it." Sprinklings and ablutions clean the body. The soul is purified by contemplation of the perfection of the sacrificial victim: "For if you observe this with your reason rather than with your eyes you will proceed to wash away the sins and defilements with which you have besmeared your whole life ... For you will find that all this careful scrutiny of the animal is a symbol representing in a figure the reformation of your own conduct" (The Special Laws 1:259-60). As to the purification of the body from contamination by death, the rule that one must await seven days and be sprinkled twice is alluded to, but not given a higher meaning.

The water of purification is mentioned, along with the rites of dipping hyssop and sprinkling with it: "Moses would have those who come to serve him ... first know themselves and of what substance these selves are made" (Special Laws 1:263). The body consists of earth and water, so is purged by ashes and water, which are not worthy of esteem.[1] If a man recognizes this, he will turn away from self-conceit and pride. The earth and water say to the man undergoing purification, "We are the substance of which your body exists, and to which you will return." Philo describes the rite of the red heifer, saying that he elsewhere explains the allegory, though no such passage is in his preserved works. "Thus," Philo says, "those who mean to resort to the Temple must needs have their bodies made clean and bright, and before their bodies, their souls... The mind is cleansed by wisdom, and

[1] The same idea occurs in Midrash Tanḥuma Ḥuqat 14. But compare Naso 5.

the truths of wisdom's teaching which guide its steps to the contemplation of the universe..." (Special Laws 1:269-70; On Dreams 1:209-212). The sanctuary is the true home, and the worshipper there presents himself as victim. "In bringing themselves they offer the best of sacrifices, the full and truly perfect oblation of noble living" (Special Laws 1:271-2), an idea that will recur in Hebrews. In respect to the sacrifice of the Passover, finally, Philo explains that to prevent the unworthy and unclean hands of the Egyptians from touching the remains, "He handed them over to an undefiled king, the fire" (Questions and Answers on Exodus, 1:18). The fire is a means of purification, an idea present in the Gospel's theory of eschatological purification, and possibly beginning with Malachi 3:2-4, "But who can endure the day of his coming ... for he is like a refiner's fire."

The allegorization of other rules of cleanness tends to move beyond the appeal to live a "blameless life" and maintain the right attitude. For instance, the uncleanness imparted by a corpse, to every open vessel under the same roof (Num. 19:15), is explained as follows: This implies "that wretchedness is due to the different parts of the soul having been left loose and gaping and unfastened, while proper ordering of life and speech is the result of those being kept close and tight" (The Worse Attacks the Better 103; Confusion of Tongues 166-7). That the Nazir is defiled if someone dies suddenly beside him (Num. 6:9, 12) produces an observation on the difference between voluntary and involuntary sin (On Husbandry 175-7). The high priests shall not go into any dead soul (Lev. 21:11). The Hebrew means, "shall not go into a house in which there is a dead body," but Philo allegorizes, "Death of soul is a life in the company of vice, so that what is meant is that he is never to come into contact with any polluting object, and of these, folly always stinks" (On Flight and Finding, 113). Mourners, made unclean by a corpse, are banished from the sacred precincts, but afterward they are readmitted—this in respect to the second Passover (Moses 2:228-231). This law teaches that those who have touched the dead are regarded as unclean, so as to guard against anyone's helping to bring about the death of another (Special Laws 3:205). The vessels and furniture in the house of a corpse are unclean: "For a man's soul is a precious thing, and when it departs to seek another home, all that will be left behind is defiled, deprived as it is of the divine image. For it is the mind of man which has the form of God, being shaped in conformity with the ideal archetype, the Word that is above all" (Special Laws 3:206-7). Whatever touches the corpse is unclean, and this applies to the temperament and characteristics of soul, "For the unjust and impious man is in the truest sense unclean" (Special Laws 3:209).

The reason a menstrual woman is unclean is that a man will "remember the lesson that the generative seeds should not be wasted fruitlessly for the sake of a gross and untimely pleasure" (Special Laws 3:32).

Philo treats numerous details of the law of leprosy (Lev. 14:57ff.) with greatest care. For example, one must remove the houses on which the leprosy-signs appear, because, "When diverse qualities, the handiwork of pleasure and desires and passions ... press and weigh down the whole soul ... lowering its level, we are to get rid of the principles which cause the infirmity and introduce in their place good healthy principles by means of a training under the law or indeed of a good education" (The Worse Attacks the Better 16). Lamech's name means being brought low. This name has two meanings. The former kind of "being brought low" is a species of leprosy: "For when the uniform and healthy appearance of the flesh is impaired and the mischief is visible below the surface, the lawgiver says that the cruel disease of leprosy has set in [Lev. 13:3]" (The Posterity and Exile of Cain 47). If a living color ("raw flesh") arises in the leper, he is defiled (Lev. 13:14-15). Now this is opposed to the natural view. Normally, one supposes the healthy are corrupted by diseased or dead things; but the healthy and living do not corrupt their opposites. However, the lawgiver thereby teaches, "It is the healthy and living which produce the condition which is tainted with pollution. For the healthy and living color in the soul, when it makes a genuine appearance upon it, is Conviction. When this Conviction comes to the surface, it makes a record of all the soul's transgressions and rebukes ... it almost without ceasing. And the soul when thus convicted sees in their true light its practices ... which were contrary to right reason, and then perceives that it is foolish and intemperate and unjust and infected with pollution" (The Unchangeableness of God, 123-6). The paradox is continued: The leper who is only partially a leper is unclean, but if the leprosy spreads throughout, he is clean (Lev. 13:11-13). Through this paradox the lawgiver shows that "such wrongdoings as are involuntary ... are pure and devoid of guilt ... but voluntary sins, even though the space they cover be not large, are convicted by the judge within the soul" (Unchangeableness of God, 127-8). Further, the two-natured leprosy, which flowers into two colors, shows voluntary wickedness, "For the soul has within it the healthy, lively upright reason, and yet does not use it as its pilot ... But the leprosy which changes into a single white appearance represents involuntary error, when the mind is throughout bereft of reasoning power..." (Unchangeableness of God, 129-130).

Then there is the leprosy of a house, with the curious provision in the law that before the priest declares the house is unclean, it is not unclean. So before the priest goes in, the things within are clean; after his declaration they are unclean. Therefore everything should be taken out before the priest goes in, to prevent uncleanness. "Yet we should have expected just the opposite, that when a man who has been purified ... has come within the house, its contents should thereby be bettered and pass from impurity to purity. But here we find that they do not even remain in the same position as before, but actually shift into the inferior region at the entrance of the priest." What this means is, "For so long as the divine reason has not come into our soul ... all its works are free from guilt, since the priest ... who alone can admonish and bring it to wisdom, is far away ... But when the true priest, Conviction, enters us, like a pure ray of light, we see in their real value the unholy thoughts which were stored within our soul ... So Conviction, discharging his priest-like task, defiles all these and bids them all be cleared out and carried away, that he may see the soul's house in its natural bare condition and heal whatever sicknesses have arisen in it" (Unchangeableness of God 131-5).

The state of repose, "because it is a stand-still of the vices and passions in the soul (which are figured by leprosy), is exempt from indictment, while the state of motion and progression is rightly held liable to arraignment. That is why Moses ruled that if the leprosy spread, it is unclean, but if it is quiescent, it is clean" (On Sobriety 49). Leprosy is a changeful disease, which assumes many different forms; it symbolizes "lack of firmness of judgment and an unstable, agitated life" (On Dreams 1:202).[1]

---

[1] Further explanations of purity-laws include these:

The uncleanness of the creature which crawls on its belly (Lev. 11:42) is assigned to "the lover of pleasure... always going after the belly and the pleasures of the adjoining parts...Accordingly a man is unclean who is given up to the one thing, pleasure..." (Allegorical Interpretation 3:139). This is a fairly obvious homily.

Noah leads into the ark seven clean beasts but only two of the unclean because the hebdomad is pure but the dyad impure, for by nature the number seven is truly pure, but two is impure, "because it is not empty and not dense" (Questions and Answers on Genesis 2:12). The clean beasts (Gen. 8:20) "are the sense and the mind of the wise man" (Questions and Answers on Genesis 2:52).

Before Moses could receive the Torah, he had to be clean in soul and in body,

In his extensive discussion of the Essenes and Therapeutae, Philo only once alludes to purity. He states that the Essenes show their love of God by a multitude of proofs, "by religious purity *(hagneia)*," as well as other virtues (Every Good Man Is Free 84). At no point does he make reference to purity-rules or rites, lustrations or other rituals of purification, sources of impurity, and the like in his description of the Essenes. F. A. Colson, however, asserts that Philo "indicates knowledge" of the Essenes' ceremonial ablutions by the single word *hagneia*.[1]

The founders of the *yaḥad*, the community at Qumran, were Temple priests, who saw themselves as continuators of the true priestly line, that is, the sons of Zaddok.[2] For them the old Temple service was invalidated because it was defiled. The deliverance would begin with the rise of the sect and the coming of the teacher. They further rejected the calendar then followed in Jerusalem. They therefore set out to create a new Temple until God would come and, through the Messiah in the line of Aaron, establish the Temple once again. The Qumran community believed that the presence of God had left Jerusalem and had come to the Dead Sea. According to Bertil Gärtner, the *community* now constituted the new Temple, just as some elements in early Christianity saw the new Temple in the body of Christ, in the Church, the Christian community. In some measure, this represents a "spiritualization" of the old Temple, for the Temple now is the community, and the Temple worship is effected through the community's study and fulfillment of the Torah.

While purity is a central issue for the *yaḥad*, the ideas associated with it do not form an equivalently important concern.[3] The Admonition

to have no dealings with any passion, purifying himself from all the calls of mortal nature, food and drink and intercourse with women (Moses 2:68). The people likewise had to be pure, so they cleansed themselves with ablutions and lustrations for three days and washed their clothes and dressed in white (Decalogue 45).

The water used to test the suspected adulteress is to be pure and living, since, if the woman is guiltless, her conduct is pure and she deserves to live (Special Laws 3:59).

[1] *Philo*, Vol. IX (Cambridge, 1954), p. 515.

[2] The *Yaḥad* as a priestly community: Frank Moore Cross, Jr., *The Ancient Library of Qumran* (N. Y., 1961), pp. 94-5, 101, 128; J. T. Milik, *Ten Years of Discovery in the Wilderness of Judaea* (London, 1959), pp. 83, 95, 105; and especially, Bertil Gärtner *The Temple and the Community in Qumran and the New Testament* (Cambridge, 1965), pp. 1-15, esp. pp. 12-13.

[3] Translations follow, for the Damascus Covenant (CD), Chaim Rabin, *The Zadokite Documents* (Oxford, 1958); for the other passages, G. Vermes, *The Dead Sea Scrolls in English* (Harmondsworth, 1970), and A. Dupont-Sommer, *The Essene Writings from Qumran*, trans. G. Vermes (Cleveland and N.Y., 1957). Note also the CD fragment in J. T. Milik, "Fragment...du document de Damas...," *Revue*

of the Zadokite Fragments refers (CD 3:17) to the generation of the wilderness, which was defiled with impiety of man and menstrual impurity (DRKY NDH). Isaiah's prophecy, "Fear and the pit and snare are upon thee," (Is. 24:17) refers to "whoredom, wealth, and conveying uncleanness to the sanctuary." The one leads to the other (CD 4:17-8). Isaiah refers to *paḥad*, *paḥat*, and *paḥ*, the third meaning "snare." But spelled *pakh*, the word means a flask or jar, very frequently used for oil-jars. Since Josephus says the sect regarded oil as impure (War 2:123), perhaps the basis for the exegesis before us is a play on the words *pakh* and *paḥ*.

As to the defiling of the Jerusalem sanctuary, this is explained (CD

---

biblique 73, 1966, pp. 105-6, which seems to indicate leprosy is caused by an evil spirit.

On leprosy as caused by evil spirits in Milik's fragment, I reproduce the pertinent remarks of E. Toff in the proceedings of the Harvard Divinity School New Testament Seminar XIII, for March 25, 1972, who states the matter in detail. I am grateful to Professor John Strugnell both for calling my attention to the Milik fragment and for supplying a copy of Toff's paper.

> The description of this disease is rather lengthy, perhaps more lengthy than that of the other kinds of leprosy. The lengthiness is caused partly by the nature of the disease and partly by an additional reason: The whole description of the disease is adapted to the dualistic way of thinking of the sect. The *locus classicus* for this view is the passage 1QS 3:13-4:26. The world is dominated by two spirits *(rûḥôt)*, created by God, the spirit of truth and the spirit of perversity (*ib.*, 3:18, 19). For our purpose it is important to note that the realm of disease and discovering is ascribed to these two spirits. About the spirit of perversity it is said "all men's afflictions *(n^{e}gi'ehem)* and all the moments of tribulation are due to this being's malevolent sway" (3:23; Gaster's translation). Every one who walks in the ways of the spirit of perversity gets a "multitude of afflictions at the hands of all the angels of destruction" (4:12). On the other hand, those who walk in the ways of the spirit of truth are rewarded with *marpe'* (healing, health) and *šalôm* (4:7), and God will "destroy every spirit of perversity from within his flesh" (4:21).
>
> In the context of the phenomenon of leprosy upon the head and in the beard, this view appears as the belief that the beginning of the disease occurs when the bad spirit enters the head of the beard. The use of the word *hārûāḥ* (the spirit, 1:6) should be considered as a euphemism. If the spirit is very strong the man will remain a leper. If there are no additional signs of the disease, however, and the man is declared clean, it is thought that the spirit of life dominates the body (again). The symbol of the spirit of truth is changed here to the spirit of life. This picture fits the situation better, and one may consider the spirit of life as the embodiment of the spirit of truth in individual men.
>
> The dualistic view of the disease is to be seen also in the document's stress on the matter of the living and the dead elements and the living and the dead hairs. Where the biblical and mishnaic language speak about the spread of the disease, D^{a} expresses this as the transition from the realm of life to the realm of death, or better: from the realm of the spirit of life to the realm of the spirit of perversity (death).

5:6-7), "In as much as they do not keep separate according to the Law but lie with her that sees the blood of flux" *(dam zobah:* Lev. 15:19). They also "rendered their holy spirits unclean and with a blasphemous tongue opened their mouth against the ordinances of the covenant of God" (CD 5:11-12). Those brought into the covenant are asked by God "to refrain from the unclean wealth of wickedness acquired of vowing and appropriating the wealth of the sanctuary ... to put a distinction between the unclean and the clean, the holy and the common" (6:15-18), also "to keep away from all forms of uncleanness in the manner proper for them and not for each man to defile his holy spirit, according as God taught them to distinguish" (CD 7:3-4). Making the sanctuary unclean recurs (CD 20:24), without further definition.

The Damascus Covenant's Laws refer to purification with water (CD 10:12f.). An offering to the altar may not be sent by anyone affected with any of the types of uncleanness, thus empowering him to convey uncleanness to the altar; proof of this is found in Prov. 15:8, "The sacrifice of the wicked is an abomination" (CD 11:19-21). One who comes to the house of meeting in order to pray must come in a state of cleanness (CD 11:22). No one should lie with a woman in Jerusalem so as to convey uncleanness to the sanctuary with their impurity (NDTM) (CD 12:1-2). No one should defile his soul with any living being or creeping thing by eating of them (CD 12:12). Wood and stones defiled by a corpse convey uncleanness (CD 12:16-17) like the corpse. Utensils and nails or pegs in the wall of a house containing a corpse are unclean (CD 12:18). The clean and unclean are to be distinguished as are the holy and the profane (CD 12:19-20).

One who despises the precepts of God shall receive no instruction in the "Community of his counsel:" "He shall not be reckoned among the perfect; he shall neither be purified by atonement, nor cleansed by purifying waters, nor sanctified by seas and rivers, nor washed clean with any ablution" (1QS 3:3-6). "Sins are expiated through the spirit of true counsel; he shall be cleansed from sins by the spirit of holiness ... And when his flesh is sprinkled with purifying water and sanctified by cleansing water, it shall be made clean by the humble submission of his soul to all the precepts of God" (1QS 3:8-9). God will cleanse man of all wicked deeds with the spirit of holiness: "He will shed upon him the spirit of truth like purifying waters (to cleanse him) of all abomination and falsehood" (1QS 4:5). Those who have been cleansed from their wickedness may not partake of the pure meal of the saints, for all who transgress his word are unclean (1QS 5:13-14). One who has not completed his initiation may not touch the pure meal of the congregation until a year has passed and he has been examined concerning his spirit and his deeds (1QS 6:16). Punishments are inflicted in terms of separation from the pure meal of the congregation for various periods of time (1QS 6:24-7:21). At the end (1QS 11:14) comes the following: "Through His righteousness He will cleanse me of the uncleanness of man and of the sins of the children of men ..."

The War rule (1QM 7:4-5) holds that no one smitten with a bodily impurity may march out to war ... No man shall go down with them on the day of battle who is impure because of his 'fount,' [the man with an issue: *Zab*] for the holy angels shall be with their hosts." The priests are not to approach the slain.

A hymn (1QH 6:8) says God will "purify and cleanse them of their sin, for all their deeds are in thy truth." Another (1QH 16:10-11) says, "I know thou hast marked the spirit of the just, and therefore I have chosen to keep my hands clean in accordance with [thy] will; the soul of Thy servant [has loathed] every work of inquiry." "Wallowing in uncleanness" is a metaphor for turning aside from the counsel of God's truth: "For I have been defiled by uncleanness and I have [walked] aside from [thy] assembly" (Dupont-Sommer, p. 250). The commentary on Habakkuk (1 QpHab 2:5-6; 8:13) states that the wicked priest lived "in the way of abominations amidst every unclean defilement."

What is new in the *yaḥad*'s ideas concerning purity is not the substance, but the locus of application of the laws. The priestly code clearly ruled that only the clean might enter the Temple. Cleanness involved morality, not merely taking a bath or refraining from sexual relations with a menstruating woman. Rebellion against God, as in the case of idolatry, was unclean. Water purifies; the sacrifices of the wicked are unacceptable. Creeping things defile. Corpse-uncleanness affects objects in a house. The priests cannot touch corpses. None of these assertions would have surprised the priestly lawyers. Once it is admitted that the community is subject to the purity-laws, it goes without saying that the priestly code will exclude one who despises the law or disobeys God. The cleansing of sins by the "spirit of holiness" is hardly alien to the imagery of Ezekiel. What would have surprised the priestly authors was the requirement of purity outside of the Jerusalem Temple and for a purpose other than the conduct of the Temple cult. Indeed, the *yaḥad*'s obsessive concern for purity is matched by its claim to have a monopoly on it. Only the members are pure and control the means of purification, e.g. 1QS 3:4-6. In that sense alone do we find the purity-laws used as part of a much larger metaphor, comparing the Temple to the community; but within that metaphor, purity and impurity are understood in an entirely literal way.

The second innovation in the *yaḥad*'s view of purity seems to me entirely without parallel. Its importance was pointed out to me by Prof. A. R. C. Leaney, Nottingham University, in a lecture at Brown University. The *yaḥad*'s laws treat committing a sin not as a metaphor for becoming unclean, but as an actual source of uncleanness. If one transgresses any part of the law, he is excluded from the "Purity" of the sect. It is not *as if* he were unclean, as with the biblical metaphor. He is *actually* unclean and requires a rite of purification. So the uncleanness is not metaphorical but is treated as equivalent to the impurity imparted by a corpse or a menstrual woman. So 1QS 5:13 says the wicked may not touch "the Purity of the holy, for a man is not pure unless he be converted from his malice. For he is defiled for as long as he transgresses His word." Punishments are meted out in terms of periods of uncleanness, symbolized by separation from the Purity of the community. If one speaks angrily against one of the priests, he is excluded for a year; if he speaks arrogantly, it is for six months. Three months' separation punish foolishness; ten days for interrupting the words of another. One who laughs stupidly and loudly is punished for thirty days. Afterward there is a period of purification, marked by a test of the penitent's spirit. So too in CD 12:4, if one breaks the Sabbath, he is "watched" for seven years, then allowed to enter the assembly.

Now what makes this view of purity other than metaphorical is the provision of both a specific disability consequent on sin-impurity and a rite of purification—whatever it may be. This means the impurity is regarded as affective, the man is really impure and requires cleansing from impurity before he may have contact with the pure objects of the community. This innovation seems to be the ultimate result of the comparison of impurity with sin: it is no longer a matter of simile at all. One who sins is impure and requires purification; the impurity of the menstrual woman and that of the arrogant person are not distinguished in any way. This last stage in the development of ideas about purity carries to the logical conclusion the interpretation of the priests, both lawyers and prophets, who inaugurated the process by making use of purity as a metaphor for righteousness. For the *yaḥad*, one cannot distinguish between cultic and moral impurity. In themselves and in their consequences they are identical.

In connection with the *yaḥad*, we have to take account of the role of purity in the Book of Jubilees, for copies were discovered in the documents found at Qumran. Written sometime after 200 B.C., the Book of Jubilees interprets world-history from creation to Sinai. The author attempts to link to the story of creation at least one of the purity-rules, namely that a woman who has given birth to a male-child is impure for forty days, to a female, for eighty. The author says that in the first week Adam was created, and in the second week God showed Eve to Adam: "And for this reason the commandment was given to keep in their defilement, for a male seven days, and for a female twice seven days." After Adam had completed forty days in the land where he had been created, he was brought into the garden of Eden, but Eve was not brought in until the eightieth day, "And for this reason the commandment is written on the heavenly tablets, in regard to her that gives birth," that a male causes seven-days of uncleanness and thirty-three days in the "blood of purifying," and a female requires twice these numbers, eighty days of purification in all. (The later rabbis produced a somewhat similar story). Everything in the garden was holy. The garden was like the Temple: "Therefore there was ordained regarding her who bears a male or female child the statute of those days that she should touch no hallowed thing nor enter into the sanctuary ... This is the law and testimony which was written down for Israel in order that they should observe it all the days" (3:8-14). The analogy of the garden and the Temple is secondary to the story.

Otherwise Jubilee's interpretation of purity may be called standard.[1] That is, the biblical repertoire is drawn upon, but not significantly enhanced; impurity applies to sex, idolatry, food, and, of course, the cult. The metaphorical use of uncleanness to mean iniquity recurs. Noah commanded his sons to "guard their souls from fornication and uncleanness and all iniquity, for owing to these three things the flood came upon the earth" (7:20-21). The flood was on account of illicit sexual relations, which produced "the beginning of uncleanness." One

[1] R. H. Charles, in R. H. Charles, *op. cit.*, II, p. 1. Texts: pp. 16-17, 24, 29, 37, 42-8, 58-9, 63-4. On the calendars at Qumran and in Jubilees: J. T. Milik, *Ten Years of Discovery in the Wilderness of Judea* (London, 1959), pp. 110-112, 117-118; G. Vermes, *The Dead Sea Scrolls in English* (Harmondsworth, 1962), pp. 42-4; and A. Jaubert, "Le Calendrier des Jubilés et les jours liturgiques de la semaine," *Vetus Testamentum* 7, pp. 35ff.; but compare Matthew Black, *The Scrolls and Christian Origins* (N.Y., 1961), p. 199.

should not shed blood, which pollutes the earth, "for the earth will not be clean from the blood which has been shed upon it until it is purified" by the blood of him who shed it (7:33). Malignant spirits assisted in making graven images "and seduced them into committing transgression and uncleanness" (11:4). The Sodomites defiled themselves through fornication and "worked uncleanness on the earth" (16:5). Abraham warned his sons to refrain from "fornication and uncleanness" (20:3, 6) and from "idols and their uncleannesses" (20:7).

He further warned Isaac, "And at all times be clean in thy body and wash thyself with water before thou approachest to offer on the altar, and wash thy hands and thy feet before thou drawest near to the altar; and when thou art done sacrificing, wash again thy hands and thy feet" (21:16-17). This washing of the hands and feet, unknown to the priestly law-givers, has nothing to do with purity at an ordinary meal. It is explicitly linked to the cult and the act of sacrifice. However, it may well be the source of the later Pharisaic-rabbinic requirement to wash hands before eating. The Pharisees saw eating as a cultic act and transferred to the home and table many of the laws that had originally applied to the Temple and altar.

Abraham further tells Isaac to "turn away from all the nations' deeds and their uncleanness and observe the ordinance of the Most High God" (21:22-3). Unrighteousness and impurity moreover are equated (22:14). Isaac warns Jacob, "Remember my words and observe the commandments of Abraham, thy father: Separate thyself from the nations, and eat not with them, and do not according to their works, and become not their associate, for their works are unclean, and all their ways are a pollution and an abomination and an uncleanness" (22:16). These ways are then spelled out: the nations sacrifice to the dead, worship evil spirits, eat over graves. Again, Isaac warns Jacob to remove himself "from their uncleanness and from all their error, and beware ... of taking a wife from any seed of the daughters of Canaan" (22:19-20). Here impurity is sexual. An evil generation is going to come, whose works are "uncleanness and fornication" (23:14). "They shall defile the holy of holies with their uncleanness and the corruption of their pollution" (23:21), possibly a reference to Maccabean times, or to the "wicked priest" of the Qumran Habakkuk commentary. The deed of the Shechemites is cited, along with the warning not to defile one's seed by marrying gentiles (30:10-12), "for this is unclean and abominable to Israel. And Israel will not be free from this uncleanness if it has a wife of the daughters of the gentiles" (30:13-14). The consequence will be "plague upon plague and curse upon curse."

Anyone who defiles the sanctuary likewise will see no blessing (30:16). At the advent of the new moon Jacob tells his family, "Purify yourselves and change your garments, and let us rise and go up to Bethel" (31:1).

After Bilhah has sexual relations with Reuben, she tells Jacob, "I am not clean for thee, for I have been defiled as regards thee, for Reuben has defiled me and has lain with me in the night" (33:6-7). On this account, the author says, the heavenly tablets ordained "that a man should not lie with his father's wife ... for this is unclean ... for they have wrought uncleanness on the earth. And there shall be nothing unclean before our God in the nations which he has chosen for himself for a possession" (33:10). Fornication again is described as an "uncleanness, abomination, contamination, and pollution ... There is no greater sin" (33:19-20). This usage is familiar from Leviticus.

None of the foregoing views of purity greatly develops the biblical concepts. What is striking is that the larger number of biblical laws is not even alluded to. After the citation with which I began, no further effort is made to draw upon their details for homiletical purposes, nor is the author interested in adducing other examples of the way in which the biblical purity-laws relate to the story of the creation, the Patriarchs or the Exodus and Sinai. But the fact that the author refers to purity as much as he does is important.

The materials on purity in Jubilees raise the problem of assigning the work to a particular group within ancient Judaism. R. H. Charles attributes Jubilees to a Pharisee between 135 and 105. Despite his repeated assertion that the author was a Pharisee, Charles does not give decisive reasons for supposing so, except correspondence between Pharisaic legal "strictness" and that in Jubilees. But Jubilees has a different date from that of the Pharisees for the Feast of Weeks and knows nothing about the Pharisaic regulation about pouring water on the altar on Tabernacles. The "midrashic tendency" cannot have been limited to Pharisaic authors. Charles states, "Since our author was an upholder of the everlasting validity of the law and held the strictest views on circumcision, the Sabbath, and the duty of complete separation from the gentiles, since he believed in angels and demons and a blessed immortality, he was inquestionably a Pharisee of the strictest sect." Such traits as these would equally have characterized a member of the *yaḥad*, and it is not unlikely that other, ordinary folk, not members of any sect, would have shared many of them. Charles's considerations are not decisive.

Moreover, the discovery of Jubilees in the Qumran library, while not definitive evidence that the document is Essenian or produced by the *yaḥad*, allows us to suppose the materials before us were favorably received by that group. Jubilees' and the *yaḥad*'s view of purity have in common an obsessive interest in menstrual impurity. The calendar of each is virtually identical to that of the other. The Scrolls accuse the Jerusalem priests of engaging in sexual relations with menstruating women and so defiling Jerusalem and the Temple (not to mention themselves). The related concern for basing the associated taboo, against the woman after childbirth, within the foundations of creation-story is revealed in Jubilees, which combines an explanation of a detail of the cultic law with the larger theme of cultic purity—natural for the priestly circles of Qumran. Secure attribution of a work to a party can only be made when one of the absolutely peculiar characteristics of the party can be shown to be an essential element in the structure of the whole work. No reliance can be placed on elements which appear in only one or another episode, or occur in several episodes but are secondary and detachable details in all instances. Such things may be accretions. Motifs which are not certainly peculiar to one sect cannot prove that sect was the source. The best sort of evidence is something technically peculiar and structurally essential. On this criterion the common calendar allows definitive assignment of Jubilees to the *yaḥad*. It may to be sure have been written earlier and taken over by the *yaḥad*. But its main ideas on purity surely exhibit a striking affinity to those of the *yaḥad*.

The study of the history of Judaism comprehends a considerable part of early Christian experience, simply because for a long time in Palestine, as well as in much of the diaspora, the Christian was a kind of Jew and saw himself as such. Moreover, the Christians, whether originally Jewish or otherwise, took over the antecedent holy books and much of the ritual life of Judaism. For our purposes New Testament Christianity therefore is a form of Judaism, one which differed from the rest primarily in regarding the world as having been redeemed through the cross of Jesus. But one must hasten to stress the complexity of the Christian evidences, which cannot be simplified and regarded as essentially unitary.

Like the Qumranians, many Christians criticized the Jerusalem Temple and its cult. Both groups in common believed that the last days had begun. Both believed that God had come to dwell with them, as he had once dwelled in the Temple. The sacrifices of the Temple were replaced, therefore, by the sacrifice of a blameless life and by other spiritual deeds. But some Christians differed on one important point. To them, the final sacrifice has already taken place; the perfect priest has offered up the perfect holocaust, his own body. Christ on the cross completed the old law and inaugurated the new. This belief took shape in different ways. For Paul in I Cor. 3:16-17 the Church is the new Temple. Christ is the foundation of the "spiritual" building. The deuteropauline Ephesians 2:18ff. has Christ as the corner-stone of the new building, the company of Christians constituting the Temple. It is within this context that the role of purity in early Christianity is to be interpreted.

The first evidence on Christian views of purity derives from Paul and the Pauline writers. The symbol of purity is routinely alluded to in Romans 1:24, where impurity is spoken of as "dishonoring their [the transgressors'] bodies," and in 6:19, which equates impurity and iniquity, as against righteousness for sanctification. The use of purity and impurity in reference to food occurs in Romans 14:14-23. Here Paul says, "I am persuaded in the Lord Jesus that nothing is unclean in itself, but it is unclean for anyone who *thinks* it unclean"—a highly rabbinic conception as we observed (p. 16). The context is eating: "For the kingdom of God does not mean food and drink but righteousness and peace and joy in the Holy Spirit. Everything is indeed clean, but it is wrong for anyone to make others fall by what he eats." I Cor. 6:12-13 and Gal. 2:11 likewise allude to the lawfulness of all food; 8:1-13 concerns food offered to idols. If a person has a weak conscience and regards the food as really offered to an idol, the conscience is infirm, for food has no relationship to God. Idolatry as a source of impurity is already familiar. The centrality of intention in the determination of an impure state is, as noted, known in Talmudic law. Children may be "unclean" (I Cor. 7:14); the child is "holy" if one parent is a believer, and the couple stays together. Similarly, immorality and all impurity or covetousness are compared with one another; but here the meaning is simply filthiness. I Thes. 4:7 contrasts uncleanness with holiness, the context being marital relations. Paul therefore uses the symbol of purity chiefly in respect to food and sex. The former is no longer subject to impurity, but the latter certainly is. In Romans and Corinthians, Paul consistently argues that food is not intrinsically pure or impure, though an individual may not eat anything he thinks he should not. There can be no doubt that Paul regards the impurity decreed in biblical food-laws as suspended. The allusions to purity otherwise fall wholly within the established biblical framework of interpretation.

The Synoptic Gospels treat purity in three aspects: bodily afflictions, unclean hands and food, and ethics. The stories about Jesus emphasize the first, the sayings attributed to him stress the second and third.

The Synoptic narratives include Jesus's healing lepers by a touch (Mk. 1:40-44, Mt. 8:2-4, 10:1, 8, 11:5, Lk. 5:12-14, 17:22, 17:11-19). The issue of impurity does not enter the narrative. Though by touching the leper, Jesus becomes impure, he might in any event purify himself before going to the Temple and is not represented as a priest declaring the leper pure, but as a wonder-worker healing the disease itself. He is portrayed as telling the lepers to go to a priest for purification. Similarly, the woman with a continual flow of blood (Mk. 5:24-34, Mt. 9:20-22, Lk. 8:43-8) touches Jesus's garments and the hemorrhage ceases. The woman, discovered to have touched the garments, was frightened, perhaps because she had made the man unclean by her touch. Both sorts of stories take for granted that the diseased are healed by Jesus, but say nothing of the uncleanness which has been imparted to him or of his removing that impurity. The healing of people from unclean spirits in like manner lays no stress on the matter of impurity.

Far more curious is the silence about Jesus's staying in the home of Simon the leper in Bethany (Mk. 14:3, Mt. 26:6) before going to Jerusalem for Passover. This should have been explained, for merely coming under the same roof as a leper defiles a person. Jesus ought to have remained pure, since he planned the next day to celebrate the Passover. If impure, he would have had to wait a whole month before keeping the Passover. The detail occurs in Matthew, and since Matthew held that the law remained valid, one cannot maintain that the detail was meant to indicate that Jesus had annulled the purity laws in respect to either the Temple or leprosy. One might suppose Simon was no longer a leper, having been healed; if so, it is not clear why he is still called a leper. More important, Luke 7:36-50 places Jesus in the home of a Simon, and also has the story of the woman's pouring out the flask of oil on Jesus. So the setting cannot be different. But Bethany is dropped, so is the occasion of the Passover, and Simon is no longer a leper. Luke therefore has dropped a detail given in Mark and Matthew. This should mean the detail was of some negative consequence to Luke. But if the story-teller intended to claim that by staying with a leper on the eve of the Passover, Jesus intended to annul the laws of purity in the cult—or to annul the cult entirely, taking it over into his Church—*that* rather significant claim has then not been spelled out and therefore cannot be inferred on the basis of a single curious detail. John 12:3-8 knows the story of the woman (Mary) and the oil, but not Simon or his leprosy. It is remarkable that neither Mark, who has an important discussion of Jesus' attitude to the purity laws in Chap. 7, nor Matthew, who is positive about the *halakhah*, is bothered at all by the question of whether Jesus was pure or impure at Passover. The simplest solution is that all the NT writers saw "the leper" as referring to the man's former state, not his present status, and therefore never recognized the problem I have raised. The pericope itself probably was not connected to Passover before Mark inserted it into the passion-narrative, so at an earlier stage the question of uncleanness would not have arisen in any event.

Mark does claim that Jesus annulled the purity-rules, that is, the custom of the Pharisees. The disciples eat with "defiled, that is, unwashed hands." Jesus is asked why his disciples do not live according to the tradition of the elders, which is defined as eating with clean hands. Jesus contrasts obedience to God with the tradition of men, then, ignoring the issue of the cleanness of *hands*, declares the rules about the cleanness or uncleanness of *food* are invalid (!). There is nothing outside a man which by going into him can defile him, but the things which come out of a man are what defile him (Mk. 7:15). This is explicitly assigned to the problem of food—(7:19) "Thus he declared all foods clean." Then the cleanness of food is contrasted with the unclean things in the heart of man which come out and defile: evil thoughts, fornication, theft, murder, and so on. The composite pericope thus links two entirely separate aspects of uncleanness, one concerning the Pharisaic tradition about the hands and washing, the other the biblical rules of food and eating; the former is (correctly) declared to be the works of man, the latter to be unimportant by contrast to inner uncleanness. The metaphorical use of uncleanness to refer to iniquity recurs. But the literal and concrete aspect—the actual uncleanness of certain foods—is at the same time rejected, consistent with the picture given by Paul.

Matthew is mostly in harmony with Mark on these points, though he drops the gloss that Jesus had declared all food clean. The washing of the hands is not a divine commandment (Mt. 15:1-3). It is treated as separate from the cleanness of foods, still in the same context (Mt. 15:10-19). But then ignoring their differences—the *hands* as a Pharisaic custom, the food as a biblical injunction—Matthew links the two in a curious fusion, "These [namely, iniquitous deeds which come out of a man] are what defile a man, but to eat with unwashed hands does not defile a man." Mark was appropriately silent on the supposed connection between the customary washing of the hands and the Mosaic rules on the cleanness of foods, which Matthew has confused. Mk. 7:23 concludes the pericope, which Mt. 15:23 further embellishes. It seems to me Matthew has supplied nothing more than a redactional improvement, linking—and mixing up—two quite separate matters in his concluding summary. But the antecedent pericopae will have kept them distinct and, correctly, treated them as entirely separate issues. Washing was never part of God's will—the Torah; unclean food was part of the Torah but was meant to teach a moral lesson, and not to be interpreted in a literal way.

Matthew 23:25-6 (Lk. 11:39-41) and 23:27-28 take up and develop the contrast between inside and outside. The Pharisees clean the outside of the cup and plate, but inside they are full of extortion: "First clean the inside of the cup, that the outside also may be clean." Similarly, the scribes and Pharisees are like whitewashed tombs, outwardly beautiful, but inwardly full of uncleanness. Luke 11:40 adds that God made both the inside and the outside of the cup and dish, a pointless homily. The contrast between impurity and iniquity and purity and righteousness is commonplace. What is more interesting is the problem of the division of the parts of the cup into the insides and the outsides. For Jesus we have here only a metaphor for inner against outer purity. What is to be kept pure is the inside of the man—a play on the theme already introduced in the cleanness of foods. Later rabbinic law distinguished between the inside of the cup, which was highly susceptible to ritual impurity and which, when unclean, rendered the whole cup unclean, and the outside, which was less susceptible and would not impart impurity to the inside. That the same distinction between inside and outside occurs in both rabbinic and Christian material suggests that it was early, but does not indicate what use was made of it in earlier periods. To be sure, the saying attributes to Jesus the strict view that the inside had to be clean. But the whole saying seems to me solely a metaphor for moral purity and is not built upon exact knowledge of the (possibly later) Pharisaic purity-rule in this connection. If

Jesus was supposed to have known the rule and to have treated it literally, and if the Pharisaic law then was the same as the well-attested rule Yavnean later, he could not have told the Pharisees first to cleanse the inside of the cup. That was their rule to begin with. The figurative sense likewise is lost if one really does clean the inside of the cup first of all.

The one important addition is the reference to baptism with fire (Lk. 3:16-17), a metaphor of a form of purification known to Josephus as an eschatological image of judgment. The other claim of Luke-Acts, which is quite routine, is that Paul purified himself before going to the Temple, but was alleged to have brought unclean people there (Acts 21:17-28). Acts 21:25 imposes food laws on gentile-Christians. Otherwise Acts' references to purity—10:9-23 (11:4-12), the revelation to Peter that cleanness no longer applies to foods, because "What God has cleansed you must not call common," and 15:9, God's cleansing the gentiles' hearts by faith—are already familiar.

James 4:8, like Ps. 24:4, compares clean hands to a pure heart. Revelation 21:27, which says nothing unclean shall enter Jerusalem, sees cleanness as a symbol of inner sanctity. Otherwise purity plays no articulated role in other literature of the early Church, except for Hebrews. To be sure John and the Johannine literature are not silent on the question of purity. I Jn. 3:25, 13:10, 15:2, and Jn. 1:7, 9 hold the disciples of Jesus are clean because of their association with Jesus.

The author of Hebrews, like Philo, is a noteworthy philosopher of the purity-rules.[1] The reason is his view of the abiding importance, even after 70, of the Christians' relationship to Temple, cult, and priesthood. Like Philo, the author of Hebrews treats the purity-rules as metaphorical or figurative of a higher reality. His interpretation is imaginative, original, and wide-ranging. In the important part, Chapters 8-10, the author emphasizes the superiority of Jesus' sacrifice in the heavenly sanctuary to the Levitical priests' sacrifice in the earthly one. In the setting of this extended argument, the author contrasts the sprinkling of defiled persons with the blood of goats and with the ashes of a heifer, which sanctifies for the purification of the flesh (Hebrews 9:13): Then: "How much more shall the blood of the Mes-

[1] James Moffatt, *A Critical and Exegetical Commentary on the Epistle to the Hebrews* (N.Y., 1924), pp. 121ff.; Hugh Montefiore, *A Commentary on the Epistle to the Hebrews* (N.Y., 1964), pp. 150ff.; C. Spicq, *L'Épître aux Hébreux* (Paris, 1952), II, pp. 246ff.

siah, who through the eternal Spirit offered himself without blemish to God, purify your conscience from dead works to serve the living God!" (9:14). Jesus' sacrifice here is represented as superior to the sacrifice of the red heifer, which produced the ashes to be mixed with the water for the ceremony of purification. The earthly priests have only the ashes and water. But Christ is the sacrificial animal itself. He therefore will more surely effect purification.

The author further alludes to the purity-rite, which was effected by a sprinkling of blood: "Indeed under the law almost everything is purified with blood, and without the shedding of blood there is no forgiveness of sins." The allusions to the priestly law are then given their new meaning: Christ offered himself not repeatedly, but once alone; the blood was not that of a goat, but his own. What is wrong with the earthly cult is that the worshipers, once cleansed, ought no longer have any consciousness of sin (10:2): "But in these sacrifices there is a reminder of sin year after year." Here the author of Hebrews regards purification as a rite having to do with sin, not with impurity, except as impurity is regarded as a metaphor for sin. He moreover explicitly draws out the ambiguity of the symbol of the blood. Blood-excretions of a human being and of a corpse are a source of impurity, not of purification. The blood of the sacrifice serves to achieve atonement. But the blood of Jesus does *not* defile. It purifies like that of the sacrificial animal: "Let us draw near with a true heart in full assurance of faith, with our hearts sprinkled clean from an evil conscience and our bodes washed with pure water" (10:22). This is part of Hebrews' larger paradox, that the priest serves also as the oblation.

The third group to whom the laws of purity were important is the Pharisees. Their commune, called *ḥavurah*, which may be translated "fellowship," is described in the law-codes produced by later rabbinic Judaism. We know very little about the Pharisees before the time of Herod. During Maccabean days, according to Josephus, our sole reliable evidence, they appear as a political party, competing with the Sadducees, another party, for control of the court and government. Afterward, as a group they all but fade out of Josephus's narrative. But the later rabbinical literature fills the gap with fanciful stories about Pharisaic masters from Shammai and Hillel to the destruction of the Temple. It also ascribes to pre-70 authorities numerous sayings, particularly on matters of law, both to the masters and to the Houses of Shammai and of Hillel. These circles of disciples seem to have flourished in the first century, down to 70 and for a few years beyond.

The legal materials attributed by later rabbis to the pre-70 Pharisees are thematically congruent to the stories and sayings about Pharisees in the New Testament Gospels, and I take them to be accurate in substance, if not in detail, as representations of the main issues of Pharisaic law. After 70, the masters of Yavneh seem to have included a predominant element of Pharisees, and the rabbis after 70 assuredly regarded themselves as the continuators of Pharisaism. Yoḥanan ben Zakkai, who first stood at the head of the Yavnean circle, was later on said to have been a disciple of Hillel. More credibly, Gamaliel II, who succeeded Yohanan as head of the Yavnean institution, is regarded as the grandson of Gamaliel, a Pharisee in the council of the Temple who is mentioned in Acts 5:34 in connection with the trial of Paul.

The dominant trait of Pharisaism before 70 is depicted both in the rabbinic traditions about the Pharisees and in the Gospels as concern for certain matters of rite. In particular, the rite was of eating one's meals in a state of ritual purity as if one were a Temple priest, and carefully giving the required tithes and offerings due to the priesthood. The Gospels' references to Pharisaism also included fasting, Sabbath-observance, vows and oaths, and the like, but the main point was keeping the purity laws outside of the Temple, where the priests had to observe purity when they carried out the requirements of the cult.

The Pharisees, like the Dead Sea commune, believed that one must keep the purity laws outside of the Temple. Other Jews, following the plain sense of Leviticus, supposed that purity laws were to be kept only in the Temple. The priests also had to eat their Temple food in a state of purity, but lay people did not. To be sure, everyone who went to the Temple had to be pure, but outside of the Temple, as I said, it was not required that noncultic activities be conducted in a state of Levitical cleanness.

The Pharisees held, to the contrary, that even outside of the Temple, in one's own home, a person had to follow the laws of purity in the only circumstance in which they might apply, namely, at the table. They therefore held one must eat his secular food, that is, ordinary, everyday meals, in a state of purity *as if one were a Temple priest*. The Pharisees thus arrogated to themselves—and to all Jews equally—the status of the Temple priests and did the things which priests must do on account of that status. The table of every Jew in his home was seen to be like the table of the Lord in the Jerusalem Temple. The commandment, "You shall be a kingdom of priests and a holy people," was taken literally. The whole country was holy. The table of every man possessed the same order of sanctity as the table of the cult. At this time, apart from the *yaḥad*, only the Pharisees held such a viewpoint, and eating unconsecrated food as if one were a Temple priest at the Lord's table thus was one of the two indications that a Jew was a Pharisee, a sectarian.

The other was meticulous tithing. The laws of tithing and related agricultural taboos may have been kept primarily by Pharisees. Here we are not certain. Pharisees clearly regarded keeping the agricultural rules as a chief religious duty. But whether, to what degree, and how other Jews did so, is not clear. Both the agricultural laws and purity rules in the end affected table fellowship: *How and what one may eat.* That is, they were "dietary laws."

The Dead Sea Sect, the Christian Jews, and the Pharisees all stressed ritual in connection with the eating of meals. The Qumranians and the Christians tended to oppose Temple sacrifice and to prefer to achieve forgiveness of sin through repentence, and, in the case of the Christians, "baptism," a ritual bath. The immersions of the Qumran group were not thought to remove sin but only to give bodily cleanliness, provided the recipient had previously repented and been cleansed by the spirit; on this the Manual of Discipline is explicit and emphatic. By contrast, the Pharisees before 70 continued to revere the Temple and its cult. While the early Christians gathered for ritual meals, and made them the climax of their group life, the Pharisees did not. What expressed the Pharisees' sense of self-awareness as a group apparently was not a similarly intense communion-meal. So far as we know, eating was not endowed with mythic elements, even though the Pharisees had liturgies to be said at the meal. No communion-ceremonies, or rites centered on meals, or specifications of meals on holy occasions characterize Pharisaic table-fellowship.

Pharisaic table-fellowship was a quite ordinary, everyday affair. The various fellowship-rules had to be observed in a wholly routine circumstance—daily, at every meal, without accompanying rites, other than a benediction for the food. Unlike the Pharisees, the Christians' myths and rituals rendered not their table-fellowship, but the special communion meals, into a much heightened spiritual experience: *Do this in memory of me.* As to their regular meals, Christians differed considerably. Many held that the eating of things sacrificed to idols and of animals not slaughtered according to Jewish rules was prohibited, but these rules were gradually, over the first three centuries, abandoned.

The use of a blessing before meals remained customary. The Pharisees told no stories about purity laws, except (in later times) to account for their historical development (e.g., who had decreed which purity-rule?). When they came to table, so far as we know, they told no stories about how Moses had done what they now do, and they did not "do these things in memory of Moses our rabbi."

In the Dead Sea commune, table-fellowship was open upon much the same basis as among the Pharisees: appropriate undertakings to keep purity and to consume properly grown and tithed foods. As we know it, the Qumranian meal was liturgically not much different from the ordinary Pharisaic gathering. The rites pertained to, and derived from, the eating of food and that alone. Both Christians and Pharisees lived among ordinary folk, while the Qumranians did not. In this respect the commonplace character of Pharisaic table-fellowship is all the more striking. The sect ordinarily did not gather *as a group* at all, but in the home. All meals required purity. Pharisaic table-fellowship took place in the same circumstances as did the meals of outsiders. Pharisees were common folk, who ate everyday meals in an everyday way, among ordinary neighbors, not members of the sect. They were engaged in workaday pursuits like everyone else. The setting for law-observance therefore was the field and the kitchen, the bed and the street. The occasion for observance was set every time a person picked up a common nail, which might be unclean, or purchased a *se'ah* of wheat, which had to be tithed—by himself, without priests to bless his deeds or sages to instruct him. Keeping the Pharisaic rule did not require an occasional, but exceptional rite at, but external to, the meal. Instead, it imposed the perpetual "ritualization" of daily life, that is, the imposition of the cultic rules outside of the Temple, on the one side, and the constant, inner awareness of the communal order of being, on the other.

Earlier I pointed out that the *yaḥad* regarded the commission of a sin as a direct cause of uncleanness, so that a person who spoke arrogantly was regarded as impure and could not touch the pure food or water of the community. The later rabbinic description of the laws pertinent to the *ḥavurah* includes a significant detail. The second-century rabbis say that certain classes of people may not be admitted into the *ḥavurah* to begin with, and if a member of the *ḥavurah* enters such a class, he is thrown out. Judah b. Ilai alleges (M. Demai 2:3) that a member of a *ḥavurah* may not rear small cattle, be profuse in vows or levity, or contract uncleanness because of the dead (which means he is like a priest); moreover he should serve the sages. Judah's contemporaries correctly claimed that not all of these considerations entered into the original definition of the *ḥaver*. Obviously, Judah has anachronistically assigned to the *ḥavurah* ideas—such as study of Torah and service of the sages, or not rearing goats—important only later on. Of greater interest is the rule (Tos. Dem. 3:4) that a member of a *ḥavurah* who becomes a tax-collector is expelled from the *ḥavurah* for so long as he holds that office. Once he leaves the office, he is readmitted into the status of a novice *(ne'eman)*. Now this conception formally is not different from the notion that a person who is arrogant or malicious is impure. The effect is the same. But the substantive difference seems to me important. The Tosefta's rule does not allege the man is regarded specifically as *unclean;* he may not join in the communal meal, to be sure, but the reason that he has been expelled from the *ḥavurah* is not explicitly that he has made himself unclean by his profession or deeds. An explicit statement appears in the *yaḥad*'s rule. Exclusion from the common meal may come on account of failure to tithe, and this has nothing to do with purity. The specific allegation of the *yaḥad* is that he who sins is literally *impure*. Tosefta's rule seems to me to know nothing of that conception.

The response of the Pharisees to the destruction of the Temple is known to us only from rabbinic materials, which underwent revision over many centuries. A story about Yoḥanan ben Zakkai and his disciple, Joshua ben Ḥananiah, tells us in a few words the main outline of the Pharisaic-rabbinic view.

> Once, as Rabban Yoḥanan ben Zakkai was coming forth from Jerusalem, Rabbi Joshua followed him and saw the Temple in ruins.
>
> "Woe unto us," Rabbi Joshua cried, "that this, the place where the iniquities of Israel were atoned for, is laid waste."
>
> "My son," Rabban Yoḥanan said to him, "be not grieved. We have another atonement as effective as this. And what is it?"
>
> "It is acts of loving kindness, as it is said, 'For I desire mercy and not sacrifice' [Hos. 6:6]."
>
> (The Fathers according to Rabbi Nathan, Chap. 6)

How shall we relate the arcane rules about ritual purity to the public calamity faced by the heirs of the Pharisees at Yavneh? What is the connection between the ritual purity of the "kingdom of priests" and the atonement of sins in the Temple?

The will of God demanded deeds of loving kindness. "I desire mercy, not sacrifice" (Hos. 6:6) meant to Yoḥanan, "We have a means of atonement as effective as the Temple, and it is doing deeds of loving kindness." Just as men would contribute bricks and mortar for the rebuilding of a sanctuary, so they ought to contribute renunciation, self-sacrifice, love, for the building of the sacred community. Earlier, Pharisaism had held that the purity observed in the Temple should be observed everywhere, even in the home and the hearth. The table of the ordinary man was to be kept pure as the altar. Admittedly, I am reading into the requirement to observe purity at home the view that the home consequently was compared to the Temple. The extension of the Temple purity rules to the household might be seen as an expression of extreme piety. "As his presence is everywhere, so we should always behave as if we were in the Temple, that is, in his presence." This *as-if* attitude would explain why the functions of the altar are not attributed to the table before 70; until then it did not atone.

Now Yoḥanan taught that sacrifice greater than the Temple's must characterize the life of the community. If one were to do something for God in a time that the Temple was no more, the offering must be the gift of selfless compassion. The holy altar must be the streets and marketplaces of the world, as, formerly, the purity of the Temple had to be observed in the streets and marketplaces of Jerusalem. By making the laws of ritual purity incumbent upon the ordinary Jew, the Pharisees already had effectively limited the importance of the Temple and its cult. The earlier history of the Pharisaic sect thus had laid the ground work for Yoḥanan ben Zakkai's response to Joshua ben Ḥananiah. It was a natural conclusion for one nurtured in a movement based upon the priesthood of all Israel.

Clearly, the *yaḥad* and the *ḥavurah* shared the view that meals were to be eaten in a state of purity. But at the outset the *yaḥad* claimed that its community constituted the Temple, while nothing in the Gospels' references to the Pharisees or in the rabbinic traditions about the Pharisees explicitly reflects a negative view of the cult of the Jerusalem Temple. We have no grounds to suppose, therefore, that the Pharisees claimed they formed a "new Temple," or that the old one was not holy. The *ḥavurah* therefore clearly differed from the *yaḥad* in its interpretation of its *own* observance of the purity-laws. The Pharisees may have criticized the present priesthood, but that criticism did not lead them to reject the cult. They held one should be pure *both* in the Temple and at table, while for the *yaḥad*, the latter was equivalent to the former. This seems to suggest the Pharisees would not have "spiritualized" the cult or regarded the purity-laws as metaphorical, as was the case for the author of Hebrews. That fact makes all the more curious their requirement that the purity-laws be kept at home. They thereby extended to the home the application of the Temple's purity rules, yet without declaring in abeyance the cult itself, thus combining a literalistic with a figurative view of purity. One should keep the concrete laws in the worldly Temple. One should also keep those laws, in a practical way, at the table at home, which is therefore regarded as more than a mere metaphor for the Temple altar. If these surmises are correct, then the Pharisees may be seen as in an intermediate position, between the *yaḥad*, which in a literal way kept the purity-laws *but* regarded its community as a new Temple, on the one side, and, on the other, the Christian community, which gradually dropped the laws and regarded its special communion meal as a sacrifice superior to the Temple's. To be sure, the early Christians did not reject the cult while it stood; Acts reports that the early disciples were assiduous in it, even Paul was willing to participate, and James is said to have been famous for his piety. To 66, therefore, Jerusalem Christians presumably continued to be practicing Jews.

The difficult question before us, however, is, What ideas or interpretations did the pre-70 Pharisees associate with the preservation of purity for ordinary meals? Later rabbinic literature preserves sayings appropriate for such an interpretation of purity, for example, "As long as the Temple stood, the altar atoned for Israel, but now a man's table atones for him."[1] But this saying takes for granted that the cult is no more and is attributed to Yoḥanan [b. Nappaha] and Eleazar [b. Pedat], third-century masters. Clearly, the idea behind the Pharisaic stress on purity in ordinary meals is that the table is to be compared to the altar, the meal to the cultic service. C. Rabin suggests, "The blessings pronounced before and after the meal correspond to the prayers before and after the sacrifices."[2] But without literature written by pre-

[1] b. Berakhot 55a.

[2] C. Rabin, *Qumran Studies* (Oxford, 1957), pp. 34-5. Rabin rightly points out that in later rabbinic Judaism eating one's food in a state of Levitical purity remained an ideal, and signified outstanding piety. Abraham was alleged to have eaten his food in a state of purity (b. Bava Meṣi'a' 87a) as was Saul (Pesiqta Rabbati 68a). In the early third century Ḥiyya advised his nephew Rav to eat his ordinary food in purity throughout the year, or at least during the days between the New Year and the Day of Atonement (y. Shabbat 1:5), cited by Rabin, pp. 35-6. But these are exceptional instances. Evidence that purity at meals was widely observed even in rabbinical circles is very sparse.

70 Pharisees, we cannot take for granted that is how they saw things. Nor do we know the origins of their specific practices.[1]

---

[1] Isidore Lévy, *La légende de Pythagore de Grèce en Palestine* (Paris, 1927), pp. 275f. supposes the Pharisaic rite derives from Pythagorean sources. Washing before meals, he says, is difficult to find in the ancient world, other than the Pythagorean usage:

> ...se tenant le matin à l'écart du monde, ils vaquent l'après-midi aux affaires profanes, font une promenade, puis prennent un bain après lequel a lieu le repas.

It seems difficult to see in common more than the fact of washing; but the reasons adduced for doing so are apt not to have had anything at all in common—whatever those reasons may have been. The notion that the Pharisees and Essenes derived their discipline and ideas from the Pythagoreans seems certainly false. Lévy did not take account of the extent to which those ideas had become common property in the Hellenistic world. The legend of which he speaks was probably more a creation of popular Hellenistic piety than of Pythagoreanism, as Morton Smith points out in his part of *Heroes and Gods* (N.Y., 1965), pp. 101-105.

CHAPTER THREE

PURITY IN TALMUDIC JUDAISM

The surviving literature produced by the rabbis of the first to the seventh centuries exceeds in quantity the whole of the Jewish literature deriving from the period of the Second Temple. We therefore should not be surprised that Talmudic literature on the subject of purity yields a great many more comments. These comments are considerably more imaginative than anything that preceded. To be sure, this may reflect merely the result of the accident of survival of a large corpus of writings. A second reason, however, is that the rabbis took more seriously than did antecedent groups the legal part of biblical literature. They accordingly invested much effort in the detailed elucidation and application of legal materials, which, except for Philo, are practically neglected by antecedent groups and individuals.

Rabbinic ideas about purity are to be derived from both legal and non-legal parts of Talmudic literature. We shall not survey ideas which may stand behind the legal passages, for these, while authoritative and normative, are imbedded in the law itself and difficult to extract from that context. It may be shown, for example, that certain Mishnaic pericopae take for granted a priestly and cultic setting, while others assume the law is to be kept at home by ordinary people, not priests. These assumptions constitute two important and divergent interpretations of purity and probably indicate the laws derive from different sources. But to uncover the total ideological or theological foundations of the law requires comprehensive studies of the individual laws themselves, item by item. Before such studies in detail, we cannot draw reliable conclusions. We therefore concentrate on the ideas about purity revealed in non-legal Talmudic literature, for these are more readily accessible and may be easily summarized. I must stress the following picture of Talmudic thinking about purity is partial.

The rabbis' primary hermeneutical interest lay in the ethical or moral lessons to be derived from the purity-rules. Their secondary interest was in the historical foundations of those rules, meaning, which biblical or earlier "rabbinic" authority was responsible for making them? When and how had they been applied in biblical antiquity? In its fundamental method, their hermeneutic does not differ from that of Philo or the author of Hebrews; they interpreted one set of ideas or rules in terms of another set of ideas or rules, that is, allegorically. But while Philo's allegory drew upon intellectual traits, and Hebrews' upon the Christian myth, the rabbis' interpretation drew upon practical ethical and social qualities. Thus for Philo the laws of leprosy "really" referred to a serene spirit, while for the rabbis they spoke of gossip or arrogance. The rabbis' concrete interpretation is part of their larger conception of the sacred community as the Temple, so impurity will be assigned to social vices, just as Temple rites will be regarded as figured in rabbinic practices, the priest in the rabbi, the sacrifice in the study of Torah. This is the main result of the inquiry before us.

While the modes of thought do not differ in fundamental approach to the interpretation of biblical laws, they otherwise have nothing in common. Philo's ethical thinking is more systematic and is tied to an external system, as worked out by generations of Stoic, Neopythagorean, and Middle Platonist philosophers, and worked into a connection with Scripture by generations of Alexandrian Jews. The rabbis' ethics tended to be less reflective and more like common law. The imaginative, figurative interpretation attempted by Philo has its counterpart in the more mechanical, less subtle reference of rabbis to either moral lapses or historical events. The two literatures also have in common repetitiousness and a certain tedium.

How shall we justify the treatment of the various and multifaceted sayings found in Talmudic and Midrashic literature as a single chapter in the history of Judaism? There are two reasons.

First of all, rabbinic literature yields an internally consistent and nearly seamless fabric of ideas, developing along a single path from beginning to end. We can easily distinguish modes of expression different in Talmudic from Midrashic literature, but these consist chiefly of literary style, rather than of exegetical or conceptual principles. The differences derive from the nature of the literature, not from the historical period or intellectual setting in which the literature was produced. The earlier Midrashic collections come from the Amoraic period, ca. 200-500, in which the legal literature of the Talmuds also was created. Many of the same authorities occur in both Talmudic and Midrashic literature. The fundamental ideas exhibited in the Mishnah, Tosefta, and Talmuds recur in the Midrashic compilations, though there they are spelled out differently. As in the biblical legacy we here observe a striking correspondence between legal and non-legal ideas.

What the law expresses in its way, the ethical or theological or exegetical sayings tend to formulate in theirs.

Second, the fundamental consistency within the rabbinic interpretations of purity, from the earliest to the latest strata of the literature, has its counterpart in the ideologically monolithic character of the rabbinic movement as a historical and institutional phenomenon. From the beginnings of rabbinic Judaism in the aftermath of the destruction of the Temple down to the Middle Ages and beyond, the rabbinic movement exhibits, amid many kinds of interesting changes, elaborations, and developments, remarkable stability in its main theological traits. Institutional support for the stability of rabbinic values derived partly from the system of training disciples through imitation of the masters' deeds and memorization of their words, which left little room for divergence in fundamental matters. The rabbinic movement was disciplined also by belief that the legacy of the masters derived from divine revelation at Sinai, and that in imitating the way of the rabbi they followed the model established by God for Moses "our rabbi." The consequence of this stability for intellectual history will be seen in the unfolding of rabbinic ideas about purity, which exhibit remarkable consistency and at the same time leave ample room for individual imagination and later elaboration and augmentation.

Our inquiry provides a good opportunity to investigate one aspect of the intellectual antecedents of rabbinic Judaism. No one supposes that when, as is alleged, Yoḥanan ben Zakkai began to bestow the title, "rabbi," upon his disciples, rabbinic Judaism was created, fully developed and utterly without roots in traditions formed before 70. On the contrary, it is generally, and rightly, supposed that rabbinic Judaism preserves a considerable legacy deriving from various sources, not all of them Pharisaic, in Second Temple times. But rather than engage in abstract argument as to the nature of that legacy, we shall look for concrete affinities between what we find within the rabbinic interpretation of purity and what we have already observed.

To state the result at the outset: we shall see that, like all other groups, rabbinic Judaism focused on the Bible, at the same time bringing to the interpretation and application of Scripture its own set of concerns and values. These concerns and values, however, in striking measure were shaped within biblical literature itself. But they do not exhibit significant correspondence with the antecedent ideas of other groups, except so far as both bodies of interpretation begin in the Hebrew Scriptures. The central question is whether rabbinic Judaism reveals a range of ideas which, in general or in detail, is independent of biblical thought but is already familiar from the consideration of the literature of Judaism in the period of the Second Temple. The answer is that it does not. I discern little evidence that ideas important to Talmudic views of purity begin in post-biblical, but prerabbinic circles; there is virtually no correspondence. The sole continuity is from Pharisaism to rabbinism, on the one side, and—obviously—from biblical literature, on the other.

The rabbinic view of purity forms part of a much larger, and quite independent effort to justify the fate of Israel. Whatever God does is just, and the suffering of individuals is justified, in a measure, by their ethical failures, as the sufferings of the people result from its moral lapses. This fundamental theodicy, shaped in the aftermath of the disaster of 70 and, in the case of the interpretation of purity, that of 135, provides the larger context for the concrete and episodic sayings about the meaning of impurity. It is a hermeneutic quite characteristic of, and unique to, the rabbinic movement, while deriving from the legacy of biblical literature. Yet, in the application to purity of that larger body of commonplace ideas on theodicy—known to Leviticus and Deuteronomy, as well as Ezekiel and Jeremiah—the rabbis stand wholly by themselves, as we shall observe when we review the whole corpus of data, for the issue of theodicy simply has not surfaced in the ideas about purity we have already surveyed.

We shall consider the history of rabbinic thinking about purity in three parts.

The first under consideration is Mishnah and Tosefta, documents which are generally believed to have reached their present form in the early third century. Alongside but separately considered are sayings of those same first- and second-century rabbis (Tannaim) as are represented in Mishnah and Tosefta but attributed to them by other, somewhat later collections, in particular the Midrashic compilations attributed to Tannaim, and sayings in their names in the Babylonian and Palestinian Talmuds. These sayings in the matter of purity are consistent with those found in the more reliable documents.

The second stage is examination of the sayings of the Amoraic authorities in the Palestinian and Babylonian Talmuds; and the third is sayings of authorities in the Midrashic literature of the same period, chiefly Leviticus Rabbah, Tanḥuma, the Pesiqta's, and other more or less contemporary documents.

The corpus of rabbinic sayings and stories on purity is huge. I have selected items representative of the main outline of rabbinic thought and then given, in the main, only one example of each idea or interpretive tendency. My effort is to lay out the primary lines of development, beginning with what is indubitably the earliest stratum of rabbinic literature, ending with the latest. Within the several strata the differentiation according to specific authorities plays no role in the historical account of the development of the idea of purity. We shall observe some important signs of development, from one period to the next, both in actual, detailed interpretation, and in the *mode* of interpreting purity. To establish that these developments actually were sequential, it is sufficient to divide the literary materials in the way I have described.

My claim is not, and cannot be, that if a saying is first attributed to a given authority, it must begin with him, or that ideas appearing for the first time in a later stratum cannot have been available to the authorities represented in an earlier one. We do not know that as fact. It will be possible to show in a few instances that an idea first occurring in rabbinic circles in the name of a late authority had already been stated in non-rabbinic circles much earlier. There we may take it as fact that the idea is both earlier and not Pharisaic or rabbinic in origin. It rather has been taken over, by what means we do not know, by the rabbinic tradition. Whether or not it has been changed in the transmission to rabbinic circles will be an interesting question for some future generation. In other instances we may be fairly certain that a given mode of interpretation both characterizes a later generation and is wholly absent in an earlier one; here we may reliably suppose that the mode is original to the later generation. The fact of first occurrence in a given stratum may therefore become significant, but only if what first occurs is a very substantial, and evidently innovative, mode of interpretation, not merely an isolated and episodic notion. Our inquiry is into the broad outlines of development in the interpretation of purity. We cannot suppose that random thoughts, not formed according to a larger pattern of interpretation, begin at the point of their first appearance in the preserved remains.

The first important view of purity in the Mishnah-Tosefta is contained in the following story, which preserves the familiar polemic against the preference for purity over higher ethical requirements:

> A. The story is told of two priests of equal rank, who were running up the ramp. One pushed the other when he was within the four cubits [of the altar]. The other took a knife and stabbed him in the heart.

B. R. Ṣadoq came and stood on the steps of the hall and said, "Hear me, House of Israel, our brethren! Lo it says, 'When a corpse is found ... [and it is not known who killed him] and your elders and judges will go forth and measure ... [to which village is the corpse nearer, and that village has to bring the heifer in penitence—Deut. 21:1-2]. Come and let us measure to see who has to bring the heifer—the sanctuary or the courtyards."

They all groaned and wept after him.

C. And afterward the father of the youth came and said to them, "My brethren, I am your atonement.

"His [my] son is still writhing, and the knife is therefore not unclean."

D. This teaches you that the uncleanness of the knife was more disturbing to Israel than the shedding of blood.

E. And so Scripture says, "And also Manasseh shed very much innocent blood, until he had filled the whole of Jerusalem from one end to another" (I Kings 21:16).

F. On this basis it was said that for the sin of bloodshed the Presence of God departed, and the sanctuary was made unclean.

(Tos. Kippurim 1:12, Lieberman, pp. 224-225, ls. 55-64 [= Tos. Shavuʿot 1:4, y. Yoma 2:2, b. Yoma 23a. Compare Tos. Kelim B. Q. 1:6; Sifré Num. 161])

The story is in two parts. In the first, A + C, two priests fight for precedence. One kills the other, showing that the priesthood was hotheaded and violent, just as Josephus says of the Sadducees. Then comes a separate element, B, the sarcastic homily of Ṣadoq, which is irrelevant to A + C and out of place. The murderer is known, so Deut. 21:1-2 does not apply. So far, purity plays no role in the account. As with Josephus' failure to allude to the purification of corpse-impurity, so here the impurity of the cult is not an issue. C makes it an issue. The father tells the people not to worry. Since the dying man has not expired, the knife for the sacrifice at the altar has not been contaminated through the corpse-uncleanness of the son. D draws out this point: The priests—"Israel"—cared more for ritual than for morality. They were more disturbed at the uncleanness of the knife than at the murder of the boy. E supplies a Scriptural precedent; but F says the point of the story and text is that murder caused the divinity to depart from the sanctuary, made unclean by bloodshed, both in 586 and in 70.

Obviously, before us in A + C — F is a rabbinic polemic against the priesthood, comparing impurity and priestly morality. That polemic reflects the tension, after 70, between the rabbinical leadership and the surviving priesthood, revealed in the extensive stories about Yoḥanan ben Zakkai's and others' struggles with the priesthood. But it is a theme which, in the interpretation of purity, does not recur, and this suggests that the priests posed to the rabbis a less formidable problem in the second century and afterward.

Purity without morality is contrary to God's will. The idea is a very old one. We saw in earlier literature numerous examples of the same contrast. More interesting: what the rabbis have to say about the priests is pretty much what the Synoptics' Jesus says about the Pharisees, John's Jesus about "the Jews", and Paul about the Law. The contrast between outward and inward purity is a routine formulation of the biblical notion. Here the story-teller has relied upon the more general distinction between cultic ritual and ethics, but the point is not much different. So it is hardly surprising that the biblical view of purity persists. The intersectarian polemics all draw upon that view; one party will accuse its opponents of a gross misinterpretation of the divine will. Purity therefore serves as an instrument of vilification in the common polemic; it does so because it forms one of the common concerns of the religious life. When cultic purity is a distant memory, in the third century and afterward, the contrast between purity and morality will no longer form an important aspect of the interpretation of purity. Then it is taken for granted either that impurity is a metaphor for immorality, or that a specific form of bodily impurity in itself signifies that a particular sin has been committed. But that development derives from a theological perspective different from the one which perceives tension between cultic purity and ethical impurity.

A second, utterly different view of purity, in a saying assigned to Pinḥas b. Yair, places purity in a larger scale of values. Instead of the negative contrast between ethics and ritual, we have a strikingly affirmative view of purity, though the focus of purity—cultic or otherwise—is not defined. It rather is made into a station in the way toward the resurrection of the dead:

> Pinḥas b. Yair says, "Heedfulness leads to [physical] cleanliness, cleanliness to purity, purity to separateness (*perishut*), separateness to holiness, holiness to humility, humility to the shunning of sin, the shunning of sin to saintliness, saintliness to the Holy Spirit, the Holy Spirit to the resurrection of the dead."[1]

---

[1] M. Sotaḥ 9:15, y. Sheq. 3:3; compare b. ʿAvodah Zarah 20b, M. Sheq. 4:6, Midrash Tannaim to Deut. 23:15. The link between purity and holiness is supplied by Lev. 16:19. Note also A. Büchler, *Types of Jewish-Palestinian Piety from 70 B.C.E. to 70 C.E. The Ancient Pious Men* (1922; reprint N.Y., 1968). The saying varies in its several occurrences, but the view of purity as part of the scale of values leading to sanctity is consistent throughout.

The idea that holiness leads to humility bears some resemblance to Philo's interpretation of the heifer-sacrifice; man sees the ashes and water and recalls that he is made of the same, so he is humbled and therefore will not sin.

Pinḥas begins with heedfulness, the opposite of indifference or laxness. This will produce cleanliness in the ordinary sense. Cleanliness will further lead to purity in what I take to be the cultic sense. Purity produces separateness *(perishut)*, which leads to holiness, and onward. What is remarkable is the wholly positive view of purity, which serves not to contrast cultic with ethical behavior or as a metaphor for sin, but as an autonomous, independent value, important in its own right, and leading to a still higher stage. Also remarkable is the low, elementary position of purity in this series. Other versions of the saying have purity lead directly to sanctity, just as purity is linked to sanctity by the priestly lawyers. Separateness sometimes is regarded as equivalent to holiness, as in Sifra Qedoshim (Pereq 11:21 = Shemini Pereq 12:3): "As I am holy, you be holy. As I am separate *(parush)*, so you be separate *(perushim)*." In the preceding saying separateness leads to holiness, so the two, although distinguished, are connected. The differing versions do not yield contrary attitudes to purity. This is the closest we shall come in rabbinic theories of purity to what history suggests should have been the Pharisaic interpretation of the matter. From what we have seen above, the Pharisees ought to have equated purity with holiness or sanctity, as in the Sifra passages about God as separate *(parush)*.

This cannot have been the view of cultic priest, for whom purity was incidental to the sacrificial service. Remarkably, for Pinḥas the sacrificial service plays no role in the path to the eschaton, nor is it restored at the end. Sacrifice is not among the stages; the end is not the reintroduction of the cult but the resurrection of the dead. So Pinḥas's saying curiously treats purity entirely apart from its cultic setting, just as the Pharisees divorced the purity-laws from the cult. But, as we noted, Pinḥas then does not treat purity as a metaphor for sinlessness. It is attached, on the one side, to hygienic cleanliness, on the other to separateness and holiness—a quite separate, and evidently unique, interpretive framework from the one which centers on ethics or morality.

The saying is puzzling, therefore, for it has no antecedents in biblical viewpoints, let alone among those reviewed in the literature deriving from the period of the Second Temple. And it produces no subsequent sayings or stories: Pinḥas's view of purity simply does not recur. It therefore is not a quintessentially "rabbinic" viewpoint. But it is, as I said, remarkably appropriate to the Pharisaic program. We cannot confuse versimilitude with authenticity and suppose that, because this is what Pharisees should have said, it is what they did say. We justifiably may claim, however, that the saying is not characteristic of the rabbinic viewpoint, which we saw in the story about the priests and shall now examine in further detail.

Professor Wayne Meeks points to one pertinent source, however, which presents a closely related view of purity in linking it with the eschatological times. It is Zech. 14:20-21: "And on that day there shall be inscribed on the bells of the horses, 'Holy to the Lord.' And the pots in the house of the Lord shall be as the bowls before the altar; and every pot in Jerusalem and Judah shall be sacred to the Lord of hosts, so that all who sacrifice may come and take of them and boil the flesh of the sacrifice in them ..." The foregoing passage proposes that at the end of days every pot in Jerusalem and Judah—not merely in the sanctuary—will be holy. I take it for granted that included in holiness here is antecedent cultic purity or cleanness, despite the absence of explicit use of the cultic language of purity. Any other interpretation is unthinkable. If the pre-70 Pharisees believed one should preserve purity outside of the Temple, even in the home, and if they also saw themselves as living on the threshhold of the eschaton—at the stage of cleanness, in Pinḥas's saying—then the prophecy in Zechariah would have supplied an important proof-text for their theological position. The achievement of purity outside of Temple precincts then would mark a stage in the eschatological process, and the Pharisees would have kept the laws as they did because of their larger conception of the requirements of the eschaton. We do not, however, know how the pre-70 Pharisees interpreted the events of their day, therefore cannot say whether they shared the view of the *yaḥad* and of the Christian community concerning the imminent advent of the eschaton.

A third theme is that uncleanness is not a metaphor for, but a sign of, sin, and despite both the Israelites' uncleanness and the sin thereby connoted, still "God is in their midst";

> [The Lord said to Moses, "Command the people of Israel that they put out of the camp every leper ... that they may not defile their camp] in the midst of which I dwell" (Num. 5:1-3).
>
> Israel are beloved, for even though they are unclean, the Presence of

God is among them, and so Scripture says, "Who dwells with them in the midst of their uncleanness" (Lev. 16:16) ... and Scripture says, "That they may not defile their camp in the midst of which I dwell," and likewise, "And they not defile the land in which you dwell, in the midst of which I dwell" (Num. 35:34).

R. Yosé the Galilean says, "Come and see how strong is the power of sin, for before they put forth their hands in transgression, there were not found among them people unclean through having a discharge and lepers, but after they put forth their hands in transgression, there were among them people unclean through having a discharge and lepers. So we learn that these three things happened on the same day."

(Sifré Num. Naso 2)

Yosé and his contemporaries treat uncleanness differently from the prophets. To them it is not a metaphor for sin. Yosé does not claim that cleanness is somehow figurative of ethical purity. The presence of uncleanness in a concrete and this-worldly sense itself *signifies* the antecedent commission of sin. Impurity as a symptom here is connotative; it is inseparable from its consequence and indicative of the presence of sin. It may be claimed that, as in the *yaḥad*, the biblical metaphor has here been brought to its logical conclusion: impurity is like sin, sin therefore causes impurity. But while the rabbis say impurity connotes the commission of sin, they do not then follow the *yaḥad* in saying that committing certain sins automatically imposes a period of impurity.[1] This is in the hands of Heaven. No rabbi ever declared a gossip to be impure with the same impurity as a leper, for example. The rabbinical conception therefore is structurally not similar to that of the *yaḥad*. I am not certain that the metaphor inexorably produces the connotation discerned by the rabbis; it certainly did not lead the prophets to the same conclusion, nor did anyone except the *yaḥad* in the period of the Second Temple claim that sin causes impurity, though many, like Jesus, supposed that impurity might serve as an analogy for sin. So Yosé's saying does not suggest he has, like Philo, taken a metaphor and supplied it with a second level of meaning, as with Philo's progression: leprosy → uncleanness → instability. That is, leprosy is a metaphor of uncleanness, which further serves as a metaphor of instability. To take a different example from Philo, he sees the purification-rite as the figure for humility, thus: water and ashes → purity → humility. For Yosé, the progression is reversed: Actual

[1] The Damascus Covenant fragment published by J. T. Milik in (*Revue biblique* 73, 1966, p. 105) seems to hold that an evil spirit causes leprosy, so 4Q 226 Da 1 XVII. But this seems to me a quite different conception from that of the second-century rabbis. See above, p. 51, n. 3.

transgression → *metaphor:* moral impurity → *divine punishment:* physical impurity. Qumran drops stage two. The progression is thus: transgression → material impurity. In the *yaḥad* sinners are declared impure as an immediate consequence of their sin. For Yosé sin is punished by God, who sends on the sinner a condition that causes impurity. Yosé the Galilean thus presents the general principle that the presence of sin causes uncleanness. To others of his generation are attributed more concrete illustrations of that same principle.

The biblical metaphor comparing sins to uncleanness nonetheless recurs, as one might expect, in the earliest strata of Talmudic literature. Lev. 16:30, "For on this day shall atonement be made for you to cleanse you; from all your sins you will be clean before the Lord," is assigned to the High Priest's prayer on the Day of Atonement.[1] But the early rabbis went on to say something not explicitly claimed in biblical or intertestamental literature: violation of certain specific rules of purity will be punished just as sin in general is punished, therefore, conversely, just as in general the presence of punishment will indicate the antecedent commission of a sin, so the presence of certain specific sins will prove that particular purity-laws have been violated. Yosé the Galilean stops short of that assertion, which actually is stated, in most extreme form, in the claim that women die in childbirth for not keeping the laws of the menstruant.[2] A later master, R. Isaac, explained, "She transgressed through the chambers of her womb, therefore she is punished through the chambers of her womb."[3] Still later Amoraim explain why it is in particular on the occasion of childbirth that the woman perishes. "Measure for measure" is thus explained in entirely concrete and specific terms.

A further illustration of the general conviction that punishment, such as illness or death, must signify the antecedent commission of a particular sin is the saying, attributed to Tannaim, that dropsy is a sign of sin, jaundice is a sign of causeless hatred, poverty is a sign of conceit, and croup is a sign of slander.[4] Croup is further discussed. Judah b. Ilai explains, "Though the kidneys counsel, the heart gives understanding, and the tongue gives form, yet the mouth completes it. Therefore croup signifies that the mouth has spoken slander."[5] Eliezer

[1] M. Yoma 3:8.
[2] M. Shabbat 2:6.
[3] b. Shabbat 31b.
[4] *ibid.*, 33a.
[5] *ibid.*

b. R. Yosé, of the same generation, says croup comes because "unclean food is eaten with the mouth."[1] So to Eliezer the eating of unclean food is comparable to slander and produces the same punishment others assign to the latter.

Leprosy is likewise said to be caused by slander or pride. This is the most commonplace assertion linking a particular sin to a specific form of uncleanness. The connection with slander is based upon the case of Miriam, the connection with pride on that of Uzziah:

> ["Take heed, in an attack of leprosy to be very careful to do according to all that the Levitical priests shall direct you ...] Remember what God did to Miriam" (Deut. 24:9).
>
> What has one thing to do with the other?
>
> But it teaches that she was punished only on account of gossip.
>
> And is it not an argument *a fortiori*? If this happened to Miriam, who did not speak in such a way in Moses' presence, one who speaks of his fellow in his very presence, how much the more so!
>
> R. Simeon b. Eleazar says, "Also leprosy comes on account of arrogance, for so we find concerning Uzziah, about whom Scripture says: 'But when he was strong, he grew proud, to his destruction. For he was false to the Lord his God and entered the Temple of the Lord to burn incense on the altar of incense. But Azariah the priest went in after him, with eighty priests of the Lord who were men of valor; and they withstood King Uzziah and said to him, 'It is not for you, Uzziah, to burn incense to the Lord, but for the priests the sons of Aaron, who are consecrated, to burn incense. Go out of the sanctuary, for you have done wrong, and it will bring you no honor from the Lord God.' Then Uzziah was angry. Now he had a censer in hand to burn incense, and when he became angry with the priests, leprosy broke out on his forehead ...'" (II Chronicles 27:16-19).
>
> (Sifra Meṣoraʿ Parashah 5:9 [Tos. Neg. 6:7; Sifré Deut. 275[2]])

The rabbinic view that leprosy is caused by gossip or slander ("evil speech") depends upon the interpretation of Miriam's behavior. In Num. 12:1ff., Miriam and Aaron are guilty of criticizing Moses because of his wife and of saying that they are capable of prophecy just as much as he: "Has the Lord indeed spoken only through Moses? Has he not spoken through us also?" So Moses' authority is called into

[1] *ibid.*, 33b.

[2] See also Sifré Zuṭṭa to Num. 11:14, Midrash Tannaim to Deut. 24:9; Sifré Num. 106; Sifra Meṣoraʿ 1:11. On Uzziah: b. Moʿed Qaṭan 7b—Uzziah had sexual relations while a leper, so Ḥiyya and Judah the Patriarch. See also Meir, Sifra Meṣoraʿ Parashah 5:11, "The evil person, not the righteous one, is unclean by leprosy." and Sifra Meṣoraʿ Parashah 5:4, Judah b. Ilai says the announcement of the coming of leprosy was not good news.

question, and the divine response is to declare Moses' prophecy of a higher order than theirs. Then Miriam is turned into a leper. The issue of "gossip" therefore is hardly obvious. To the rabbinic eisegetes, the rebellion against Moses is of no consequence, the criticism of his marriage is central. Then this criticism is interpreted as slander, *lashon hara'*, and the rest follows.

Simeon b. Eleazar has a better case, for II Chron. 27:16ff. says clearly that Uzziah was made a leper because of his intervening in the cult, and he did so because of pride. Both views of the origin of leprosy take for granted the established notion that the punishment of impurity signifies the commission of an antecedent crime; and the punishment will exactly fit the crime. Later on this latter idea will generate efforts to show *why* the punishment is fitting to the crime. Then all the other biblical references to leprosy will be tied to specific sins. In the first stage of rabbinic thought on the subject, the attempt to spell out this correspondence produces only Judah b. Ilai's and Eliezer b. R. Yosé's explanations for the association of croup with the mouth.

Further specific details of the purity laws elicit explanation. To Simeon b. Yoḥai is attributed a reason for the requirement that a woman after childbirth must bring a sacrifice. He evidently understand the *ḥaṭa'at* as a sin, rather than a purification-offering. To Meir is attributed the following explanation for the menstrual taboo:

> R. Simeon b. Yoḥai was asked by his disciples, "Why did the Torah ordain a woman after childbirth should bring a sacrifice?"
>
> He replied, "When she kneels in bearing she swears impetuously that she will have no intercourse with her husband. The Torah, therefore, ordained that she should bring a sacrifice."
>
> "And why did the Torah ordain that in the case of a male [the woman is clean] after seven days and in that of a female after fourteen days?"
>
> "[On the birth of a] male with whom all rejoice she regrets her oath after seven days, [but on the birth of a female] about whom everybody is upset she regrets her oath after fourteen days."
>
> It was taught: R. Meir used to say, "Why did the Torah ordain that the uncleanness of menstruation should continue for seven days? Because being in constant contact with his wife [a husband might] develop a loathing towards her. The Torah, therefore, ordained: Let her be unclean for seven days in order that she shall be beloved by her husband as at the time of her first entry into the bridal chamber."
>
> (b. Niddah 31b, trans. W. Slotki, pp. 218-9 [Sacrifice: Tanḥuma Tazri'a 6])

Both masters draw upon a this-worldly and rational hermeneutic. Simeon's alludes to the woman's oath, taken during birth-pangs, not to have more children. She has to atone for that oath, which she will regret. After the birth of a male, the woman quickly reverses the oath; after a female it takes a while longer. Similarly, Meir's view of the menstrual taboo is apparently drawn from the everyday realities of marriage. We may contrast Simeon's explanation of the difference between the rules of offering after a male and a female with that of Jubilees (p. 55), which seeks the foundation of the law in the history of creation itself and says that the difference is due to the different time of entry into the Garden of Eden.

The Fathers according to Rabbi Nathan, a work attributed to Tannaitic authorities, makes use of the purity-rules to illustrate sayings of the Tannaim. Thus "making a fence around the law" is exemplified in the separation of husband and wife during menstruation. That the people should keep these laws is taken for granted and cited as evidence that Israel will, through keeping them, merit the world to come:

> "Hedged in by lilies" (Song of Songs 7:3) teaches this: When Israel put them into practice, they are led thereby to the life of the world to come. How so? A man's wife in her menses is alone with him at home. If he is so minded, he cohabits with her; if he is otherwise minded, he does not cohabit with her. Does then anyone see him, or does anyone know to tell him aught? He fears only Him who commanded against contact with a menstruant.
>
> (Again), one has suffered a pollution. If he is so minded, he bathes; if he is otherwise minded, he does not bathe. Does anyone see him, or does anyone know to tell him aught? He fears only Him who commands ritual immersion ...
>
> What is the hedge which Moses made about his words? Lo, it says, "And the Lord said unto Moses: Go unto the people and sanctify them today and tomorrow" (Exod. 19:10). Moses the righteous did not wish to speak to Israel the way the Holy One, blessed be He, had spoken to him. Instead, this is what he said to them: "Be ready against the third day; come not near a woman" (Exod. 19:15). And of his own accord Moses added one day for their sake. For thus reasoned Moses: If a man cohabits with his wife and on the third day semen issues from her, they will be unclean; in that event Israel will receive the words of the Torah from Mount Sinai in impurity. I shall therefore add a day for their sake, so that no man shall cohabit with his wife, on the third day no semen will issue from her, and they will be clean. And thus Israel will receive the words of the Torah from Mount Sinai in purity."
>
> (The Fathers According to Rabbi Nathan, Chap. 2, trans. Goldin, p. 18)

Accordingly, keeping the laws is rewarded in the world to come. No one is going to know whether a couple keeps or violates the rules.

God knows, however, and will act accordingly. Moses is praised for his strictness in adding to the divine requirements of keeping the laws.

The view of the purity-rules revealed here is that of the rabbinic lawyer. He assumes the laws are valid and should be observed. He therefore provides reasons for people to keep the laws even when not forced to do so. The same could be said of numerous other laws. The menstrual and related rules are useful illustrations because whether they are kept or violated is wholly a private matter. Standing outside of the power of the rabbinical courts or even the influence of public opinion, purity-rules are the sort of laws which best illustrate the homily that God will enforce laws men cannot.

The same source presents a story to illustrate this same point. A certain man who had studied much Torah died in middle age, before his time. His wife complained to the rabbis that he had been a loyal disciple of the sages, yet had died young. No one knew the reason. Finally Elijah heard the story and asked, "During the first three days of your impurity, how did he conduct himself in your company?" She replied that the man did not touch her and told her to touch nothing "lest it become of doubtful purity." "During the days of your impurity, how did he conduct himself. She replied that the couple ate and drank and slept together, and their flesh touched, but they did not engage in sexual relations. "Blessed be God who killed him," Elijah exclaimed, "For thus it is written in the Torah, 'Also thou shalt not approach unto a woman as long as she is impure by her uncleanness' (Lev. 18:19)." Here failure to observe not the law but an acknowledged addition to, or extension of, the law ("hedge") produces the most severe punishment. Again the story about a purity-rule serves as an illustration of another, more fundamental matter. Impurity is not a metaphor for immorality, nor does death signify that one particular purity-rule has been violated. Dying in middle age may signify the antecedent commission of any of a number of sins, not the particular one at hand. So purity law is not essential to the operative details of the story, but is merely an element of the plot, for which some other element with the same consequence could be substituted.

Stories and sayings such as these leave no doubt that, so far as the rabbis who told them were concerned, the purity-rules were an integral part of the divine will. They were not to be turned into metaphors. Their value was not made to depend upon some other, "higher" ethical value. They were to be kept literally and carefully; if they were not kept, God would punish the law-breakers. Here ethics is not contrasted to purity. Impurity is not a metaphor for sin. It is a state to be avoided, and deliberate failure to avoid it is a sin in and of itself. Purity is not made solely into a symbol of sinlessness. Both purity and impurity are concrete and literal facts of life.[1]

How shall we characterize the first stage in the rabbinic interpretation of purity? We found four major themes.

First comes the enigmatic saying of Pinḥas b. Yair, which stands by itself and, as I said, seems to refer backward to the viewpoint appropriate to Pharisaism before 70.

Second is the general assertion that impurity comes on account of sin. While not in Mishnah-Tosefta, the saying is a generalization of the specific allegation, which does occur in that literature, that women die in childbirth for transgressing menstrual rules, and that leprosy is a sign that a person is guilty of having gossiped, or, as in Simeon's saying in both Tosefta and Sifra, a sign of arrogance. So Yosé the Galilean's viewpoint in a somewhat later compilation is entirely consistent with the better-attested opinions.

Third, we find the effort, attributed primarily to the Ushan masters, to elaborate the assignment of reasons for specific forms of impurity or of sacrifices required on account of impurity. Meir says the requirement of separation is to keep alive the interest in marital sex—a far-cry from the taboo in which the menstrual separation is apt to have originated. Simeon b. Yoḥai explains in this-worldly terms the sacrifice after childbirth and the difference between the time of the sacrifice for a male, and for a female child. These explanations set the style for what will follow. If it is asserted in Tannaitic literature that women die in childbirth for not observing the menstrual laws, then, in later times, the specific connection between violating the law and dying in childbirth will be spelled out. This is the sort of linear development which justifies treating the rabbinic corpus as a unity.

The final view of purity, in *The Fathers According to Rabbi Nathan*, stands quite separate from the foregoing, because there is no effort to explain or interpret the laws, simply an effort to persuade people to keep them. Keeping the laws will produce a reward in the world to come. One might have told exactly the same stories in connection with any other law. The specific traits or meaning of purity-laws play no important role. What is striking is the saying assigned to Elijah that it was right for God to kill the man in his middle-age. One might

---

[1] Avot deR. Nathan, Chap. 2, Goldin, p. 17.

suppose that the homily and story were told in response to laxness on the part of ordinary folk, but that is by no means a necessary conclusion.

I should regard the first three modes of interpreting the laws as reliably attributed to Tannaitic authorities and laying foundations of the later development of rabbinic ideas on the subject. Of the three certainly-Tannaitic approaches, the second and third seem to me entirely unique to the rabbis, therefore illustrative of their special viewpoint. The innovation of earlier rabbinic Judaism is the view of impurity—leprosy—not as a metaphor for sin in general, but as a sign that a *specific* sin has been committed. As I said, this then will generate the effort to show the reasonable relationship between a particular form of punishment, on the one side, and a specific sin on the other, an approach to be richly elaborated later on.

This mode of thought is part of a larger rabbinic view that suffering comes primarily in consequence of human failings. "Measure for measure" characterizes divine justice. The employment of purity-laws in this connection therefore constitutes part of the rabbinic accounting for and justification of the fate of the Jewish people after the destruction of the Second Temple and, in particular, the disaster of the Bar Kokhba War—the time of Meir, Yosé, Simeon b. Yoḥai, and Simeon b. Eleazar. Just as the people were told they had sinned but could achieve regeneration through atonement and good behavior, so in the specific and very ordinary instances of disease or early death one might try to show a particular sin lay at the origin of the suffering. The purity-rules provide an explanation for individual suffering because the impurity—leprosy, menstruation—afflicts the private person. So through their interpretation of the purity-laws, the early post-70 rabbis' generalized allegation, that Israel suffered on account of sin, after 135 is made precise and concrete in the life of the private person. The emphasis on the individual and his personal impurity is consistent with the stress of the priestly prophet, Ezekiel, that the individual bears the burden of his own guilt. The person who sins will die, but his family will not. Ezekiel's view of purity is part of the larger priestly ideology; but the stress on the individual—in connection with either sin or uncleanness—seems to have been at first Ezekiel's peculiar contribution, for priestly law commonly views sacrifices as collective. Ezekiel introduces his notion of individual retribution as a novelty, given him by revelation and contradicting the common opinion.

I think this broader theological task provides the context in which to understand the detailed sayings before us. If the rabbis of second century Usha occur most commonly, it is because after the disaster of the Bar Kokhba War the problem of theodicy and the application of the peculiarly rabbinic solution proved most pressing for ordinary folk, who suffered in the general debacle far more severely than was the case after 70. But the general outlines of their answer, linking suffering to sin, of course had been well-established for many generations.

The rabbinic theodicy of individual suffering occurs within a still larger conception, beginning with Pharisaism before 70 and carried forward by rabbinism afterward. As we saw, the Pharisees before 70 extended the Temple's sanctity to the affairs of ordinary folk, requiring that people eat their meals in a state of purity appropriate for the sanctuary and preserve their food from impurity originally pertinent only to the cult and priesthood. After 70 the rabbinical continuators of Pharisaism treated sacrifice itself as something to be done in everyday life, comparing deeds of lovingkindness to the sacrifices by which sins were atoned for. So it was an established trait of Pharisaism and later rabbinism to apply cultic symbols to extra-cultic, communal matters, thus to regard the Temple's sanctity as extending to the streets of the villages. This was done after 70 by assigning ethical equivalents to Temple rites, on the one side, and by comparing study of Torah to the act of sacrifice and the rabbi to the Temple priest, on the other. It is in this context that the interpretation of the purity-rules was undertaken. By locating ethical lapses as the cause of impurity, beginning with the view that leprosy is a sign that one is guilty of having gossiped, the second-century rabbis simply carried forward the established trait of rabbinism and the antecedent Pharisaism. Just as earlier, cultic purity was extended to the home, and, later on, study of Torah was substituted for cultic sacrifice and deeds of lovingkindness for sin-offering, so it now was natural to take over the purity-rules and to endow them with ethical, therefore with everyday, communal significance, instead of leaving them wholly within the cult. It was a continuation of an earlier tendency to ethicize, spiritualize, and moralize the cult by treating the holy people—the community of Israel—as equivalent to the holy sanctuary. This tendency to be sure had already been present in a vague and general way in the biblical treatment of purity as a metaphor for righteousness and impurity for sin. But it was now greatly elaborated and extended to the minutiae of daily life, as was normal for rabbinism in many other ways.

The Amoraic stratum—ca. 200-500—in the Talmuds develops ideas set forth in the Tannaitic sayings, particularly of the notion that uncleanness is a sign of sin. One new theme is the inquiry into the history of the purity-laws, though this may have been adumbrated in the second-century circles.

Mar Zuṭra or R. Ashi (fifth-century Babylonians) explained the saying of Haggai, "This people and all the works of its hands and that which they offer are unclean" (Hag. 2:13) to mean, "Because they perverted their actions, the Scriptures stigmatize them *as though* they offered up sacrifices in uncleanness."[1]

Of considerably greater interest is the following, which vastly expands the idea of leprosy as a sign of one's having committed a particular sin:

> R. Samuel b. Naḥmani said in the name of R. Yoḥanan, "Because of seven things the plague of leprosy is incurred: [These are:] Gossip [slander], the shedding of blood, vain oaths, incest, arrogance, robbery and envy....
>
> [2.] "For blood-shed, as it is written: 'And let there not fail from the house of Joab one ... that hath an issue or that is a leper' (II Sam. 3:29).
>
> [3.] "For a vain oath, as it is written: 'And Naaman said, be content, take two talents' (2 Kings 5:27), and it is written: 'The leprosy therefore of Naaman shall cleave unto thee' (II Kings 5:27).
>
> [4.] "For incest, as it is written: 'And the Lord plagued Pharaoh ... with great plagues' (Gen. 12:17).
>
> [5.] "Because of arrogance, as it is written: 'But when he was strong, his heart was lifted up so he did corruptly, and he trespassed against the Lord, his God ... and the leprosy broke forth in his forehead' (II Chron. 26:16ff.).
>
> [6.] "Because of robbery, as it is written: 'And the priest shall command that they empty the house' (Lev. 14:36), in connection with which a Tanna taught: 'Because he had gathered money that was not his own, the priest comes and scatters it.'
>
> [7.] "And because of envy, as it is said: 'Then he that owneth the house shall come' (Lev. 14:35), referring to which the school of R. Ishmael taught: 'He who would reserve his house for himself.'"
>
> (b. ʿArakhin 16a, trans. Leo Jung, p. 91)

Yoḥanan, a third century master, thus picked up the idea that leprosy is a sign of having committed a sin. The most striking items come at the end. A house which displays the signs of mildew has to be emptied out. So, a Tanna taught, the man has to show everything in the house, emptying out all its contents, and thus the dishonestly acquired pos-

[1] b. Pesaḥim 17a.

sessions are displayed to the world. The same circumstance produces a further homily. Because a man wants to keep his house to himself, he loses the use of the house entirely. The emphasis on gossip recurs in the following:

> R. Samuel b. Elnadab asked of R. Ḥanina, or as others say, R. Samuel b. Nadab, the son-in-law of R. Ḥanina, asked of R. Ḥanina—or, according to still others, asked of R. Joshua b. Levi—"Wherein is the leper different that the Torah said: 'He shall dwell alone; without the camp shall his dwelling be'? (Lev. 14:4). He separated a husband from his wife, a man from his neighbor, therefore said the Torah: 'He shall dwell alone.'"
>
> R. Joshua b. Levi said, "Wherein is the leper different that the Torah said, 'Two living clean birds' (Lev. 14:4 [he should bring] so that he may become pure again? The Holy One, blessed be He, said, 'He did the work of a babbler, therefore let him offer a babbler as a sacrifice.'"
>
> (b. ʿArakhin 16b, trans. Leo Jung, p. 93)

Through gossip, the guilty party separated people from one another, therefore he is separated from society. Joshua b. Levi derives the same lesson from the use of birds in the sacrifice; just as birds chirp, or babble, so did the common gossip. Still later, the "exile" of the leper will be turned into an allegory for the exile of the whole Jewish people. The public, collective suffering, explained as the consequence of communal sin, produces a similar interpertation of individual ailments. And this, in turn, will ultimately be applied to the condition of the community—a full and exhaustive exploitation of the original metaphor.

Conversely, avoiding uncleanness is taken to be a sign of divine approval. This will occur, for example, in the absence of nocturnal emissions and of consequent impurity, assigned to Ezekiel:

> "Then said I, 'Ah Lord God! behold my soul hath not been polluted; for from my youth up even till now have I not eaten of that which dieth of itself [*nebelah*], or is torn of beasts [*trefah*]; neither came there abhorred flesh into my mouth' " (Ezek. 4:14).
>
> [And it has been interpreted as follows:] 'Behold my soul hath not been polluted,' for I did not allow impure thoughts to enter my mind during the day so as to lead to pollution at night.
>
> (b. Ḥullin 37b, trans. Eli Cashdan, p. 201; for Elisha: Lev. R. 24:6)

Thus Ezekiel has it to his credit that he avoided uncleanness.[1]

A further effort to explain the claim that women die in childbirth

[1] For the same idea, y. Yevamot 2:4.

for ignoring the menstrual laws is the following, which in a remote way recalls the homily of Jubilees:

> The First Man was the blood of the world ... and Eve brought death upon him. Therefore the commandment concerning the menstrual rules was given to the woman.
>
> (y. Shabbat 2:6; Tanḥuma Noaḥ to Gen. 3:19)

The woman's very liability to those laws is her own fault, therefore she will be put to death for ignoring them.

In addition to the effort to assign specific sins to particular kinds of uncleanness to particular sins, as in *The Fathers* we find the effort to encourage people to keep the laws on account of other bad results of ignoring them:

> When R. Dimi came [from Palestine] he reported, "The omission to wash the hands before the meal caused one to eat swine's flesh, and the omission to wash the hands after the meal caused a separation of a wife from her husband."
>
> When Rabin came [from Palestine] he reported, "The omission to wash before the meal caused one to eat *nebelah*, and the omission to wash after the meal caused a murder."
>
> R. Naḥman b. Isaac said, "[In order to remember the statements of each bear in mind] the following mnemonic: 'R. Dimi came [first] and separated her, and then Rabin came and killed her.' "
>
> R. Abba reported the graver result in each case.
>
> (b. Ḥullin 106a, trans. Eli Cashdan, p. 587; Tanḥuma Balaq 24)

The story to which Dimi and the others refer concerns a person who entered an inn and sat down without washing his hands. He was assumed to be a gentile and was given pig's meat.

The second story tells about rabbis' entrusting their purses to a man who later denied he even knew them. They noticed that the man had traces of lentils on his upper lip. They went to his house and asked his wife for the purses, saying the husband had told them to tell her to return them. She asked what evidence they had to support their story. They said that her husband had told them he had eaten lentils that day. She gave them their purses. When the husband came home and heard what the wife had done, he divorced her; in another version of the story, he killed her. But if he had washed his hands (and face) after the meal, he would not have divorced or killed his wife.[1] Rabin's version changes the first story slightly, and his second version has murder instead of divorce. Then Naḥman b. Isaac provides a

---

[1] b. Yoma 83b.

mnemonic to keep the two versions separate. Abba held that in the first instance the man had eaten pig's meat, in the second, the wife had been murdered. This sort of sermon would have encouraged people to wash their hands before they ate, a rite connected with purity-laws, not only hygiene, as we have observed. (The connection of the purity-laws with hygiene in the saying of Pinḥas is exceptional.)

To the Amoraim, the cult, including its purity-laws, was part of the history of the people and the hope for the future, but it had no concrete reality for the present. One natural interest lay in assigning to historical figures responsibility for the Temple's laws. It was taken for granted that biblical heroes had been rabbis, just like those of the present, and that they had studied Torah and explained its meaning and laws just as did the contemporary masters. Doeg and Ahitophel (II Sam. 16:23) were in particular believed to have been masters of the laws of *Ohalot*, the uncleanness conveyed by a corpse in a tent:

> Samuel found Rab Judah leaning on the door-bolt weeping. So he said to him: "O, keen scholar, wherefore does thou weep?"
>
> He replied, "Is it a small thing that is written concerning the Rabbis: 'Where is he that counted, where is he that weighed? Where is he that counted the towers?' (Is. 33:18)
>
> "'Where is he that counted?'—for they counted all the letters in the Torah.
>
> "'Where is he that weighed?'—for they weighed the light and the heavy in the Torah.
>
> "'Where is he that counted the towers?'—for they taught three hundred laws concerning a 'tower which flies in the air.'
>
> "And R. Ammi said, 'Three hundred questions did Doeg and Ahitophel raise concerning a tower which flies in the air.'
>
> "Yet we have learned, 'Three kings and four commoners [including these "rabbis"] have no share in the world to come. What then shall become of us?"
>
> Said Samuel to him, "O, keen scholar, there was impurity in their hearts."
>
> R. Ammi said, "Doeg and Ahitophel propounded four hundred problems with respect to 'a tower flying in the air,' and not one was solved."
>
> (b. Sanhedrin 106b, trans. H. Freedman, p. 725 ff., also Tanḥuma Meṣoraʿ)

R. Ammi said, "Doeg did not die until he forgot his learning, as it is written, 'He shall die without instruction, and in the greatness of his folly he shall go astray' (Prov. 5:23)."

R. Ashi said, "He was smitten with leprosy, for it is said, 'Thou hast destroyed all them that go awhoring from thee' (Ps. 73:27) ... And we learned: The only difference between him who is a *meṣora' muḥlaṭ* [definitely a leper] and one who is locked up [for observation] is in respect of letting the hair grow wild and tearing the garments."

(b. Sanhedrin 106b)

A second sort of historical inquiry was to locate in biblical legislation the origins of contemporary laws.

R. Simeon b. Pazzai said, "Where is there an indication in the Torah that gravesides should be marked?

"In the instructive text: '[And when they pass through ... the land] and one seeth a man's bone then shall he set up a sign by it' (Ezek. 39:15)."

Said Rabina to R. Ashi, "But who told us that before Ezekiel came?"

[Said the other], "It was first learned as an oral tradition, and then Ezekiel came and gave us a textual basis for it."

R. Abbahu suggested that it may be derived from this [text]: "And he shall cry, 'Unclean! Unclean!' (Lev. 13:45). [That is], impurity cries out [to the passer-by] and tells him, 'Keep off!'"

And R. 'Uzziel, the grandson of the elder R. 'Uzziel said the same, "Impurity cries out and tells him, 'Keep off!'"

But was this [text] intended for this lesson?

It is not required for what has been taught:

"And he shall cry 'Unclean! Unclean!" [This teaches that] one must make his distress known to many, that many pray for mercy on his behalf?

If that be so, let the text read 'Unclean' [but once]; why has it 'Unclean,' 'Unclean' twice over? Infer [from it] the two points.

(b. Mo'ed Qaṭan 5a, trans. H. M. Lazarus, pp. 23-24)

The history of purity-laws included the assignment of particular rules to specific authorities. We shall rapidly review elements of that "history." Abbaye (fourth century Babylonian) said that Ezra had ordained the law that a healthy man whose emission is involuntary must use nine *qavs* of water for his purification.[1] R. Naḥman b. Isaac, of the same period, said that the earlier rabbis held a gentile child to be a source of defilement by gonorrhoea so that an Israelite child would not practice sodomy with him.[2] Jacob instituted baths for Shechem (Gen. 33:18).[3]

While the earlier rule had been that a clean person should not eat with an unclean one, the first-century authorities were credited by the Amoraim with the rule that two unclean people should not eat with one another.

[1] b. Berakhot 22b.
[2] b. Shabbat 17b.
[3] b. Shabbat 33b.

In reference to the destruction of Shiloh the Temple court cried out, "Let the sons of Eli, Hophni and Pinḥas, depart hence for they defiled the Temple" (I Sam. 2:17-22).[1]

Abraham and Saul ate ordinary meals in a state of ritual purity.[2]

Yosé b. Yoʿezer and Yosé b. Yoḥanan (second century B.C.) were supposed to have declared the foreign countries to be unclean and made glassware susceptible to uncleanness. Simeon b. Sheṭaḥ (first century B.C.) imposed uncleanness upon metal utensils. Shammai and Hillel (first century B.C.) decreed that uncleanness applies to the hands.[3] Likewise it is alleged that Solomon had instituted the practice of washing the hands before meals:

> Rav Judah said in Samuel's name, "When Solomon instituted ... the washing of the hands, a Heavenly Echo came forth and declared, 'My son, if thine heart be wise, My heart shall be glad, even mine,' (Prov. 23:15) and 'My son, be wise, and make my heart glad, that I may answer that reproacheth me' (Prov. 27:11)."
>
> (b. Shabbat 14b)

Another tradition, attributed to Yosé b. Ḥalafta, a second-century authority, held that uncleanness was imposed on foreign countries and on glassware eighty years before the destruction, that is, long after the time of the two Yosé's.[4]

The compilations of Midrashim produced in Amoraic times, represented principally by Leviticus Rabbah, a Palestinian collection possibly completed in the sixth or seventh century, as well as those collections deriving from medieval times, tend to repeat, tediously and without much variation, the ideas already before us. They greatly elaborate them, however, and expand their range of Scriptural prooftexts and illustrations in numerous formulations. We shall therefore select the more important illustrations, rather than, as heretofore, citing or alluding to nearly all passages concerning the significance of purity. What is entirely original is not the ideological framework, but the novel literary expression of already familiar ideas. At the end we shall consider the two entirely new developments of the Midrashic literature deriving from Amoraic authorities, one in the literary use of the idea of purity, the other in its interpretation.

---

[1] b. Keritot 28a. This of course cannot have been Solomon's, let alone Herod's, Temple.

[2] Abraham: b. Bava Meṣiʿa' 87a. Saul: Midrash on Psalms 7:2, Pesiqta Rabbati 15:3.

[3] b. Shabbat 14b.

[4] b. Shabbat 15a.

As in the Amoraic sayings in the Talmud, also in Midrashic literature, uncleanness continues to serve as a metaphor for sin in general. In the following, Israel is called "sick," like a woman in her menstrual period, but, just as a woman is purified, so too Israel will attain salvation:

> R. Yoḥanan said in the name of R. Eliezer b. R. Yosé the Galilean, "Seeing that a woman, just becauses he keeps herself in separation for two or three days, is called by the Torah 'sick' [or 'suffering'], surely the term applies all the more to us who have been separated from the House of our Life and from the House of our Holiness and our Glory, so many days and so many years, so many terms and so many epochs."
> (Lev. R. 19:5, trans. J. Israelstam, pp. 244-5)

Committing a transgression is now actually said to make a man unclean so as to require purification, but this is probably a literary conceit, not a practical law. The context suggests the uncleanness is merely metaphorical:

> "... Every man who commits a transgression is as unclean as though he had touched a dead body and must be purified with hyssop. So, too, David said, 'Purge me with hyssop and I shall be clean' (Ps. 51:9)."
> Did David actually fall into uncleanness? No, but into an iniquity whereby his soul was wounded unto death.
> (Midrash on Psalms 51:2, trans. W. B. Braude, I, p. 472)

This view has no impact on the law; we have no equivalent to the *yaḥad*'s rule.

The idea that uncleanness is a sign of sin is most fully spelled out in the following:

> ... When Israel came out of Egypt the vast majority of them were afflicted with some blemish. Why? Because they had been working in clay and bricks and climbing to the tops of buildings. Those who were engaged in building became maimed through climbing to the top of the layers of stone; either a stone fell and cut off the worker's hand, or a beam or some clay got into his eyes and he was blinded.
> When they came to the wilderness of Sinai, God said, "Is it consonant with the dignity of the Torah that I should give it to a generation of cripples? If, on the other hand, I wait until others take their place, I shall be delaying the Revelation. What, then, did God do? He bade the angels come down to Israel and heal them ...
> "I will put none of the diseases upon thee, which I have put in Egypt" (Ex. 15:26). Thus you have proof that they were healed.
> When, however, they committed that crime of calf-worship, their blemishes returned to them, and they became afflicted with gonorrhoea and with leprosy, in which condition Moses beheld them; for it says,

'And Moses saw that the people were broken loose'—*paru'a* (Ex. 32:25), and *paru'a* can only allude to the leprous, as you read, 'And the leper in whom the plague is ... the hair of his head shall go loose' (*paru'a*)" (Lev. 13:45).

Said God to Moses, "When you [Israel] had not yet made the Tabernacle, I had contact with you merely through speech, and those afflicted with gonorrhoea or leprosy mingled with you, but now that you have made the Tabernacle and I am causing my Presence to dwell among you, you must separate them from yourselves; let them, 'Put out of the camp every leper, and every one that hath an issue, and whosoever is unclean by the dead.' For what purpose? 'That they defile not their camp, in the midst whereof I dwell' (Num. 5 3)."

(Num. R. 7:1, trans. J. J. Slotki, pp. 178-9; Lev. R. 18:4 in the name of Simeon b. Yoḥai)

Josephus would not agree that the generation that went out of Egypt was afflicted with leprosy.

A related, but somewhat different view is that leprosy is an affliction of the nations, not of Israel. This opinion is without counterpart in the remainder of Talmudic and Midrashic interpretations of purity, which stress the interrelationship between Israel's wickedness, in general or in some special aspect, and uncleanness, again in particular in Israel's life. Further, we have already observed the claim that these ailments are reserved for Israel and are a mark of its close relationship to God. The following, therefore, stands by itself:

Another exposition of, "When a man shall have in the skin of his flesh a rising" (Lev. 15:4). This is alluded to in what is written, "Judgments are prepared for the scorners, and stripes for the back of fools" (Prov. 19:29).

"Punishments are prepared for the scoffers": Usually when a man rides an ass, if it is recalcitrant, he beats it, and if it plays pranks with him, he beats it [but not otherwise]. In this instance, however, "For the scorners judgments are prepared."

"And stripes": This may be compared to the case of a lady of rank who, on entering the king's palace, saw whips hanging [around], and was terrified; but the king said to her, "Be not afraid; these are meant for the male and female slaves, but you are here to eat and drink and make merry."

So, too, when Israel heard the section of Scripture dealing with leprous affections, they became afraid. Said Moses to them: "These are meant for the wicked nations, but you are intended to eat, drink and be joyful," as it is said, "Many are the sufferings of the wicked; but he that trusteth in the Lord, mercy compasseth him about" (Ps. 32:10).

(Lev. R. 15:4, trans. J. Israelstam, p. 191; compare Tanḥuma Meṣora' 15 to Lev. 18:19)

As with Philo, so in the Midrashic literature the association of specific sins with particular forms of uncleanness centers on the several forms of leprosy. The leprosy associated with houses is explained in two ways. First, it is seen as an act of favor for the Israelites themselves:

> It is written, "And I shall give the plague of leprosy in a house of the land of your possession" (Lev. 17:6).
>
> R. Ḥiyya[1] taught, "Was it then a piece of good news for them that plagues were to come upon them?"
>
> R. Simeon b. Yoḥai taught: "When the Canaanites heard that the Israelites were approaching, they set to and hid their valuables in the houses and in the fields. Said the Holy One, blessed he He: 'I promised their [i.e. the Israelites'] forefathers that I would bring their children into a land full of all that is good,' as it is said, "And houses full of all good things" (Deut. 8:11).
>
> "What did the Holy One, blessed be He, do? He brought plagues upon a house of one of them [the Israelites], so that when he would pull it down, he would find a treasure."
>
> (Lev. R. 17:6, trans. J. Israelstam, pp. 220-1)

Second, the leprosy of houses is seen as a punishment for Israelites' own selfishness;

> This [i.e. the lesson to be derived] is indicated by what is written, "The increase of his house shall depart, his goods shall be dragged away in the day of His wrath" (Job 20:28). [The latter clause means], They will drag it out. When? In the day that the Holy One, blessed be He, will stir up His wrath against the man concerned. How is this to happen?
>
> A man says to his friend, "Lend me a *qab* of wheat." And the other says, "I have none." Or one asks for the loan of a *qab* of barley, and the other says, "I have none." Or one asks for a *qab* of dates, and the other says, "I have none." Or a woman says to her friend, "Lend me a sieve," and the other says, "I have none." Or one says, "Lend me a sifter," and the other says, "I have none."
>
> What does the Holy One, blessed be He, do?
>
> He causes leprosy to light on his house, and as the owner takes out his household effects, people see and say, "Did he not say, 'I have none?' See how much wheat is here, how much barley, how many dates! Cursed be the house with such cursed inmates!"
>
> (Lev. R. 17:2, trans. J. Israelstam, pp. 214-5)

Leprosy is caused in a new-born child by the mother's failure to observe the purity laws concerning menstrual separation:

> "If a woman produce offspring, bearing a male child, she shall be unclean seven days" (Lev. 12:1). What is written after this? "When a man shall have in the skin of his flesh a rising" (Lev. 13:2).

[1] This is attributed, in Sifra Meṣoraʿ Parashah 5:4, to Judah b. Ilai.

What has one subject to do with the other [that they should be juxtaposed]?

Said R. Tanḥum b. Ḥanilai, "This may be compared to a sheep which was sick and was cauterized, and her foetus emerged with a cauterization mark. What caused it to come out with a cauterization mark? The fact that its mother was cauterized. Likewise, who causes a new-born child to be leprous? Its mother, who did not observe her period of separation." (Lev. R. 15:5, trans. J. Israelstam, p. 193)

Perhaps the single most influential interpretation of leprosy is Yoḥanan's allegation (p. 90) that leprosy is caused by a whole range of transgressions. This produces extended homilies, as in the following:

For ten things [i.e. sins] does leprosy come upon the world: (1) idol-worship, (2) gross unchastity, (3) bloodshed, (4) the profanation of the Divine Name, (5) blasphemy of the Divine Name, (6) robbing the public, (7) usurping [a dignity] to which one has no right, (8) overweening pride, (9) evil speech [gossip], and (10) an evil eye [greediness].

1. [We learn that it comes] for idol-worship, from the [experience of the] Israelites who testified falsely against the Holy One, blessed be He, and said of the Golden Calf, "These be thy gods, O Israel, which brought thee out of the land of Egypt" (Ex. 32:4). Whence [do we know] that they were smitten with leprosy? From the fact that it is said, "And Moses saw the people that they were *paru'a*" (*ib.* 25), i.e. leprosy had broken out *(parah)* among them.

2. [We know leprosy comes] for unchastity, from [the experience of] the daughters of Zion, of whom it is said, "Because the daughters of Zion are haughty, and walk with stretched-forth necks and ogling eyes" (Is. 3:16ff.). Whence [do we know] that they were smitten with leprosy? Since it is said, "Therefore will the Lord smite with a scab the crown of the head of the daughters of Zion" *(ib.* 17).

3. [We know that leprosy comes] for bloodshed, from [the experience of] Joab, of whom it is said, "Let it fall upon the head of Joab, and upon all his father's house; and let there not fail from the house of Joab one that hath an issue, or that is a leper" (II Sam. 3:29).

4. [We know that leprosy comes] for the profanation of the [Divine] Name, from [the experience of] Gehazi, as it is said, "But Gehazi, the servant of Elisha the man of God, said: Behold, my master hath spared this Naaman the Aramean, in not receiving at his hands that which he brought; as the Lord liveth, I will surely run after him, and take something from him" *(me'umah)* (II Kings 5:20). What does 'something' *(me'umah)* mean? It means, Of the blemish *(mum)* that he [i.e. Naaman] had had. Whence [do we know] that he was smitten with leprosy? Since it is said, [Elisha said to Gehazi:] "The leprosy therefore of Naaman shall cleave unto thee" *(ib.* 27).

5. [We know that leprosy comes] for blaspheming the [Divine] Name, from [the experience of] Goliath, of whom it is said, "And the Philistine cursed David by his God" (I Sam. 17:43). Whence [do we

know] that he was smitten with leprosy? Since it is said, "This day will the Lord enclose *(sagar)* thee" *(ib.* 46). The term *sagar* is used here in precisely the same sense as in relation to leprosy, where it is said, "And the priest shall shut him up *(sagar)*" (Lev. 13:5ff.).

6. [We know that leprosy comes] for robbing the public, from [the experience of] Shebna, who derived illicit personal benefit from property of the Sanctuary. Whence [do we know] that he was stricken with leprosy? Since it is said, "Behold, the Lord ... will wrap thee round and round" (Is. 22:17). *Wrap thee round* must refer to a leper, of whom it is said, "And he shall wear a wrapping over his upper lip" (Lev. 13:45).

7. [We know that leprosy comes] for usurping a dignity to which one has no right, from [the experience of] Uzziah [who tried to usurp the priesthood], of whom it is said, "Uzziah the king was a leper unto the day of his death" (II Chron. 26:21).

8. [We know that leprosy comes] for overweening pride [from the same,] since it is said of him, "But when he became strong, his heart was lifted up, so that he did corruptly and he trespassed against the Lord his God" *(ib.* 16).

9. [We know that leprosy comes] for evil speech, from [the experrience of] Miriam, of whom it is said, "And Miriam ... spoke against Moses" (Num. 12:1). Whence [do we know] that she was stricken with leprosy? Since it is said, "And when the cloud was removed from over the Tent, behold Miriam was leprous" *(ib.* 10).

10. [We know that leprosy comes] for an evil eye, from [the person described in the verse], "And that keeps his house to himself shall come to the priest, saying, It seems to me there is something like a plague in the house," [this is] one who confines his house to himself, and is not willing to permit others to have any benefit from it.

(Lev. R. 17:3, trans. J. Israelstam, pp. 215-217; compare 16:1, which properly assigns the whole to Yoḥanan; see also Num. R. 7:5)

Through what did Israel become liable to issues and leprosy?

R. Huna said in the name of R. Hoshaiah, "Because they cast aspersions on their great men, saying: 'Is not this family one of lepers?' This is to teach you that leprosy comes as a punishment for slander."

R. Tanḥuma said, "Because they cast aspersions on the Ark of the Covenant, saying: 'This Ark kills its bearers,' and leprosy comes as a punishment for slander. It is because of this that Israel became subject to issues and leprosy."

The rabbis said, "Because of the [worship of the Golden] Calf, since it is written, 'And Moses saw that the people was loosed *(paru'a)*' (Ex. 32:25), which means that leprosy broke out among them, as it is said, 'And his hair shall be loosed *(paru'a)*' (Lev. 13:45)."

R. Simon said, "On account of the 'murmurers,' since it is said, 'Until it comes out of your nostrils, and it be a thing loathsome to you' (Num. 11:20)."

(Lev. R. 18:4, trans. J. Israelstam, pp. 231-232)

Both Scriptural proof-texts and a play on words again make the point that leprosy is linked to gossip or slander:

> "This shall be the law of the leper" (Lev. 14:2). This is alluded to in what is written, "Who is the man that desireth life" (Ps. 34:13).
>
> This may be compared to the case of the peddlar who used to go round the towns in the vicinity of Sepphoris, crying out, "Who wishes to buy the elixir of life?" and drawing great crowds round him. R. Yannai was sitting and expounding in his room and heard him calling out: "Who desires the elixer of life?"
>
> He said to him, "Come here, and sell me it."
>
> The peddlar said, "Neither you nor people like you require that [which I have to sell]." The rabbis pressed him, and the peddlar went up to him and brought out the Book of Psalms and showed him the passage, "Who is the man that desireth life." What is written [immediately] thereafter? "Keep thy tongue from evil, depart from evil and do good."
>
> R. Yannai said, "Solomon, too, proclaims, 'Whoso keepeth his mouth and his tongue keepeth his soul from troubles' (Prov. 21:23)."
>
> R. Yannai said, "All my life have I been reading this passage, but did not know how it was to be explained, until this hawker came and made it clear, *viz.*, 'Who is the man that desireth life ...? Keep thy tongue from evil.'"
>
> It is for the same reason that Moses addressed a warning to Israel, saying to them, "This shall be the law of the leper" *(meṣora')*, i.e. the law relating to one that gives currency to an evil report *(moṣi shem ra')*.
>
> (Lev. R. 16:2, trans. J. Israelstam, pp. 203-4)

> R. Joshua b. Levi said, "Five times is the word 'law' *(torah)* used with reference to leprosy, *viz.* 'This is the law of the plague of leprosy' (Lev. 13:59); 'This shall be the law of the leper' (Lev. 14:2); 'This is the law of him in whom is the plague of leprosy' (Lev. 14:32); 'This is the law for all manner of plague of leprosy' (Lev. 14:54); 'This is the law of leprosy' (Lev. 14:57). [Since, as we have seen], 'This shall be the law of the leper' *(meṣora')* means, '...of him that utters evil reports,' it [i.e. the five-fold repetition of Torah in this matter] is intended to teach you that if one indulges in a calumny, it is as if he transgresses the Five Books of the Torah. For this reason did Moses warn Israel, 'This shall be the law of the leper.'"
>
> (Lev. R. 16:6, trans. J. Israelstam, pp. 207-8)

One entirely new treatment of purity in Midrashic literature is literary. Here, for the first time in rabbinic literature, Scriptures concerning purity serve wholly as an allegory, interpreted in terms entirely separate from their original or metaphorical meaning in respect to cultic impurity. An example is the following:

> "A rising *(se'et)*" (Lev. 15:9) alludes to Babylon, since it is said, "Thou shalt take up this parable against the king of Babylon and say:

> How hath the oppressor ceased! The exactress of gold *(madhebah)* ceased!" (Is. 14:4).
>
> "A scab *(ṣappaḥat)*" alludes to Media, which reared Haman who inflamed *(shaf)* the people [of Media] like a snake, of which it is said, "Upon thy belly shalt thou go" (Gen. 3:14).
>
> "A bright spot *(baheret)*" alludes to Greece [i.e. Seleucid Syria] who made herself conspicuous by her decrees against Israel, saying to them, "Write on the horn of an ox that you have no share in the God of Israel."
>
> "The plague of leprosy" alludes to Edom [i.e. Rome], because it[s power] is derived from the strength of the blessing of the old man, Isaac.
>
> (Lev. R. 15:9, trans. J. Israelstam, p. 197. See 18:5, compare Num. R. 7:10).

Here the Scripture on leprosy is made to refer to the four conquerors of Israel: Babylon, Media, Greece, and Rome. All reference to actual leprosy or to leprosy as a sign of some closely-related sin is lost. But the comparison of the situation of the leper to the "exile" of Israel had been made earlier and provided the point of departure for the allegorical use of leprosy to refer to the conquerors.

A second allegory, in a late compilation, treats leprosy as a symbol of idolatry, but does not claim that leprosy is the punishment for idolatry:

> "Every leper, and every one that hath an issue, and whosoever is unclean by the dead" (Num. 5:2).
>
> He intimates to them that if Israel will commit the following three transgressions—idolatry, immorality, or bloodshed—they will incur the penalty of exile. *Leper* alludes to idolatry: as a leper communicates defilement by entry, so does idolatrous sacrifice. *One that hath an issue* alludes to immorality, for both communicate defilement by means of a flux of semen. *Unclean by the dead* alludes to those who shed blood and so defile themselves and defile the land by bloodshed.
>
> (Num. R. 7:10, trans. J. J. Slotki, p. 197; compare Midrash Zuṭṭa to Song of Songs 2:15)

The law serves in a figurative way, as in Philo. But, strikingly, the same sins for which impurity serves as a metaphor in biblical literature are specified here.

A further interpretation takes the purification-rite as referring to Nebuchadnezzar and the heroes of Daniel. But the foregoing opinion is preserved, which takes uncleanness as an allegory for the sins that entailed the exile of Israel. Now, however, the Israelites are symbolized by the ashes of the heifer. At the end comes a mixture of allegory and metaphor:

"And ... shall take" (Num. 19:6)—that is, the wicked Nebuchadnezzar shall take "cedarwood, and hyssop, and scarlet" (Num. 19:6), [meaning] men such as Ḥananiah, Mishael, and Azariah.

"And cast it into the midst of the burning of the heifer" (Num. 19:6): "The flame of the fire slew those men" (Dan. 3:22).

"And a man that is clean shall gather up all the ashes of the heifer" (Num. 19:9).

That is, the Holy One, blessed be He, will gather them up, for of Him it is written "He will set up an ensign for the nations, and will assemble the dispersed of Israel" (Is. 11:12).

By *man* in the previous verse is meant the Holy One, blessed be He, of whom it is written "The Lord is a man of war" (Exod. 15:3).

By *that is clean* is meant the Holy One, blessed be He: "Thou that art of eyes too pure to behold evil" (Hab. 1:13).

The ashes of the heifer are the dispersed of Israel.

"And lay them up without the camp in a clean place" (Num. 19:9) —that is to say, they will be assembled in Jerusalem, which is clean.

"And [the mixture of ash and water] shall be kept for the congregation of the children of Israel" (Num. 19:9). In this world things are pronounced clean or unclean by the mouth of a priest. But in the time-to-come it will not be so. The Holy One Himself, blessed be He, will cleanse Israel of all their sins and from all their uncleanness, as is said, "And I will sprinkle clean water upon you, and ye shall be clean; from all your uncleannesses, and from all your idols, will I cleanse you" (Ezek. 36:25).

(Pesiqta Rabbati 14, trans. W. B. Braude, p. 295;
Midrash Tanḥuma Ḥuqat 28;
compare Pesiqta deR. Kahana, ed. Mandelbaum, p. 76, 1s. 3ff.)

It would be interesting to speculate on the occasion for the allegorization of purity. But we do not have a clear idea as to when the development toward complete allegorization began. We also do not know whether this process went on alongside the interest in specifying punishment through impurity for specific sins. They occur in the same document, Leviticus Rabbah. The mode of interpretation which stresses measure for measure clearly comes early in the history of rabbinic theology, beginning among Ushans, and continuing in the names of third-century masters. The allegorical approach is not assigned to specific authorities. We cannot, therefore, be certain it represents a successive stage. Nor do we know whether these modes of thought represent separate rabbinical circles or different settings of rabbinic discourse. We cannot be sure, for instance, that one kind of interpretation characterized academic discourse, another, synagogue homilies (if, indeed, rabbis regularly preached in synagogues at all). None of these questions may now be answered.

In the following late homily, ʿAqiba draws out a lesson from the laws of purity. While he compares uncleanness to sin and cleanness to a good deed, the lesson depends not on the well-established metaphor of purity for moral uprightness, but rather on the treatment of the cleanness-rule as a generalized allegory for the moral life overall:

> "He that doeth these things shall never be moved" (Ps. 15:5). Whenever Rabban Gamaliel read this verse he would grieve, saying: "What man can do all of these things?" But R. ʿAqiba, reading this verse, or the verses in Ezekiel beginning, "But if a man be just, and do that which is lawful and right" (Ezek. 18:5-6), did not grieve but rejoiced.
>
> Rabban Gamaliel asked him, "Why do I grieve while thou rejoicest?"
>
> R. ʿAqiba replied, "Note that it is written, 'These are they which are unclean to you among all that creep; whosoever doth touch them ... shall be unclean' (Lev. 11:31), and so it might be argued that for a man to be unclean, he would have to touch all these creeping things, whereas if he touched only one of them he would not be unclean. Yet in truth, like the 'bright spot' of leprosy which makes all the leper's garments unclean, the touch of one creeping thing—even a portion of it no larger than a lentil—can make him unclean.
>
> "Note also that at the end of the chapter which contains regulations concerning defilement it is written, 'Defile not yourselves in all of these things' (Lev. 18:24), and again it might be argued that only a man guilty of all such defilements becomes unclean.
>
> "Yet the truth is that a man becomes unclean if he touches any of these sins even by a touch as light as the weight of a lentil.
>
> "Now consider: what measure is greater? The measure of goodness or the measure of punishment? Clearly, the measure of goodness is five hundred times greater than the measure of punishment. And so if a man who touches a single creeping thing, even a portion of it no larger than a lentil, thereby becomes as unclean as though he had touched all creeping things, does it not follow that if a man does a single one of these good deeds, it is as though he had done all of them?
>
> "And does it not also follow that just as the word *These* specifies the creeping things and defilements to indicate that a man touching any one of them touches them all, so a man who does any one of the good things of which it is written, 'He that doeth these things shall never be moved,' yea, does any one at all of them—it is as though he had done all of them."
>
> Thereupon Rabban Gamaliel said to R. ʿAqiba, "Thou has comforted me, ʿAqiba, thou hast comforted me."
>
> (Midrash on Psalms 15:5, trans. W. B. Braude, pp. 194-5)

Once impurity is so completely divorced from its ordinary meaning as well as from its metaphorical significance, it becomes available for any sort of use in condemnation. In other passages the four kinds of leprosy now are symbols of the four exiles. All that is left is the final step, of denying to the actual rites any real efficacity so as to make them merely exercises in obedience to the divine will, however empty of rational or metaphorical meaning that may seem.

This last development of the interpretation of purity is contained in the following story, which first appears in the latest strata of Midrashic literature and may not be assigned with complete confidence to Talmudic times at all:

> A pagan asked R. Yoḥanan b. Zakkai, "These deeds which you do look to me like hocus pocus. You bring a heifer and burn it, and crush it, and take its ashes, and if one of you is defiled by a corpse, you sprinkle him in the third and seventh day of his uncleanness, and say to him, 'You are purified.'"
>
> He answered, "Has a wandering spirit ever entered into you?"
>
> "No."
>
> "But have you ever seen a man into whom a wandering spirit has entered?"
>
> "Yes."
>
> "And what did you do for him?"
>
> "You put smoking roots under him, and throw water over him, and the spirit flees."
>
> He said, "Listen then with your ears to what your mouth speaks! This is a spirit of uncleanness, as we learn in Zechariah (13:2), 'And also I shall cause the spirit of uncleanness to pass away from the earth.' You sprinkle on him waters of purification, and it flees."
>
> After the man left, the disciples said to Yoḥanan, "Master, this man have you driven off with a broken reed. What will you reply to us?"
>
> He answered, "By your lives! It is neither the corpse which renders a man unclean nor the waters which purify, but the Holy One said, 'A statute have I enacted, an ordinance have I ordained, and you are not permitted to transgress my commandment,' as it is said [with reference to the heifer], 'This is the *ordinance* of the Torah' (Num. 19:2)."
>
> (Tanḥuma Ḥuqat 26: Pesiqta deR. Kahana, ed. Mandelbaum, p. 74, 1s. 2-12; Num. R. 19:4; compare Midrash on Psalms to Ps. 9:2)

The allegation that Yoḥanan b. Zakkai, the founder, in 70 A.D., of the rabbinic center at Yavneh, first had declared the rite of purification to be without reason may not be a late invention. It may flow from a tradition originating earlier, for M. Yadaim 4:6 attributes to Yoḥanan the opinion that the reason Holy Scriptures are regarded as a source of uncleanness is functional, merely to protect them from mishandling. No material uncleanness is present. This saying, first occurring in the stratum of Mishnah-Tosefta, deals with a non-biblical decree in respect to the uncleanness of the Scriptures; it is a long way indeed from providing a rational explanation for a decree of historical authorities to denying that the revealed law on the purification-rite bore any relation to material reality, indeed had no meaning whatsoever except as a discipline in the obedience to the divine will. As we have seen, other authorities were able to find meaning in the preparation of the heifer and the use of the ashes, among such authorities Philo himself, while, by contrast, Yoḥanan is represented as seeing no meaning whatever, concrete or figurative, in the rite. I am inclined to think the story comes at the end of a long period of development, rather than at the outset of the rabbinic tradition, as would be the case if Yoḥanan himself had actually said what is here attributed to him. If Yoḥanan had really said such a thing, then his opinion was everywhere ignored for the next four or five centuries and played no part in the interpretation of purity through most of Talmudic times. This to be sure is not a decisive argument, for his pro-gentile sayings were similarly ignored.

The saying establishes a fitting conclusion to the history of Talmudic thought on purity. The rabbinic movement began with the assertion, first appearing in the second century, that specific sins stand behind particular forms of uncleanness. That assertion, while an extraordinary innovation when compared to antecedent opinions, came in the context of biblical thought, which had seen purity as a metaphor for righteousness, impurity for sinfulness. It represented the making concrete of what until then had been an abstract and undeveloped assertion. Once the concrete assignment of particular sins to specific uncleannesses had entered the rabbinic system, the process of conserving and repeating that idea began. But it seems from the evidence before us to have been limited to the leprosy of fluxes. We have found no sayings that any particular sins cause defilement by dead bodies, impure animals, impure food, copulation, or childbirth.

We therefore observe three independent phenomena: (1). Speculation as to which sins cause certain types of impurity, and conversely, which impurities entail certain types of punishment. (2). Allegorical interpretations of purity laws, like allegorical interpretations of the histories, the prophecies, and much else in the Hebrew Scriptures—for the rabbis a literary exercise which never entailed any doubt as to the plain, literal meaning of the laws and the fact that they were to be obeyed. (3). Speculations as to the reasons for the laws (not for the impurities nor for the resulting punishments, in contrast with No. 1). Such speculations on the reason for the laws are a distinct class of material. Some of them end, as did Maimonides, with the despairing conclusion that human reason can never solve the problem; the law is a decree of the king. This obviously brings us close to "Yoḥanan's" saying. But that saying is not a logical consequence of the earlier modes of speculation. Perhaps it is his, for such a surprising and original saying should have come from an original and unconventional man. Whoever said it was a deep, critical thinker, but a conservative and observant Jew. If it was not Yoḥanan, it surely was someone—wherever and whenever he lived—much like Yoḥanan.

What is attributed to Yoḥanan is, to be sure, not really new. Paul had told the Romans nothing is intrinsically unclean. But he did not believe the laws of the Torah remained valid as a mode of salvation. And every rabbi believed exactly that. Yoḥanan's saying derives, after all, from a movement that affirmed the Torah as the continuing and permanently valid will of God. The purity laws were part of God's will. To regard them, however, as merely that, and not as a means of determining, avoiding and removing an unfortunate bodily condition, is remarkable. One cannot forget, after all, that the rabbinic explanations for various diseases, while justifying the ways of God and affirming his justice, left for sick people the uncomfortable burden of their own guilt for their unsavory afflictions.

CHAPTER FOUR

THE IDEA OF PURITY IN ANCIENT JUDAISM

Two important ideas about purity and impurity come down from ancient Israel: first, purity and impurity are cultic matters; second, they may serve as metaphors for moral and religious behavior, primarily in regard to matters of sex, idolatry, and unethical action. Purity furthermore closely relates to holiness. The land is holy, therefore must be kept clean. It may be profaned by becoming unclean. The sources of uncleanness are varied and hardly cultic: certain animals, the woman after childbirth, skin ailments, mildew in a house, bodily discharges, especially the menses and seminal flux, sexual misdeeds, and the corpse. In general, as I said, these are things which evidently seemed loathsome. Reference to the symbols of purity and impurity comes chiefly in priestly writings, whether legal, or prophetic, or historical.

In the literature produced in the four centuries before the destruction of the Temple, purity occurs as an important symbol not at random, but according to a predictable pattern. The specific language of purity and impurity will be important in two settings: in Palestine before 70, both as a polemical theme for sectarian discourse, and as a means of defining a sectarian community's relationship to the Jerusalem Temple; in the diaspora before 70 and in Palestine after 70, as a basis for moralistic allegory.

Purity therefore, first, serves as an important mode of differentiation and definition for the sects known to us in the first century B.C. and A.D., and, second, provides for Philo and the later rabbis an important set of laws for allegorical interpretation and source of ethical homilies. The several sects have in common direct, close relationship to the actual Temple. Allegory, by contrast, occurs primarily among those for whom the Temple is not a physical presence, because of distance either of space, as with Philo, or of time, as with the later rabbis. We may generalize that nearness to the cult will yield concrete and socially significant interpretations of purity, while distance from the Temple will result in the interpretation of purity-rules in terms other than of cultic symbols. In groups remote from the cult the term "purity" will generally be used metaphorically, while the sectarian claim to replace the Temple will result in discussion of whether or not, where, and how literally to observe the biblical purity rules and in production of new purity rules to suit the new needs of the sects.

The destruction of the Temple by itself will not attract attention to the symbolism of purity and impurity. We observed that the use of unclean and clean is not common for Jeremiah, while it is prominent in Ezekiel. Similarly, II Baruch and IV Ezra, who are obsessed by the destruction of Jerusalem in 70, are strikingly silent on the matter of the consequent pollution, cultic or otherwise. The Temple is the major motif for Baruch; its contamination is not even alluded to. The reasons of the restoration of the Temple and the resurrection of the dead are not accompanied by reference to the purification of the altar. At best we find a passing allusion: "Nor shall there by any remembrance of the present time, which is defiled with evils" (II Baruch 44:9). Israel is polluted by sin (60:2). The fire devours, it does not purify (II Baruch 48:43). Josiah to be sure was pure and cleansed the land from idols and hallowed the polluted vessels of the Temple (II Baruch 66:1ff.). The references to cultic purity therefore come chiefly within the context of biblical allusions to the Temple in times past. Purity in the apocalyptic age is not mentioned. It is surely taken for granted. But the absence of concrete references and the failure to employ purity as a primary image for the eschaton contrasts with the importance of purity to the apocalyptic community formed by the *yaḥad*, even to the Johannine writers of the New Testament. IV Ezra conforms to the pattern established in II Baruch. The collection is written in full awareness of the destruction of the Temple. But the pollution of the Temple, so important to Josephus, is passed over silently. The evil of man is not even compared to pollution (e.g., IV Ezra 7:62-74). The use of defilement is routine: the creatures have defiled the name of him who made them (8:60). The destruction of the Temple likewise means "our holy things are defiled," parallel to "the name that is called upon us is profaned" (10:22). But the vision of the heavenly Jerusalem (10:25-8) does not then include the purification of the vessels or the holy name. These collections come from writers who were actually contemporary with the destruction, who regard the loss of the Temple as a grievous calamity, and who envision its restoration—but not its purification! The symbols of pollution and purification turn out to be utterly useless to them.

The absence, or near-absence, of the idea of purity therefore is also significant. As we just noticed, purity plays a very small role in some apocalyptic writings in the Apocrypha and Pseudepigrapha, such as Enoch, IV Ezra, and Baruch. But it is important in the New Testament and apocalyptic writings, and central for the *yaḥad*. Where reference to purity does occur, as in the Maccabean histories, purity applies to the Temple; impurity is an issue because of the concrete deeds of the Seleucids in Jerusalem. Purity here is in no way turned into a metaphor or developed outside of the biblical framework of interpretation. Here proximity to the Temple therefore will not satisfactorily explain the importance of purity in inter-sectarian polemic, or in the self-definition of sects. Purity clearly is important to the *yaḥad* and the *ḥavurah*, the former an apocalyptic context. It certainly was of great importance in the early days of the Maccabean movement, even though it is not prominent in the histories. To be sure, we cannot be misled by the mere absence of the words "purity" and "impurity" to suppose the idea unimportant if it is not often mentioned. But this still seems to call for some comment, for the language of purity is a significant vehicle for Josephus's polemic against the Zealots, Jesus's polemic against the Pharisees, and Paul's against the Law, but not much used, or used only in perfectly routine ways, in the bulk of the literature surviving from the fourth, third, and second centuries B.C. The most likely explanation is that this literature comes from groups which took observance of the purity laws for granted and therefore were not arguing about them. We cannot suppose people always discuss matters of most importance to them. Usually they do not. So the silence of Baruch or IV Ezra or the Maccabean historians on the question of Temple pollution indicates only that they did not propose to say what was obvious. Purity comes up for discussion primarily for people to whom it is, for one reason or another, highly problematic.

In the writings collected as Apocryphal and Pseudepigraphic literature, only Jubilees, fragments of which were uncovered at Qumran, pays much attention to purity. Even here, apart from the linking of the impurity of the woman after giving birth to the Garden of Eden, impurity is interpreted entirely within the limits of the biblical repertoire of ideas. These things are called impure: fornication, bloodshed, unrighteousness, and idolatry—just as in Scriptures. Abraham tells Isaac to be pure when approaching the altar, which does not much elaborate the Levitical law. The sanctuary may be polluted by intermarriage, the sole somewhat unusual usage, but a development of Ezra's idea simply by treating intermarriage as fornication. In all, Jubilees' interest in purity, while by and large routine in contrast to that of the later rabbis, or of Philo, or of the authors of Hebrews and the Synoptic traditions, stands apart and is considerable when compared to that of the other Apocryphal and Pseudepigraphic books. It is probably significant that in this literature sins are called impure more often than impurities are called sinful. This means that "impure" is the more effective term of abuse. Many sources of impurity, particularly bodily fluxes, were repulsive. This sort of usage illustrates that fact and shows the strong hold the dislike of impurity and the desire for purity had in the minds of the expected readers. To discredit major sins the authors call them impure.

It cannot be supposed that the prominence of purity in the first century writings of Philo and Josephus, and in the sectarian traditions of Qumran, Christianity, and Pharisaism, came in response to historical stimuli not present in the earlier centuries in which the bulk of Apocryphal and Pseudepigraphic literature came forth. In each of the centuries under study we find the capture and pollution of the Temple—by the Seleucids after 170 B.C., by the Romans under Pompey in 63 B.C., and again by the Romans under Vespasian in 70 A.D. The Temple was many more times violated and made into a battlefield. As I said, the revision and elaboration of the idea of purity did not characterize either the historians or some apocalyptics. For Daniel, for instance, the words "purity" and "impurity" play no articulated role whatsoever, though the fate of the Temple under the Seleucids predominates. Yet this means little. The book starts off with the blessing on those who keep the food laws and refers to the abomination of desolation. In this connection, Josephus's silence on the purification of the Temple after its pollution by gentiles also is probably misleading.

Both the issue of the purity of the Temple and the reinterpretation of purity in non-cultic settings thus tend to occur primarily in connection with sectarian strife within the Jewish community—even within Josephus's narrative itself! When gentiles profane the Temple, the language of cultic purity is not apt to enter into the description of the event nor to predominate in the interpretation of its meaning. But when Jews accuse other Jews of doing the wrong thing in the Temple or in connection with the cult, they are apt to phrase their indictment, in part, through accusations of polluting the sanctuary or entirely misunderstanding the meaning of purity. To put it another way, purity is likely to elicit original speculation, not limited to the established biblical perspective, specifically in response to issues within the Jewish sectarian environment.

Since Josephus and the founders of the *yaḥad* were priests, it would be tempting to suggest that purity becomes important specifically for intra-priestly disputes. But the Pharisees do not claim to have been priests (though it may be that the sect first took shape because of differences about purity-laws between the Temple priesthood and dissenters), and the early Christians certainly did not include many important Temple authorities or disgruntled and excluded priests. So in sectarian discourse the issue of purity is not introduced primarily by priests. The three pre-70 sects important in our study, *yaḥad*, Church, *ḥavurah*, and the post-70 rabbis have in common not origin within the priesthood, but the claim, for the first two, to constitute the Temple, or, for the third, to share in the Temple's sanctity and to take over the priestly prerogatives. A fourth sect, that formed by the Zealots, has left us no literature. They evidently modeled themselves after the Maccabees and claimed that they would purify the Temple from its present impurity. But we do not know how they interpreted the idea of purity and impurity, or whether they regarded impurity in terms other than those set forth in Scriptures, as did the three sects about which we do know something.

The reason that purity bulks so large in the inter-sectarian polemics therefore is that, as with their approach to the Temple's other symbols and meanings, the several sects all determined to define their relationship to the established Temple and to come to terms with, and to take over, its rules, either by reinterpreting them or by rejecting them. The three sects struggled with one another because they were so much alike, and because their claims in respect to the Temple brought them into direct conflict. But the specific use of purity and impurity within the polemic is not uniform. To be sure, what the Synoptics have Jesus say about the Pharisees is pretty much the same as what the later rabbis say about the priesthood: the opposition lays stress on the outward aspect of purity, to the neglect of the true purity of the moral life. But when the *yaḥad* accuses the Jerusalem priesthood of impurity, the intent is that the priests were impure in a narrowly Levitical sense. This is made explicit in terms of the accusation that the Jerusalem priests had sexual relations with menstruating women and then came to the Temple itself. Josephus's polemic against the Zealots is equally standard and makes no figurative use of the concept. It also is noteworthy that, so far as the sources now permit us to determine, the sects' polemics do not seem reciprocal. The Synoptics' Jesus criticizes the Pharisees, but we have no counterpolemic. The rabbis' Pharisees criticize the priesthood; the *yaḥad* condemns the Jerusalem priests. We do not know how the Temple priests or Sadducees responded to the sectarian critique, if they did at all. We do not know whether they even knew that critique or took it to heart.

The absence of Temple and priestly writings must be stressed. All we have in hand are sectarian books and traditions. We do not know what the spokesmen of the normative religion of the country—that religion which consisted of reverence for the Temple cult and belief in the revelation of Moses, together, presumably, with *ad hoc* explanations of the latter's meaning—had to say about purity. Since the sects tend to diverge from, and to develop, the Scriptural usages, it is reasonable to suppose the priestly spokesmen and the ordinary folk alike would have understood "purity" and "impurity" pretty much as the Bible does, either as a metaphor for good or evil behavior, on the one side, or as a matter of cultic concern when going to Jerusalem, on the other. Purity in the latter sense, however, would have played a significant role in the religious life of the ordinary person. Pilgrimage seems to have been important, particularly in connection with festivals. So at least at a few points in life, ordinary people would actually have gone through a rite of purification—though we cannot be certain just what that rite might have consisted of—and so have entered into a state of purity appropriate for the cult. That was something the *yaḥad* did not do in regard to Jerusalem, and it was an issue for the early Church whether, and to what extent, one should do so. To those who undertook to be pure for the pilgrimage to the Temple, however, purity cannot have meant much more than an aspect of the cultic experience. Those to whom purity, as much else, was problematic greatly expanded the range of interpretation of the idea. I should imagine people who took the rite for granted, as part of the cult, also took its biblical meanings for granted.

This conjecture must again underline the main and consistent trait of the innovative ideas of purity before us—their sectarianism. For the period of the Second Temple, exceptional ideas about purity derive from sectarian groups or from a sectarian polemic. With the exception of Philo, whose interest in the matter is more than routine, the literature in which purity is prominent derives from small groups, who in their own day cannot have been very important. This makes all the more interesting the manifest interest of purity for the rabbis, who aimed at, and in time achieved, normative status within the Jewish community. Purity, to be sure, was part of the rabbinic inheritance from Pharisaism. But it was exploited in striking and original ways long after the rabbis had ceased to constitute an excluded, unimportant sect, but had come to dominate, if not entirely to control, the political institutions of the Jewish community both in the land and abroad. This fact remains to be explained; we shall reconsider it shortly.

The symbol of purity overall bears a strikingly limited range of meanings. The biblical use of impurity as a metaphor for sexual fornication, idolatry, and evil doings, and of purity in connection with the cult, is not much expanded in the period of the Second Temple. Indeed, it tends to contract, for some things which for the Levitical code produce impurity tend to be neglected in the interpretations of the later period. The first important metaphorical meaning of impurity is idolatry, obviously because of the Seleucid incursion into the Temple. Moral transgression, particularly sexual misdeeds, will normally produce an allusion to impurity. By contrast, the unclean animals of Leviticus 11 rarely play a role in the Palestinian writings, though they acquire allegorical meanings in Alexandria, both from the author of the Letter of Aristeas, and from Philo. Yet we know from pagan polemic that observance of some food taboos was one of the most widespread, conspicuous, and ridiculed aspects of Judaism. Here again is evidence that simply examining references to purity and impurity is not a reliable guide to their importance. But the interpretation of the laws cannot have greatly changed from biblical times. Philo treats purity as a metaphor for moral purity, but also as an allegory for self-control and other philosophical virtues. The specific sources of impurity interesting to Philo cover the gamut of the biblical rules: seminal emission, reptiles, leprosy, corpse-uncleanness, the uncleanness of mildew, and of the menstrual woman. The uncleanness of animals is the only biblical source of impurity not much exploited. Leprosy produces the most detailed and elaborate interpretations. For the literature produced by the *yaḥad*, uncleanness tends to be generalized as "all forms of uncleanness." The specific sources of greatest importance are menstrual impurity and fornication. For the Christian literature, the primary source of uncleanness is food; the secondary one (especially in Paul's writings) is fornication. Blood as a source of purity is important for Hebrews. Later rabbinical literature refers more than routinely to menstrual impurity, corpse-uncleanness, and, especially, leprosy. In the later stages of rabbinic interpretation, these recur, alongside sexual sources of impurity. The leprosy of a person or of a house is traced to a wide variety of sinful acts. These include murder, selfishness, idolatry, pride, false swearing, incest, arrogance, robbery, envy, and, especially, slander. As in biblical literature, uncleanness is taken as a sign of separation from God, and purity is a prerequisite of approaching God or of receiving (and studying) the Torah—an extension of cultic symbols to rabbinism, as was commonplace. Leprosy or gonorrhoea mark a person off from God. Uncleanness also serves as an allegory for exile, though this does not seem a major theme in the earlier stages of rabbinic thought on the subject. The course of rabbinic interpretation thus is marked by three elements: first, the view that impurity signifies that a sin has been committed; second, the elaboration of this view in terms of an ever-widening circle of sins, though leprosy is the primary source of the consequent uncleanness; third, the allegation in the name of Yoḥanan ben Zakkai that the whole system simply serves to produce obedience to God's will—neither an impurity nor a purity-rite possesses intrinsic power.

What we know about the idea of purity in ancient Judaism therefore concerns two aspects: the place in which one is to be pure—the Temple or some context compared to the Temple such as (for the rabbis) the holy community; and the larger meanings associated with purity and impurity—sin, particularly of a sexual or religious character. What we do not know is what conceptions lay *behind* the idea of impurity. That impurity was a matter merely of status, therefore neutral, comes clear chiefly in rabbinic law (p. 16). For Talmudic Judaism impurity was wholly neutral, entirely a metaphor deprived of its substantive, "real" character. The theological treatment of impurity as a sign of the antecedent commission of sin, rather than of contact with demons or other autonomous forces of evil, represents the counterpart to the legal treatment of impurity as relative and not substantive. This, I think, stands behind the saying attributed to Yoḥanan b. Zakkai.

What, however, was the perception of impurity before the destruction of the Temple? The answer to that question must depend upon the conclusions drawn about impurity in biblical times. For it seems to me unlikely that the view of impurity—substantive or relative and neutral—could have changed among people so utterly dependent upon, and limited to, the biblical applications, interpretations, and metaphors of purity. Certainly Philo's treatment of the subject leaves little room for doubt. He did not regard purity as something real and demonic. His mode of thought, in form, though not in substance, so close to that of the rabbis, suggests that where we do *not* find the allegorization of impurity or its use as a source for metaphors of an extreme sort (for instance, to signify the exile of Israel), there impurity is still charged with autonomous power. Limiting purity to the cult and focusing the interpretation of the matter on the life of the Temple therefore *should* mark the persistence of the ancient Israelite perception of impurity (following the view of Levine) as something dangerous. Allowing the issues of impurity to be drawn out of the cult and into the common life of ordinary folk, as with the rabbis, or into the discourse on philosophical virtue, as with Philo, strongly suggests impurity had become a symbol without a core of perceived, affective force—well-preserved but merely as a dessicated husk. To be sure, this argument, based upon the contrast between the modes of interpretation of Philo and of rabbinic Judaism and of Second Temple sectarianism, hardly decides matters. It at best may suggest that the persistence of ideas originated by Scriptures and the limitation of purity to the cult signify the persistence of the larger conceptions that lay behind the Scriptural treatment of the matter. But the sources before us, like the Scripture themselves, are strikingly reticent about the "reality" perceived to inhere in impurity and the change affected by purification. Perhaps the *yaḥad*'s view that the *Zab* may not go to war because he will offend the angels (p. 53) is the best evidence for a material conception of impurity. A decisive body of evidence for the reality of demons, including unclean ones, of course derives from the Synoptic stories about Jesus' healings. These stories leave no doubt that people in general believed in a world of spirits, malevolent, unclean, and otherwise. They strongly suggest that people believed that impurity was a material force, and that a rite of purification drove off a demon of impurity or removed the effects of one. To be sure, when Jesus heals people by exorcising demons or unclean spirits, the issue of purity then is not made explicit; nor is it significant in respect to healing lepers or women with long-standing discharges of blood. The specific sayings about the purity of foods and the purification of the hands and of cups omit reference to the underlying conceptions of impurity.

For distant Alexandria as for later rabbinism, purity remained very important. That much seems to follow from Philo's considerable interest in the matter. He believed the law should be followed, but also should be explained in a figurative sense. It seems likely that his attention to the meaning of leprosy and his explanation of the biblical rules reflect some sort of practical and everyday interest in the laws, at least in connection with food and sex. The rabbis' interest in the matter may be seen in the massive body of legal materials on purity, their working out in precise detail just what is impure and what is pure. Ordinary folk certainly believed sexual taboos were valid and obeyed them.

The variety and character of the rabbis' list of social evils yielding leprosy—gossiping, selfishness, and the rest—are routine and unexceptional. Such commonplace social vices will characterize any sort of society. What is striking is not the catalogue of sins, therefore, but the imputation of leprosy as the result of those sins. This extreme interpretation begins with nothing more than the biblical use of impurity as a metaphor for sin. The metaphor, however, is shattered. Instead of maintaining impurity is *like* gossip or fornication, or gossip or fornication is *like* impurity, the rabbis held gossip or fornication *produces* impurity. The other possible use of the broken metaphor is its transformation into allegory. This, as we have seen, is expressed in the interpretation of leprosy as an allegory for exile, or in the comparison of types of impurity with the pagan conquerors of Israel. In whichever direction the metaphor is taken, it is rendered ever more abstract. It loses its concrete traits and becomes a generalized signification of unworthiness. But the fact that metaphorical uses thus become vague does not mean that the notion of purity did so, nor the concern about it. I think the contrary is the case.

What is noteworthy therefore is the extensive rabbinic use of the symbols of impurity in connection with these social ills. Sermons against gossiping or selfishness may readily be constructed without inclusion of the claim that it is the leper in particular who has gossiped or acted selfishly. The cultic metaphor, *unclean*, and its specification in terms of leprosy or bodily discharges seem curiously inappropriate or unnatural to the specific social vices against which the rabbis inveighed. They are used by the rabbis because the community of Israel now is regarded as the Temple. What kept people out of the sanctuary in olden times therefore is going even now to exclude them from the life ot the community. The thrust of the rabbis' sermons is to remove from the community people guilty of gossiping or arrogance and the like; this very act of removal is offered by them as the *explanation* for their relating gossiping to leprosy, as we observed.

The rabbis' larger tendency to preserve, but to take over within the rabbinical system, the symbols of the Temple is herein illustrated. Just as the rabbi is the new priest, study of Torah is the new cult, deeds of lovingkindness the new sacrifice, so the community formed on the basis of the rabbinic Torah is going to be protected from social uncleanness just as the old Temple was protected from cultic uncleanness. This I think accounts not only for the preservation, but for the considerable elaboration and extension, of the cultic symbols of uncleanness. These usages after 70 were no more pertinent to, or part of the ordinary life of, the Jewish community in the land than they were before that time to Alexandrian Jewry. Two motives lie behind the rabbinic tendency to claim impurity signifies antecedent sin: first, to extend the generalized theodicy to the specific situation of ordinary folk, and second, to exploit the Temple's imagery for the rabbinic community. The second motive in general sets the context for what is done in a concrete way in the first.

To summarize: we may now rapidly trace the history of the idea of purity in ancient Judaism.

Purity in Israelite times is presented by the priestly code as primarily a cultic concern and an important source of metaphors for priestly writers. All sources of impurity according to that code produced a single practical result: one must not enter the Temple. All rites of purification aimed at one goal: to permit participation in the cult. But it cannot be supposed that the food and other purity laws in Scriptures, particularly in Deuteronomy, are intended only for priests or for persons about to sacrifice. This is probably not true. The leper was excluded from the community as well as from the Temple; he suffered all sorts of disabilities. The menstruant woman was prohibited to her husband. The *zab* if identified also suffers and causes serious disabilities. It is perfectly clear that in later times some food taboos were widely observed by people who had no expectation of entering the Temple and also were not Pharisees or Essenes. In communities where such taboos were observed, failure to keep them would result in practical excommunication. So we must not be taken in by the viewpoint of the priestly writers in the Hebrew Scriptures. Their claim that purity was primarily a cultic concern simply is false.

Uncleanness served as a metaphor for sexual misdeed, idolatry, or unethical behavior. Cleanness was compared to sexual purity, service to one God alone, and correct action. These metaphors were natural in the context of the cult, which above all else signified holiness and produced the right relation to God.

In the period of the Second Temple the biblical ideas and interpretations of purity persisted without much consequential change. Purity was no more solely a cultic matter then than earlier. Impurity served as a metaphor for fornication, idolatry, or unethical behavior. Within sectarian polemic, in particular, the right attitude toward purity was reserved for one's own party, stress on the outward, rather than the metaphorical, aspect of purity was often assigned to the chief opposition. But that polemic did not greatly expand the range of ideas associated with purity. The *yaḥad*, regarding itself as the true Temple, naturally took on the purity-discipline within the community life. The Christian community, seeing the Temple as surpassed by Christ and the cult by his sacrifice, as with Hebrews, or possessing traditions in which major authorities, Paul and Peter, as well as Jesus, had declared it unnecessary to observe the purity laws concerning foods, did not themselves wholly neglect the purity-laws for food, but adopted various compromises in actual practice and continued to make use of the metaphors of purity formerly associated with sex. The *ḥavurah*'s ideas about purity are not available; they cannot, however, have been formulated other than in relationship to the Temple, priesthood, and cult.

The two really important changes in the interpretation of purity occur in Alexandrian Judaism, on the one side, and in rabbinic Judaism, on the other. In both instances purity and impurity are interpreted entirely outside of the cultic setting. They serve for metaphors and allegories in which both the impurity and the thing to which impurity is compared have nothing whatever to do with the Temple. The substance of Philo's allegory—the philosophical life—differs from that of the rabbis, which stresses practical and ethical behavior. The modes of thought are comparable to one another. For both, however, the biblical themes and their variations in the period of the Second Temple tend on the whole to be neglected. While the cultic focus of purity is ignored, the formerly well-defined and limited use of impurity, as a metaphor for idolatry and sexual and other immorality, is vastly expanded. The very metaphorical character of that use indeed is ultimately lost.

Having considered the idea of purity within the limits of historical inquiry, let us now turn to the issues raised within current anthropological thought on the subject. The most important recent analysis of purity is Mary Douglas, *Purity and Danger*, with which we began. Our interest is not in the criticism of Douglas's ideas, for none of the data we have surveyed will decisively affect her main theses. We seek rather to construct an agendum out of anthropological thought for the further interpretation of the various expressions of the idea of purity in ancient Judaism. I shall survey points in Douglas's work pertinent to our inquiry.

We shall concentrate on four important aspects of Douglas's analysis. First is the main thesis of the book:

> ... rituals of purity and impurity create unity in experience. So far from being aberrations from the central project of religion, they are positive contributions to atonement. By their means, symbolic patterns are worked out and publicly displayed. Within these patterns disparate elements are related and disparate experience is given meaning.
>
> Pollution ideas work in the life of society at two levels, one largely instrumental, one expressive. At the first level, the more obvious one, we find people trying to influence one another's behaviour. Beliefs reinforce social pressures: All the powers of the universe are called in to guarantee an old man's dying wish, a mother's dignity, the rights of the weak and innocent. Political power is usually held precariously and primitive rulers are no exception. So we find their legitimate pretensions backed by beliefs in extraordinary powers emanating from their persons, from the insignia of their office or from words they can utter. Similarly the ideal order of society is guarded by dangers which threaten transgressors. These danger-beliefs are as much threats which one man uses to coerce another as dangers which he himself fears to incur by his own lapses from righteousness. They are a strong language of mutual exhortation. At this level the laws of nature are dragged in to sanction the moral code: this kind of disease is caused by adultery, that by incest; this meteorological disaster is the effect of political disloyalty, that the effect of impiety. The whole universe is harnessed to men's attempts to force one another into good citizenship. Thus we find that certain moral values are upheld and certain social rules defined by beliefs in dangerous contagion, as when the glance or touch of an adulterer is held to bring illness to his neighbours or his children.
>
> It is not difficult to see how pollution beliefs can be used in a dialogue of claims and counter-claims to status. But as we examine pollution beliefs we find that the kind of contacts which are thought dangerous also carry a symbolic load. This is a more interesting level at which pollution ideas relate to social life. I believe that some pollutions are used as analogies for expressing a general view of the social order ... (pp. 2-3)

It is difficult to relate Judaic ideas of purity to Douglas's primary thesis. Once purity and impurity are linked so closely to the cult, they serve to "create unity in experience" only so far as the larger social and imaginative life is lived in relationship to the cult. But this is priestly propaganda and cannot be taken to represent the larger world of

Israelite or later Judaic conceptions. The absence of writings of ordinary folk, not sectarians or apocalyptics, during the period of the Second Temple presents an almost insuperable obstacle for verifying this view. We simply do not have a clear picture of the importance of the Temple in the larger society of the land, except by accepting Douglas's view on purity (above, p. 28). We know it was exceedingly important to the sects, but, for at least one of them, the Christians, observance of purity rules in the old, cultic sense seems to have been sharply diminished. The *yaḥad* and the *ḥavurah* indeed serve to illustrate Douglas's point. The definition of the two communities' character in both instances began with the taking over of Temple purity rites. Whether these rites contributed to atonement is unclear; in the Pharisaic case, our evidence does not suggest so, and the larger issues of sin and atonement do not predominate in the *yaḥad*'s law code. In all, we may agree that for some groups within the larger society, purity functioned as Douglas says.

A more formidable reservation derives from the assertion that people try to influence behavior through pollution-laws and ideas. Once again this is true for our data only in the narrow context of the cult; but the behavior influenced by the priests by itself is not considerable. Whatever pollutions people have incurred they may remove by a single act of purification. Having to become pure in connection with a pilgrimage is hardly going to produce changes in behavior over the greater part of the year or in ordinary life. To be sure, the rabbis' appeal to sin as the cause of impurity would, if taken seriously, constitute a major deterrent to the social evils they opposed. I think Douglas would be right if she were to maintain that was among their motives. But we have no evidence that the rabbis exerted any meaningful social control by means of these particular interpretations of purity laws. We do know people consulted them about whether women's excretions constituted menstrual, thus unclean blood. But these very stories contain not a hint that in consequence of being consulted, rabbis were able then to exert some larger measure of social control than might otherwise have been available. To be sure, if they said the blood was unclean, they kept the woman from engaging in sexual relations, and that constitutes a very considerable, specific measure of social control, extending the biblical rule and applying it. But the larger effects are generalized, not specific. The rabbis' own authority was reenforced by multiplication of instances in which that authority might be accepted. So far one may follow Douglas's explanation.

But the exercise of social pressure hardly was limited to the enforcement of the sexual taboos when the occasion arose. Indeed, this was probably among the least important ways in which the rabbis told people what to do. They had a great many other modes of authority, and some of these were substantially more effective and produced greater consequence in ordinary life. So just as one cannot isolate the power to "create unity in experience" solely in rituals of purity and impurity, or, indeed, claim that whatever creates unity in experience therefore constitutes a purity-ritual (!), one also cannot suppose it was only, or primarily, through the laws and ideas of purity that rabbis legitimated their power or effected it.

It seems, to the contrary, that the specification of sins behind particular pollutions requires a more specific explanation than that offered here. True, one kind of disease is caused by gossiping—but it turns out that a whole range of sins causes that single disease, so the problem becomes, why that *particular* disease? And it is difficult to suppose that rabbis held impurity to constitute a dangerous contagion. The opposite is the case. In Second Temple times those who regarded impurity as dangerous are remarkably reticent about attempting to uphold certain moral values. Only in the *yaḥad* do we find a pertinent case: if you are arrogant, you are *unclean* for a certain period of time. But the *yaḥad* has nothing to say about the particular type of uncleanness, and the uncleanness is not regarded as disease. For ancient Judaism, therefore, we find no decisive correlation with the general theory that rituals of purity create unity in the experience of an entire community, nor evidence to support the entirely reasonable, but rather general proposal that specifically through purity laws people try to influence behavior. Throughout her work Douglas tends to speak about rituals in general, rather than about purity-rules in particular. The generalizations may be valid, but do not invariably contribute toward the elucidation of Judaic ideas of purity in detail.

The second point of special interest is Douglas's attention to the possibility of change in ideas about impurity:

> But in another sense I do not wish to suggest that the primitive cultures in which these ideas of contagion flourish are rigid, hide-bound and stagnant. No one knows how old are the ideas of purity and impurity in any nonliterate culture: to members they must seem timeless and unchanging. But there is every reason to believe that they are sensitive to change. The same impulse to impose order which brings them into existence can be supposed to be continually modifying or enriching them ... (pp. 4-5).

Here we are able to offer evidence in behalf of Douglas's view. In reviewing ideas of purity in a literate culture, appearing in sources spread over nearly a thousand years, we observe not only a remarkable persistence of the biblical ideas on the subject, but also important developments entirely outside of that framework.

But while new interpretations of impurity do occur, we have not observed augmentation of the biblical list of sources of impurity. What is regarded as impure in Leviticus remains so; the *ḥavurah* and the later rabbis do not add significantly to the things which will produce impurity. The *yaḥad*'s inclusion of ethical and moral lapses in that list is noteworthy; the covenanters will regard the effect of lying as impurity. This seems to be an outgrowth of the earlier metaphorization of the matter, but it nonetheless would constitute a new and varied set of additions to the Levitical list. Certainly nothing regarded in Leviticus as a source of impurity in the period of the Second Temple is held to be pure. The pattern in our data is for new reasons to be assigned to antecedent sources of impurity. Douglas's observation suggests the importance of that fact.

The third pertinent analysis concerns the relationship between the holy and the clean:

> ... So this is a universe in which men prosper by conforming to holiness and perish when they deviate from it. If there were no other clues we should be able to find out the Hebrew idea of the holy by examining the precepts by which men conform to it. It is evidently not goodness in the sense of an all-embracing humane kindness. Justice and moral goodness may well illustrate holiness and form part of it, but holiness embraces other ideas as well.
>
> Granted that its root means separateness, the next idea that emerges is of the Holy as wholeness and completeness. Much of Leviticus is taken up with stating the physical perfection that is required of things presented in the temple and of persons approaching it. The animals offered in sacrifice must be without blemish, women must be purified after childbirth, lepers should be separated and ritually cleansed before being allowed to approach it once they are cured. All bodily discharges are defiling and disqualify from approach to the temple. Priests may only come into contact with death when their own close kin die. But the high priest must never have contact with death ...
>
> ... We can conclude that holiness is exemplified by completeness. Holiness requires that individuals shall conform to the class to which they belong. And holiness requires that different classes of things shall not be confused.
>
> Another set of precepts refines on this last point. Holiness means keeping distinct the categories of creation. It therefore involves correct

> definition, discrimination and order. Under this head all the rules of sexual morality exemplify the holy. Incest and adultery (Lev. 18:6-20) are against holiness, in the simple sense of right order. Morality does not conflict with holiness, but holiness is more a matter of separating that which should be separated than of protecting the right of husbands and brothers.
>
> Then follows in [Leviticus] Chapter XIX another list of actions which are contrary to holiness. Developing the idea of holiness as order, not confusion, this list upholds rectitude and straightdealing as holy, and contradiction and double-dealing as against holiness. Theft, lying, false witness, cheating in weights and measures, all kinds of dissembling such as speaking ill of the deaf (and presumably smiling to their face), hating your brother in your heart (while presumably speaking kindly to him), these are clearly contradictions between what seems and what is. This chapter also says much about generosity and love, but these are positive commands, while I am concerned with negative rules ... (pp. 50-54, *pass.*).

Douglas thus explains that the breach of ritual "avoidances... unleashes danger ... The precepts and ceremonies alike are focussed on the idea of the holiness of God which men must create in their own lives." Here we find the connection between purity and holiness which seemed implicit in the biblical materials. Impurity is constituted by the violation of perfection; what is imperfect cannot be brought to the holy Temple. Douglas thereby accounts for the specificities of the Levitical rules about uncleanness.

It is curious that in the intellectual interpretations of the purity-laws we have examined, only with Philo and Hebrews do we approach this sophisticated notion. For Philo to approach the altar the soul must be purged of passion, the body of defilement, and so the two achieve perfection "like the perfection of the sacrificial victim." Everything must be kept well regulated, "close and tight." Similarly, repose is better than motion. Among the many other interpretations of impurity, general and specific, we find no hint from those writing in the land of Israel itself that the reason for keeping out women after childbirth, lepers, and those who have had bodily discharges is that they are somehow imperfect; *other* sorts of imperfections, not specified, then do not constitute pollution, though they will prevent access to the cult. For our part we may choose to perceive them as imperfect or loathsome or whatever. Since we have so considerable a corpus of explanations, however, it is remarkable that what seems central to Douglas has not been articulated by people living in proximity to the Temple and in the age in which the issues of purity were vivid. That does not seem to me a decisive argument against her interpretation of the connection between cleanness and holiness, which does not derive from, or depend solely upon, the data of ancient Judaism.

In Professor Douglas's behalf, we may observe, moreover, the importance of the distinction between manifest and latent functions. We have stressed the former, asking what people actually say. But the fact that only Philo, Hebrews, and some later rabbis actually articulate ideas pertinent to, indeed supportive of, Douglas's hypothesis of the symbolic functions of purity and impurity is not entirely to the point. If the rules really worked the way she suggests, then no one would need to articulate that fact. Second-order explanations become necessary primarily when the symbolic system is not working in its accustomed way or has been challenged by a rival set of symbols. That fact seems to account for the articulated ideas and the centrality of laws on purity located in sectarian writings, on the one side, and later rabbinic literature, on the other, but otherwise absent in a wide range of sources. As we observed earlier, the mere absence of allusion to purity proves little. The importance of the laws and the biblical legacy of associated interpretations probably is better attested in Maccabean writings and Daniel, where purity-language plays little part, than in Philo or later rabbinic sayings, where it is important. Moreover, my criticism is addressed chiefly to Douglas's descriptions of the instrumental functions of purity, while her primary interest is in its expressive purposes. As I said, our evidence neither verifies nor falsifies this latter approach. That is bound to be the case since any theory about the function of symbols in a society cannot be verified only by examination of the symbols—in our case, the actual texts—but has to have some access to the organization and workings of the society in order for us to test the alleged correlation.

The fourth and most important point for the interpretation of purity in Judaism is the relationship between cleanness and morality, uncleanness and sin. That relationship in the materials of both biblical and post-biblical origin seems the most striking. I cite Douglas at some length, because of the importance of the topic in ancient Judaism:

> ... It is true that pollution rules do not correspond to moral rules. Some kinds of behaviour may be judged wrong and yet not provoke pollution beliefs, while others not thought very reprehensible are held to be polluting and dangerous. Here and there we find that what is wrong is also polluting. Pollution rules only highlight a small aspect of morally disapproved behaviour. But we still need to ask whether pollution touches on morals in an arbitrary fashion or not ...

... The fact that pollution beliefs provide a kind of impersonal punishment for wrongdoing affords a means of supporting the accepted system of morality. The Nuer examples suggest the following ways in which pollution beliefs can uphold the moral code:

(i) When a situation is morally ill-defined, a pollution belief can provide a rule for determining *post hoc* whether infraction has taken place, or not.

(ii) When moral principles come into conflict, a pollution rule can reduce confusion by giving a simple focus for concern.

(iii) When action that is held to be morally wrong does not provoke moral indignation, belief in the harmful consequences of a pollution can have the effect of aggravating the seriousness of the offence, and so of marshalling public opinion on the side of the right.

(iv) When moral indignation is not reinforced by practical sanctions, pollution beliefs can provide a deterrent to wrongdoers ...

... So far we have discussed four ways in which pollution tends to support moral values. The fact that pollutions are easier to cancel than moral defects gives us another set of situations. Some pollutions are too grave for the offender to be allowed to survive. But most pollutions have a very simple remedy for undoing their effects. There are rites of reversing, untieing, burying, washing, erasing, fumigating, and so on, which at a small cost of time and effort can satisfactorily expunge them. The cancelling of a moral offence depends on the state of mind of the offended party and on the sweetness of nursing revenge. The social consequences of some offences ripple out in all directions and can never be reversed. Rites of reconciliation which enact the burial of the wrong have the creative effect of all ritual. They can help to erase memory of the wrong and encourage the growth of right feeling. There must be an advantage for society at large in attempting to reduce moral offences to pollution offences which can be instantly scrubbed out by ritual ...

... There are two distinct ways of cancelling a pollution: one is the ritual which makes no enquiry into the cause of the pollution, and does not seek to place responsibility; the other is the confessional rite. On the face of it one would expect these to apply in very different situations ...

... A new kind of relation between pollution and morals emerges when purification alone is taken to be an adequate treatment for moral wrongs. Then the whole complex of ideas including pollution and purification become a kind of safety net which allows people to perform what, in terms of social structure, could be like acrobatic feats on the high wire ... (pp. 129-137, *pass.*).

Douglas here treats phenomena strikingly different from those we have examined. In biblical and post-biblical literature, purity serves as a metaphor for morality, impurity for sin. It is only with the rabbis that we find full articulation of the notion that impurity both results from and punishes sin. And they do not suggest that merely undergoing a rite of purification takes away the guilt or moral effects of sin. The contrary is the case. They hold that if one sins with the notion that the Day of Atonement will effect forgiveness for the sin, the Day of Atonement does no good at all. Such a person is compared to one who takes a ritual bath while holding a reptile. The bath is of no effect.

The concept that impurity is a kind of "impersonal punishment for wrongdoing" certainly serves theoretically to support the rabbinic system of morality, as we noted earlier. But it would not be easy to demonstrate that in fact such was the case. Certainly Judaic pollution-beliefs do not accomplish the first of the four ways in which pollution beliefs may uphold the moral code. Even for the rabbis we have no evidence that leprosy proved *for legal purposes* that someone had done one particular sin. The second of the four examples is irrelevant to our data. As to the third, the things the rabbis held to be morally wrong were apt to provoke indignation not only on the part of the victim. As we have observed, pollution beliefs may have been marshalled by the rabbis as a deterrent to wrong-doers, but we have no evidence of the effect.

In ancient Judaism it would be difficult to find purification interpreted as adequate treatment for moral wrongs. Indeed, the very opposite is the case. When you want to condemn your enemy, you accuse him of regarding purity as more important than morality, hence holding the view, which is assumed to be false, that purification effects moral correction. So one again, while the ideas adduced by Douglas are illuminating, they do not bear upon the interpretation of the data before us. They seem remarkably different from the Judaic ideas of purity.

Douglas's fundamental perspective on purity, however, seems to me very suggestive. She states, "The more deeply we go ... the more obvious it becomes that we are studying symbolic systems ..." (p. 34). This I think constitutes the main result of our inquiry. We have found that ideas of purity and impurity were intimate to, and expressive of, the larger conceptions of the communities that held them. Certainly without a notion of the meaning of purity, one cannot understand either the *yaḥad* or the *ḥavurah*. As Morton Smith points out (above, p. 27), purity serves to differentiate one sect from another. Because of that fact, the ideas adduced to explain or interpret purity are going to carry implications for the larger system of which they are a part. And that fact seems to me to be admirably explained within Douglas's larger theory:

> ... Now is the time to identify pollution. Granted that all spiritual powers are part of the social system. They express it and provide institutions for manipulating it. This means that the power in the universe is ultimately hitched to society, since so many changes of fortune are set off by persons in one kind of social position or another. But there are other dangers to be reckoned with, which persons may set off knowingly or unknowingly, which are not part of the psyche and which are not to be bought or learned by initiation and training. These are pollution powers which inhere in the structure of ideas itself and which punish a symbolic breaking of that which should be joined or joining of that which should be separate. It follows from this that *pollution is a type of danger which is not likely to occur except where the lines of structure, cosmic or social, are clearly defined.* [Italics supplied.]
>
> A polluting person is always in the wrong. He has developed some wrong condition or simply crossed some line which should not have been crossed and this displacement unleashes danger for someone. Bringing pollution, unlike sorcery and witchcraft, is a capacity which men share with animals, for pollution is not always set off by humans. Pollution can be committed intentionally, but intention is irrelevant to its effect—it is more likely to happen inadvertently.
>
> This is as near as I can get to defining a particular class of dangers which are not powers vested in humans, but which can be released by human action. The power which presents a danger for careless humans is very evidently a power inhering in the structure of ideas, a power by which the structure is expected to protect itself ... (pp. 112-113).

It is curious that Douglas makes use of language akin to that of Philo: "joining," like "close and tight," seems to bear particular, symbolic meaning in the analysis of purity.

We have seen that purity was not a cultic metaphor alone. It was a term for a basic, probably unanalyzable religious experience. Various explanations—physical, demonic, social, cultic—have been advanced for that experience, both in antiquity and in modern times. Various attempts have been made to use such experience and the rules generated by it for moral purposes, both by legislation and in homiletics, by metaphors and similes. But all this is by the way. The real question is, What did the Israelites think was pure and impure, and how were those opinions gradually organized into a huge system of laws and observances? We are able to answer that question only in one aspect.

We know what the priestly writers in biblical times thought was pure and impure, and how they organized their opinions into a system of laws and observances. The consistent focus of purity on the Temple cult by the priestly writers in the Hebrew Scriptures and the stress on the language of purity and impurity within groups which saw themselves as similar to the Temple seem in the end to be traits made important solely by the priesthood and by people pretending to be priests because of their natural interest in the priesthood's own rites. If for the long period of time represented by the data we have examined—from the seventh century A.D. backward into remote antiquity—purity and impurity were associated by priests and cultic sects primarily with the Temple, the reason, following Douglas, must be that to the priests and their imitators it was the Temple in which the cosmic and social lines were clearly defined, there and no where else. And if that be true, then the full weight and meaning of the catastrophe of the Temple's destruction to the priests become evident. But its importance to non-priests was no less considerable. The difference was that to non-priests cultic details about pollution and purification would not be included in the description of what had happened or of what would in the near future take place.

The first destruction, so rapidly followed by reconstruction, must have reenforced the Temple's role as the foundation of the priestly imagination and organization of reality. Various groups in the first century claimed to have predicted the second destruction. We do not know whether these predictions came after the fact. It was surely routine, long before the first century, to predict that the Jerusalem Temple would be destroyed. The *yaḥad* certainly expected and provided for that eventuality and eagerly awaited it. What makes the *yaḥad*, the *ḥavurah*, and the Christian community, Philo, and especially the rabbinic movement interesting is their shared capacity to construct a surrogate for that foundation-stone of Judaic life. That capacity is signified by their successful arrogation of the purity-rules and the inclusion of an ideology about impurity, independent of the existing Temple, in their larger structures of thought. Obviously, they did so in different ways and by means of utterly unrelated systems of ideas.

But they all addressed themselves to what we know to have been the absolutely inescapable dilemma of their day: what to do when the Temple, the place on which, for them, the lines of cosmic and social structure converged and were clearly defined, either was no longer acceptable or would no longer exist? And these non-priestly groups all proposed the same solution: the Temple as it then was perceived no longer serves, but may be replaced by something—anything—else. The Christians, who did not care to see the Temple rebuilt, ultimately gave up on the purity-laws; the rabbis, who did, took them over, but in a form not much closer to the original than would have been produced by abandoning them altogether. In the end the two surviving groups did not greatly differ. Christ (in Hebrews) was no more like the old priest than was the rabbi; his sacrifice was no more similar to the sacrifice of the Jerusalem Temple than were acts of lovingkindness. The Temple-imagery persisted, but no longer meant remotely the same thing to the later, non-priestly groups that made use of it. Neither rabbis nor Christians ultimately relied upon the idea of impurity as the primary protection for the structure of its ideas. The profound divergence of the two groups, despite their appeal to, and use of, a common antecedent system of Temple-symbols, including ideas about purity, marked the end of the time of the service of a single cultic structure, representing society and modeled in the cosmic lines.

The concern for purity did continue, particularly in Talmudic Judaism, and for many centuries purity-laws were studied and greatly developed. This seems to me decisive testimony against the priestly view that purity ever was primarily a cultic concern. Whatever the original theory which justified the rabbis' taking over purity-rules, the fact is that the rules were important outside of the cult and ratified what was surely a widespread sense of loathing for certain things. What had long ago been associated with the cult by the priesthood persisted after the Temple was in ruins. But it is exceedingly difficult to ascertain the outlines of the huge system of law and observances, and the meanings conveyed by them, in later times. My guess is that the rabbis did what the priests had done so many centuries earlier. They took over into their system widespread attitudes and attempted to buttress their structure by enlisting those attitudes in its behalf. This was, as I said, a natural move for people who claimed to carry on after the destruction of the Temple and the cessation of the cult.

BIBLIOGRAPHY

Allon, Gedalyahu, *Meḥqarim beToledot Yisra'el* (Tel Aviv, 1957), I, pp. 121-176.

Bacher, Wilhelm, "Le baisement des mains dans le Zohar," *Revue des études juives* 22, 1891, pp. 137-8.

Baumgarten, Joseph M., "The Essene Avoidance of Oil and the Laws of Purity," *RQ* 6, 2, No. 22, pp. 183-192.

Bausani, Alessandro, *Persia Religiosa* (Milan, 1959).

Betz, Hans Dieter, "The Cleansing of the Ten Lepers (Luke 17:11-19)," *Journal of Biblical Literature* 90, 1971, pp. 314-328.

Betz, O., "Die Proselytentaufe der Qumransekte und die Taufe im Neuen Testament," *RQ* 1, 2, No. 2, 1958, pp. 213-234.

Black, Matthew, *The Scrolls and Christian Origins* (N.Y., 1961).

Blackman, Aylward M., "Sacramental Ideas and Usages in Ancient Egypt," *Proceedings of the Society of Biblical Archaeology* 40, 1918, pp. 57-66, 86-93.

——, "Some Notes on the Ancient Egyptian Practice of Washing the Dead," *Journal of Egyptian Archaeology* 5, 1918, pp. 117-124.

Blau, Joseph L., "The Red Heifer: A Biblical Purification Rite in Rabbinic Literature," *Numen* 14, 1967, pp. 70-78.

Bonnet, Hans, "Reinheit," *Reallexikon der ägyptischen Religionsgeschichte* (Berlin, 1952), pp. 631-637.

Bonsirven, Joseph, *Le judaisme palestinien au temps de Jésus-Christ. Sa Théologie. II. Théologie morale. Vie morale et religieuse* (Paris, 1935²), Vol. II, pp. 179-185.

Bousset, Wilhelm, *Die Religion des Judentums im späthellenistischen Zeitalter* (Tübingen, 1926³), ed. Hugo Gressman.

Bowman, J., "Did the Qumran Sect Burn the Red Heifer," *RQ* 1, 1958, pp. 73-84.

Boyce, Mary, "On the Sacred Fires of the Zoroastrians, "*Bulletin of the School of Oriental and African Studies* 31, 1968, pp. 52-68.

——, "The Pious Foundations of the Zoroastrians," *Bulletin of the School of Oriental and African Studies* 31, 1968, pp. 270-289.

——, "Zoroastrianism," in C. J. Bleeker and Geo Widengren, eds., *Historia Religionum* (Leiden, 1971), II, pp. 211-236.

Brandt, Wilhelm, *Die jüdischen Baptismen, oder das religiöse Waschen und Baden im Judentum mit Einschluss des Judenchristentums* (Giessen, 1910: Beihefte zur Zeitschrift für alttestamentliche Wissenschaft 18).

——, *Jüdische Reinheitslehre und ihre Beschreibung in den Evangelien* (Giessen, 1910: Beihefte zur Zeitschrift für alttestamentliche Wissenschaft 19).

Brown, Peter, "The Rise and Function of the Holy Man in Late Antiquity," *Journal of Roman Studies* 1971, pp. 80-101.

Buchanan, George Wesley, "The Role of Purity in the Structure of the Essene Sect," *RQ* 4, 3, No. 15, pp. 397-406.

Büchler, Adolf, *'Am Ha'Areṣ HaGalili* (Jerusalem, 1964), trans. by I. Eldad.

——, "The Levitical Impurity of the Gentile in Palestine before the Year 70," *Jewish Quarterly Review*, n.s. 17, 1926-7, pp. 1-82.

——, La pureté levitique de Jérusalem et les tombeaux des prophètes," *Revue des études juives* 62, 1911, pp. 201-215.

——, *Studies in Sin and Atonement in the Rabbinic Literature of the First Century* (Repr., N.Y., 1967).

Burgsmüller, Alfred, *Der 'am ha-'areṣ zur Zeit Jesu* (Marburg, 1964).

Carnoy, A. J., "Purification, Iranian," *Encyclopedia of Religion and Ethics* Vol. 10, pp. 491-493.

Carrington, Philip, *The Early Christian Church* (Cambridge, 1957), Vol. I, pp. 481-501.

Charles, R. H., ed., *Apocrypha and Pseudepigrapha of the Old Testament* (Oxford, 1913) I-II.

Cooke, S. M., "Purification, Hebrew," *Encyclopedia of Religion and Ethics* Vol. 10, pp. 489-490.

Cross, Frank M., Jr., *The Ancient Library of Qumran* (N.Y., 1961).

Cumont, Franz, *After Life in Roman Paganism* (Repr.: N.Y., 1959).

Danby, Herbert, *The Code of Maimonides. Book Ten. The Book of Cleanness* (New Haven, 1954).

Darmesteter, James, Trans., *The Zend Avesta. I. The Vendîdâd* (Oxford, 1880. Reprint: 1972).

Delcor, M., "Le sacerdoce, les lieux de culte, les rites, et les fêtes dans les documents de Khirbet Qumrân," *Revue de l'histoire des religions* 144, 1953, pp. 5-41.

——, "Repas cultuels esseniens et therapeutes, Thiases, et Haburoth," *RQ* 6, No. 23, 1968, pp. 401-426.

Delorme, J., "La pratique de Baptême dans le Judaisme contemporain des origines chrétiennes," *Lumière et Vie* 26, March, 1956, pp. 21-60.

Denis, A. -M., *Introduction aux pseudépigraphes grecs d'Ancien Testament* (Leiden, 1970).

Derenbourg, J., *Commentaire de Maimonide sur la Mischnah Seder Tohorot* (Berlin, 1887).

deVaux, Roland, *Ancient Israel. Its Life and Institutions* (London, 1961), pp. 460-8.

Dodds, E. R., *The Greeks and the Irrational* (Boston, 1957).

Döller, Johannes, *Die Reinheits und Speisegesetze des alten Testaments in religionsgeschichtlicher Beleuchtung. Alttestamentliche Abhandlungen*, ed. J. Nikel, Vol. 7 (Munster in W., 1917).

Dombrowski, Bruno W., "*HaYaḥad* in 1QS and *To Koinon:* An Instance of Early Greek and Jewish Synthesis," *Harvard Theological Review* 59, 1966, pp. 293-308.

Douglas, Mary, "Deciphering a Meal," *Daedalus*, Winter, 1972, pp. 61-82.

——, *Purity and Danger. An Analysis of Concepts of Pollution and Taboo* (London, 1966).

Duchesne-Guillemin, Jacques, *La religion de l'Iran ancien* (Paris, 1962).

——, *Symbols and Values in Zoroastrianism. Their Survival and Renewal* (N.Y., 1966).

Dupont-Sommer, André, "Culpabilité et rites de purification dans la secte juive de Qoumrân," *Semitica* 15, 1965, pp. 61-70.

——, *The Essene Writings from Qumran* (N.Y. and Cleveland, 1967) trans. G. Vermes.

——, "Le Testament de Lévi (XVII-XVIII) et la secte juive de l'Alliance," *Semitica* 4, 1951, pp. 33-54.

——, "Le problème des influences étrangères sur la secte juive de Qoumrân," *Revue d'histoire et de philosophie religieuses* 35, 1955, pp. 75-92.

Elliger, Karl, *Leviticus* (Tübingen, 1966).

Emerton, J. A., "Unclean Birds and the Origin of the Peshitta," *Journal of Semitic Studies* 7, 1962, pp. 204-211.

Epstein, J. N., *Der gaonäische Kommentar zur Ordnung Tohoroth* (Berlin, 1915).

——, *Perush Hai Gaon* (Vienna, 1912).

Fallaize, E. J., "Purification, Introductory and Primitive," *Encyclopedia of Religion and Ethics* Vol. 10, pp. 455-466.
Farmer, W. R., *Maccabees, Zealots, and Josephus* (N.Y., 1956).
Feldman, Louis H., *Josephus. IX. Jewish Antiquities Books XVIII-XX* (Cambridge, 1965).
Festugière, A. J., *La Sainteté* (Paris, 1942).
Finkelstein, Louis, "The Book of Jubilees and the Rabbinic Halaka," *Harvard Theological Review* 16, 1923, pp. 39-62. [Jubilees is not Pharisaic.]
Fowler, W. W., "Lustratio," in R. R. Marett, ed., *Anthropology and the Classics* (Oxford, 1908), pp. 169-191.

Gärtner, Bertil, *The Temple and the Community in Qumran and the New Testament* (Cambridge, 1965).
Gager, John, *Moses in Greco-Roman Paganism* (Nashville, 1972: Society of Biblical Literature Monograph Series 16).
Gispen, W. H., "The Distinction between Clean and Unclean," *Oudtestamentische Studien* 5, 1948, pp. 190-197.
Gnilka, J., "Die essenischen Tauchbäder und die Johannestaufe," *RQ* 3, 2, No. 10, 1961, pp. 185-208.
Goldberg, Abraham, *The Mishnah Treatise Ohaloth* (Jerusalem, 1955).
Gramberg, K. P. C. A., "'Leprosy' and the Bible," *The Bible Translator* 11, 1960, pp. 10-23.
Graubart, D., "Le véritable auteur du traité Kélim," *Revue des études juives* 32, 1896, pp. 200-225. [Yosi b. Ḥalafta is the author.]
Gray, Louis, H., *The Foundations of the Iranian Religions* (Bombay, 1926).

Hadas, Moses, *The Third and Fourth Books of Maccabees* (N.Y., 1953).
Hadot, Jean, "La datation de *l'Apocalypse syriaque de Baruch*," *Semitica* 15, 1965, pp. 79-96.
Haggai, S., "HaṬohorah vehaṭuma'ah eṣel Katuv Midbar Yehudah," *Maḥanayim*, Cheshvan 5722, 1961-2, pp. 80-83.
Haran, M., "The Graded Taboos of Holiness," *Sefer Segal* (Tel Aviv, 1965), pp. 33-41.
——, "The Priestly Image of the Tabernacle," *Hebrew Union College Annual* 36, 1965, pp. 191-226.
Harper, William Rainey, *The Priestly Element in the Old Testament* (Chicago, 1909).
Harrison, Jane, *Prolegomena to the Study of Greek Religion* (Repr.: N.Y., 1957).
Hauck, F., "Katharos, etc. Clean and Unclean outside the NT. I. In Primitive Religion. II. In Greek Religion," *Theological Dictionary of the New Testament*, ed. G. Kittel, Trans. G. W. Bromiley (Grand Rapids, 1965), Vol. 3, pp. 413-417.
Haupt, Paul, "Babylonian Influence in the Levitical Ritual," *Journal of Biblical Literature* 19, 1900, pp. 55-82.
Hengel, Martin, *Die Zeloten* (Leiden, 1961).
Hoenig, S. B., "Qumran Rules of Impurities," *RQ* 6, 4, No. 24, pp. 559-568.
Hoffmann, David, *Sefer Vayiqra* (Jerusalem, 1953, trans. of 1904 ed.).
Huart, Clément, *Ancient Persia and Iranian Civilization* (London, 1927).
Huppenbauer, H. W., "Tahar und Taharah in der Sektenregel (1QS) von Qumran," *Theologische Zeitschrift* 13, 1957, pp. 350ff.

Jaubert, A., "Le calendrier des Jubilés et les jours liturgiques de la semaine," *Vetus Testamentum* 7, pp. 35ff.

Katzenelson, L., "Die rituellen Reinheitsgesetze in der Bible und im Talmud," *Monatsschrift für Geschichte und Wissenschaft des Judentums* 43, 1899, pp. 1-17, 97-112, 193-210, and 44, 1900, pp. 385-400, 433-451.

Koch, K., "Haggais unreines Volk," *Zeitschrift für alttestamentliche Wissenschaft* 79, 1967, pp. 52-66.

——, *Die Priesterschrift von Exodus* 25 *bis Leviticus* 16 (Göttingen, 1959).

Krauss, Samuel, "Baden und Badewesen im Talmud," *HaQedem* 1, 1907, pp. 87-110, 171-194; 2, 1908, pp. 32-50.

Lévy, Isidore, *La légende de Pythagore de Grèce en Palestine* (Paris, 1927).

Lieberman, Saul, "The Discipline in the So-called Dead Sea Manual of Discipline," *Journal of Biblical Literature* 71, 1952, pp. 199-206.

Masani, Rustom, *Zoroastrianism. The Religion of the Good Life* (N.Y., 1962).

Mays, James L., *The Book of Leviticus. The Book of Numbers* (Richmond, 1962, 1963).

Metzger, Bruce M., *An Introduction to the Apocrypha* (N.Y., 1957).

Meyer, Rudolf, "Der ʿAm Ha-ʾAreṣ. Ein Beitrag zur Religionssoziologie Palästinas im ersten und Zweiten nachchristlichen Jahrhundert," *Judaica* 3, 1947, pp. 169-199.

——, "Clean and Unclean Outside the NT. Part II. Judaism," in *Theological Dictionary of the New Testament*, ed. G. Kittel, trans. G. W. Bromiley (Grand Rapids, 1965), Vol. 3, pp. 418-423.

Milgrom, Jacob, *Studies in Levitical Terminology. I. The Encroacher and the Levite. The Term ʿAboda* (Berkeley, 1970).

——, "Tafqid Qorban Ḥaṭa'ṭ," *Tarbiṣ* 40, 1, 1971, pp. 1-8.

Milik, J. T., "Fragment d'une source du Psautier (4Q Ps 89) et fragments des Jubilés, du document de Damas, d'un phylactère dans la grotte 4 de Qumran," *Revue biblique* 73, 1966, pp. 94-106.

——, *Ten Years of Discovery in the Wilderness of Judaea* (London, 1969).

Modi, J. J., *Ceremonies and Customs of the Parsis* (Bombay, 1937²).

Moffatt, James, *A Critical and Exegetical Commentary on the Epistle to the Hebrews* (N.Y., 1924).

Montefiore, Hugh, *A Commentary on the Epistle to the Hebrews* (N.Y., 1964).

Moulinier, Louis, *Le pur et l'impur dans la pensée des Grecs d'Homère à Aristote* (Paris, 1952).

Neusner, Jacob, *The Rabbinic Traditions about the Pharisees before 70* (Leiden, 1971), I-III.

Nikiprowetzky, Valentin, "La spiritualisation des sacrifices et le culte sacrificiel au Temple de Jérusalem chez Philon d'Alexandrie," *Semitica* 17, 1967, pp. 97-116.

Nilsson, M. P., *Greek Piety* (Oxford, 1948), trans. H. J. Rose.

——, *A History of Greek Religion* (Oxford, 1949).

Noth, Martin, *Leviticus, A Commentary* (Philadelphia, 1965).

——, *Numbers, A Commentary* (Philadelphia, 1948).

Nötscher, Friedrich, "Heiligkeit in den Qumranschriften," *RQ* 2, No. 6, pp. 163-182, and 2, 3, No. 7, pp. 315-344.

Otto, Walter F., *The Homeric Gods. The Spiritual Significance of Greek Religion* (Boston, 1964), trans. Moses Hadas, pp. 68ff.

Paschen, Wilfried, *Rein und Unrein. Untersuchung zur biblischen Wortgeschichte* (Munich, 1970: Studien zum alten und neuen Testament, 24).

Poland, Franz, *Geschichte des griechischen Vereinswesens* (Leipzig, 1909).
Proceedings of the XIth International Congress of the International Association for the History of Religions. II. Guilt or Pollution and Rites of Purification (Leiden, 1968).

Rabin, C., *Qumran Studies* (Oxford, 1957).
——, *The Zadokite Documents* (Oxford, 1958).
Refa'el, Yiṣḥaq, ed., *Torah shebe'al Peh* (Jerusalem, 1964)
Rapp, A., "The Religion and Customs of the Persians and Other Iranians as Described by the Grecian and Roman Authors," in *The Collected Works of K. R. Cama* (Bombay, 1968), Vol. I, pp. 1-84.
Reider, Joseph, *The Book of Wisdom* (N.Y., 1957).
Reinach, Theodore, *Textes d'auteurs grecs et romains rélatifs au Judaisme* (Paris, 1895).
Rendtorff, Rolf, *Die Gesetze in der Priesterschrift* (Göttingen, 1954).
Reymond, P., *L'eau, sa vie et sa signification dans l'Ancien Testament*, (Leiden, 1958: Supplements to Vetus Testamentum 6).
Rigby, Peter, "Some Gogo Rituals of 'Purification': An Essay on Social and Moral Categories," in E. R. Leach, ed., *Dialectic in Practical Religion* (Cambridge, 1968), pp. 153-178.
Rose, H. J., *Religion in Greece and Rome* (N.Y., 1959).
Rosenberg, J. A., ed., *Perush Rabenu Rav Hai Gaon 'al Seder Ṭohorot* (Berlin, 1856; repr.: Jerusalem, 1970).
Rowley, H. H., "Jewish Proselyte Baptism," *Hebrew Union College Annual* 15, 1940.

Safrai, Shemuel, *Ha'aliyah laregel bimei habayit hasheni* (Tel Aviv, 1965. English title: *Pilgrimage at the time of the Second Temple*).
Salmanowitch, H., *Das Naziräat in Bible und Talmud* (Vilna, 1931).
Shroyer, Montgomery, J., "Alexandrian Jewish Literalists," *Journal of Biblical Literature* 55, 1936, pp. 261-284.
Simon, Marcel, "The Ancient Church and Rabbinical Tradition," in F. F. Bruce and E. G. Rupp, eds., *Holy Book and Holy Tradition* (Manchester, 1968), pp. 94-112.
Smith, Morton, "The Dead Sea Sect in Relation to Ancient Judaism," *New Testament Studies* 7, 1960, pp. 347-360.
——, "The Description of the Essenes in Josephus and the Philosophumena," *Hebrew Union College Annual* 29, 1958, pp. 273-313.
Smith, Morton, and Hadas, Moses, *Heroes and Gods* (N.Y., 1965).
Smith, W. Robertson, *The Religion of the Semites* (1889; Repr.: N.Y., 1956).
Snaith, N. H., ed., *Leviticus and Numbers* (London, 1967).
Spicq, C., *L'Épître aux Hébreux* (Paris, 1952).
Stein, S., "The Dietary Laws in Rabbinic and Patristic Literature," in Kurt Aland and F. L. Cross, eds., *Studia Patristica*, Vol. II (Berlin, 1957), pp. 141-154.
Stern, Harold S., "The Ethics of the Clean and the Unclean," *Judaism* 6, 1957, pp. 319-327.
Strugnell, John, "Flavius Josephus and the Essenes Antiquities XVIII, 18-22," *Journal of Biblical Literature* 77, 1958, pp. 106-115.
Sutcliffe, E. F., "Baptism and Baptismal Rites at Qumran," *The Heythrop Journal* 1, 1960, pp. 179-188.
——, "Sacred Meals at Qumran," *The Heythrop Journal* 1, 1960, pp. 48-65.
Swellengrebel, J. L., "'Leprosy' and the Bible," *The Bible Translator* 11, 1960, pp. 69-79.

Tedesche, Sidney, *The First Book of Maccabees* (N.Y., 1950).
Teicher, J. L., "Priests and Sacrifices in the Dead Sea Scrolls," *Journal of Jewish Studies* 5, 1954, pp. 93-99.

Urbach, Ephraim E., *The Sages. Their Concepts and Beliefs* (In Hebrew) (Jerusalem, 1969).

Van der Ploeg, J., "The Meals of the Essenes," *Journal of Semitic Studies* 2, 1957, pp. 163-175. [Very important.]

Vermes, Geza, *The Dead Sea Scrolls in English* (Harmondsworth, 1962).

Von Wesendonk, O. G., *Das Weltbild der Iranier* (Munich, 1933).

Wachter, T., *Reinheitsvorschriften im griechischen Kult* (1910).

Wallington, D. H., "'Leprosy' and the Bible. Conclusion," *The Bible Translator* 12, 1961, pp. 75-79.

Williamson, Ronald, *Philo and the Epistle to the Hebrews* (Leiden, 1970: Arbeiten zur Literatur und Geschichte des Hellenistischen Judentums 4).

Zaehner, R. C., *The Dawn and Twilight of Zoroastrianism* (London, 1961).

Zimmerman, Frank, *The Book of Tobit* (N.Y., 1958).

Zussman, Jacob, *Sugyot Bavliyot liSedarim Zera'im ve Ṭohorot.* Unpublished doctoral dissertation: Hebrew University, Jerusalem, 1969. In press: Israel Academy of Sciences and Humanities.

CRITIQUE AND COMMENTARY

MARY DOUGLAS
University of London

For an anthropologist to be invited to comment on a historical work is a daunting privilege. This study of the different values attached to purity in Judaism in the centuries between 300 B.C. and 700 A.D. is offered primarily as an exercise in historical method. The author has grappled with anthropological studies of purity rules in tribal cultures. He intends to go on working on the subject of purity so that this is not his final word. All the more worthwhile therefore to try to combine two different scholarly perspectives. Yet the problems of communication across separate traditions of thought are formidable.

The unravelling of threads from various historical periods has called for impressive strictness of method. For one thing, the author assumes that the rules of purity of the biblical period, whose evidence is found only in the bible itself, cannot be taken for the views of the Hebrews at large. They are priestly propaganda, the views of the priestly editors and of no-one else, unless and until other evidence appears. Anthropologists would applaud the methodological caution. There is no-one else whose religious views the priestly books could represent. By the same token, since the Pentateuch was treated in the 3rd century B.C. as a whole, as a single unit, it must be treated by us as such. No selections from among its various teachings on purity can be made by us now. Everything on the subject has to be counted and weighed in together to discover the meaning that purity had for the editors and promulgators of the rules. The main weight of my comment on this book, which focusses principally upon the way the Talmud differs from preceding periods in its treatment of purity, will be to ask whether the purity rules in the original biblical corpus have been fully appreciated.

It is important not to fall into the trap laid by Robertson Smith in the 19th century. He imported his own distinction into the biblical rules by separating health rules from cult rules. True, he pointed out that the rules about food purity were sanctioned ultimately by the cultic restrictions laid upon those who had touched or eaten unclean things (J. N. p. 9). But this should never have entitled him to pay so little attention to the sexual, dietary and agricultural rules. Certainly we should not follow him in selecting some rules of purity and not others for examination. As J. N. declares roundly (but not till the end of his book, pp. 118-119), the emphasis on the cultic aspect of purity in the bible explains very little. Excommunication from the cult was no light matter; it would mean exile and the curse of Moses upon law-breakers. Therefore the historian with positivist inclinations must be sensitive to the reproach of picking and choosing among the purity rules, since they one and all entailed such serious consequences.

One of the terminological differences that impedes a conversation between historian and anthropologist is the meaning of the words "symbolic system." As an anthropologist I claim to find in the totality of the biblical purity rules a symbolic system. But this does not mean the same thing to the historian and to the anthropologist and I must apologise for importing a specialised meaning into the discussion. J. N. has dealt with its symbolism when he finds in each one rule or in a bunch of rules a metaphor of goodness. But this is practically tautologous when pure means fit for access to temple ritual, and such fitness means deserving of God's blessing and prosperity. The equation purity=goodness is not merely too trivial a meaning to have been worth the search. It was posited in the initial problem concerning the meaning of purity rules. Why the Bible accounted the weasel or the pig an unclean animal is not answered by citing the various explanatory metaphors used in post-biblical times. A collection of metaphors does not necessarily constitute a symbolic system. Philo and the author of Hebrews speak about purity in general as metaphors of goodness and salvation (J. N. p. 124). For them all the particular meanings enclosed originally in the multiplicity of little rules have leaked out and are lost. Both authors stood, in their different ways, apart from the society in which the meanings were once held. A symbolic system consists not at all of verbalisations about goodness. It consists of rules of behaviour, actions and expectations which constitute society itself. The rules which generate and sustain society allow meanings to be realised which otherwise would be undefined and ungraspable. The difference between a society and a miscellaneous collection of animate beings lies entirely in the presence of rules. This holds true of any society, but not all societies invoke the principle of purity to justify their constitutive rules. For some justice, for some honour, for some equality is the governing principle. But in the case of the bible, purity and impurity are the dominant contrastive categories leading to holiness. As in any social system, these rules are specifications which draw analogies between states. The cumulative power of the analogies enable one situation to be matched to another, related by equivalence, negation, hierarchy and inclusion. We discover their interrelatedness because of the repetitive formulas on which they are constructed, the economy and internal consistency of the patterns. The purity rules of the Bible, as I have argued in *Purity & Danger* (1966) and in *Daedalus*, Winter 1972 "Myth and Symbolism" (1971) set up the great inclusive categories in which the whole universe is hierarchised and structured. Access to their meaning comes by mapping the same basic set of rules from one context on to another. In this exercise the classification of animals into clean and unclean, the classification of peoples as pure and common, the contrast of blemished to unblemished in the attributes of sacrificial victim, priest and woman, create in the Bible an entirely consistent set of criteria and values. The table, the marriage bed and the altar match each others' rules, as do the farmer, the husband and the priest match each others' roles in the total pattern. So far from being able to ignore the dietary laws in the Bible, they make it possible to grasp the meaning of cultic purity and sexual purity and the agricultural rules against mixtures. Unless I can make this basic methodological assumption of my discipline clear to the historical scholar, it is unlikely that my other comments will be of interest.

This approach to the Bible enables the historian of the 1970's to avoid another pitfall. There is nothing self-evidently loathsome about mice and reptiles. Indeed the cult of pythons and crocodiles is commonly found in other parts of the world. There is nothing self-evidently defiling about sex in the Temple. Many cults require it. There may be a common loathing of leprosy and of the corruption of death. But there is nothing of itself obvious that would lump together the Levitical lists of unclean animals with skin disease and moral transgression (J. N. 19, 25 and elsewhere). To fail to see this difficulty is to shirk the analysis of what is specific to the biblical system of classification. J.N. cannot expect me to concur with him (J. N. 120-121) that the rationality of the animal classification in Leviticus is me to not related to the rational principles by which the whole Hebrew universe is experienced, since I have argued the contrary very explicitly. To seek to understand their ancient purity rules is to accept the challenge of seeing how their whole world was constituted, starting with Genesis I when the firmament, the land and the waters were separated and animals, each according to its kind, were allotted to their habitats and named. Until Philo or J. N. can say what constitutes the uncleanness of the unclean animals, they both remain outside the symbolic system under study.

Another basic principle of interpretation on which the historian and anthropologist might have difficulty in agreeing concerns the place of the temple in the society of biblical times. Obviously in the thought of the Israelites it came to hold a central place. But is the thought of the historian for that reason to stop and rest content with saying that all symbols and meanings converge on the temple? The temple is a building of stone and wood, sometimes destroyed and sometimes rebuilt. If the table and the bed and the body are all figures of the temple, as I have argued, what does the temple figure? Is there any justification for making all the lines of thought converge on the temple instead of the other way round? It is equally plausible to argue that the temple stands for the pure consecrated body of the worshipper and that the rules which protect the sanctuary from defilement repeat by analogy the rules which protect the purity of the human body from wrong food and wrong sex, and the people of Israel from false gods. Indeed, to make the meanings run the one way, from people to an object of wood and stone, is much less in the spirit of the sapiential and historical books than to trace the meanings from the Covenant to the physical object, the temple, and from it to the descendants of Abraham. But the choice of interpretation is simply not available to the anthropologist. Since it is clear that the temple rules and sex rules and food rules are a single system of analogies, they do not converge on any one point but sustain the whole moral and physical universe simultaneously in their systematic interrelatedness.

These two assumptions of anthropological interpretation enrich our understanding of the idea of purity in the biblical period as taught by the priests. The result of this line of reasoning is to weaken some of the clear contrasts J. N. discerns between later periods. What he finds to be distinctive of, say, the Pharisees, the Zealots or the Rabbis appear to this anthropologist only to be selections made from what is clearly to be found in the biblical literature itself. It is not convincing, for example, to say that no theodicy (J. N. p. 88) has surfaced from the purity rules in biblical times nor that it is distinctive of the Rabbis that they used the idea of purity to justify the fate of Israel. That very theodicy is clear in P.

Two minor misunderstandings of statements in *Purity & Danger* can perhaps be corrected. J. N. claims not to see how purity rules become instruments of coercion (pp. 127). Not to see how they arise as part of the social process is tantamount to supposing that they emerge mysteriously fully fledged and independent of the communities in which they are respected. An unlikely proposition. However, the coercive effects of the rules he describes are so obvious that I hardly need to do more than cite some of them. To inveigh, in the name of purity and holiness, against foreign cults and foreign wives, is, to use his expression, priestly propaganda. Whether it was influential or not is another matter, but the desire to influence is obvious.

As to all the manifold rules which attribute impurity to women, in menses or childbirth, if in doubt ask the Women's Liberation Movement about the intention to sustain male dominance. And to declare adultery and all improper sex impure, is not that a blow struck in defence of marriage and the family? J. N. uses this assumption himself in the last lines of his book when he sees the Talmudic ideas of purity as part of an attempt to reconstitute and "buttress" a particular kind of society (p. 130). And no-one ever said, as he contends on p. 127, that purity rules were either necessarily effective or the sole instruments of social control.

Now we turn to the general conclusions of the book, which are exceedingly interesting, plausible and suggestive.

The holiness of the Temple is a focal point of the purity rules of the biblical legacy. In the later periods, sectarian communities constituted themselves in relation to the Temple and revived purity rules to signify their apartness and holiness: so the Pharisees, the Qumran and the Zealots. For them the symbolism of the Temple does not come to rest upon a building; the temple itself signifies their godly community. The further from the Temple in time or space, the more the tendency to spiritualise and metaphoricise the rules: so Philo and Hebrews. With one modification, this is extremely convincing. Any sect tends to define itself by purity rules whether a biblical corpus lies at hand or not. I would modify the conclusion by suggesting that the further from membership of a sectarian group, the more the tendency to turn purity rules into metaphors of spiritual good instead of regulations for daily entrances and exits and rankings.

But what is not clear is the position of the Rabbinical culture in this trend. One would have thought that their great emphasis on purity rules suggests that the Rabbis too are constituting a new kind of sectarian society. But according to J. N. Talmudic Judaism takes the rules to express relative states, spiritualises their meaning and erects upon them a larger theodicy to explain the disasters of Jewish history.

In this, he would say, they are different from the Biblical priestly editors. Here I have a major methodological problem. With much anticipatory pleasure I noted that this book was addressed primarily to purity in the Talmudic period, where, I knew already, purity bulked so importantly. This is a book on method, dealing with the question of how Talmudic Judaism is to be historically investigated. Purity rules take up 25% of Talmudic thought (p. 8). But when he reaches the chapter on Talmudic Judaism the author restricts himself to the non-legal writing (p. 72). To the extent that the selection is arbitrary the conclusions based upon it are judged to be doubtful. Only by an analysis of the laws of purity can it be demonstrated that the Talmud emphasised uncleanness as deriving from faulty intention and not *ex opere operato* from the faulty association of material things. A close comparison with the biblical literature is needed to sustain the case that the Talmudic emphasis was different from that obtaining earlier in the biblical period. The source of information about Biblical ideas of purity are the rule books. The comparison with Talmudic ideas of purity does not stand unless the relevant rule books are introduced as comparable material.

One of the great interests of this book is that ix shows how a doctrine of purity, enunciated in the biblical canon before the 3rd century B.C., was subjected to different interpretations in subsequent Jewish history. At some times it was practically disregarded, so that very little appears in Josephus's history on the subject of purity; at others it was immensely extended, as by the Pharisees, always selections were made so that food, blood, or sex take the front of the stage at different points in time. Above all, the consequences of impurity differed. In the early period the prosperity of the Israelites depends upon their faithful observance; in Philo purity is given spiritual meaning; in the early Talmudic period breach of the rules has unleashed the afflictions which befell the Jewish people collectively, while later their breach is used as explanation of individual suffering, death or disease. These are important results for the anthropology of religion for which I am immensely grateful to the author. Only too often we catch ourselves supposing that a sacred text receives an identical interpretation through the centuries, even though everything else we know declares that to be improbable.

INDEX OF SCRIPTURES AND TALMUDIC PASSAGES*

I. BIBLICAL REFERENCES

Acts
5:34 65
10:9-23 63
11:4-12 63
15:9 63
21:17-28 63
21:25 63

Amos
7:17 15n

I Chronicles
23:28 22n
28:17 12n

II Chronicles
1:49 34
3:4, 8 12n
8:83-84 34
13:11 12n
23:19 22n
26:16 90, 100
26:21 100
27:16 84
27:16-19 83
30:18-19 12, 17, 18n

34:3-8 14
36:14 22n, 34

I Corinthians
3:16-17 59
6:12-13 59
7:14 59

Daniel
3:22 103

Deuteronomy
8:11 98
12:15, 22 18n
14:3-20 18n
21:1-2 77
21:23 15n
23:10 20n
24:4 14n, 15n
24:9 83
26:14 23n

Ecclesiastes
9:2 13

Ephesians
2:18 59

Exodus
15:3 103
15:26 96
19:10 85
22:4 14n
25:11 12n
25:17 12n
25:24 12n
25:29 12n
25:31 12n
25:36 12n
25:38 12n
25:39 12n
27:20 12n
28:36 12n
29:15, 30 12n
30:3 12n
31:8 12n
32:4 99
32:25 97, 99, 100
36:25 14
37:17
37:2, 6, 11, 17, 22, 23, 24, 26 12n
39:37 12n

Ezekiel
4:14 18n, 91
9:7 22n
14:11 13
18:5-6 104
20:26 13
23:17 14n
23:30 14
23:38 22n
24:11 14
24:13 14n
22:24 15n
33:26 14n
36:18 15
36:25 103
36:33 13n, 15
37-23 14n
39:12, 16 15n
39:15 94
43:7 14n
43:26 22n
44:23 12n

Ezra
6:20 22n
9:11 15n
9:11-12 14n

Galatians
2:11 59
8:1-13 59

Genesis
2:12 49n
2:52 49n
3:14 102
7:2, 8 18n
8:20 49n
12:17 90
33:18 94
34:5-13 14

* Indexes are the work of Mr. Arthur Woodman, Canaan, New Hampshire, on a grant from Brown University.

35:2 14

Habakkuk
1:13 103

Haggai
2:11-14 13
2:13 90

Hebrews
Chs. 8-10 63
9:13 63
9:14 63
10:2 64
10:22 64

Hosea
5:3 14n
6:6 68
6:10 14n
9:1-4 13n

Isaiah
1:11-15 2
1:16 13
3:16 99
3:17 99
5:16 15
6:5 13
11:12 103
14:4 102
22:17 100
24:17 51
30:22 14n
33:18 93
35:8 13
52:11 21n
53:5 37
64:5 13
66:17, 20 12

James
4:8 63

Jeremiah
2:7 15n
2:23 14
7:30 14n
13:27 14n
19:13 14
32:34 14n
33:8 13

Job
4:17 12n
14:4 12n
17:9 12n
28:19 12n

John
1:7, 9 63
3:25 63
12:3-8 61
13:10 63
15:2 63

Joshua
22:17 14n
22:19 15n

Judges
13:4-7 18n, 23
13:14 18n

I Kings
21:16 77

II Kings
5:1, 18 41
5:10-14 20n
5:20 99
5:27 90, 99
23:8-16 14

Lamentations
4:15 13

Leviticus
7:19-21 18
11 114
11:1-47 18
11:15 18
11:31 104
11:42 49n
11:44 18, 20
12:1 98
12:1-8 18
13:1 19
13:2 98
13:3 48
13:5 100
13:11-15 48
13:45 94, 97, 100
13:59 101
14:2 101
14:4 91
14:32 101
14:35, 36 90
14:54 101
14:57 19, 48, 101
15:1-33 20
15:4 97
15:9 101
15:18 43
15:19 52
16:16 20, 45, 81
16:19 21, 78n
16:30 82
17:6 98
17:15-16 18
18:6-20 124
18:19 86, 97
18:24 21, 104
19 25, 124
20:21 21
21:1-24 22
21:10 22
21:11 47
21:25 21
22:1-9 22
22:4-7 46
22:31-33 22

Luke
3:16-17 63
5:12-14 60
7:36-50 60
8:43-48 60
11:39-41 62
11:40 62
17:11-19 60
17:22 60
23:27-28 62

Malachi
3:2-4 47
3:3 13n

Mark
1:40-44 60
5:24-34 60
7 ix
7:15 61
7:19 61
7:23 62
14:3 60

Matthew
8:2-4 60
9:20-22 60

10:1, 8 60
11:5 60
15 ix
15:1-3 61
15:10-19 61
15:23 62
23 ix
23:25-26 62
26:6 60

Micah
2:10 15n

Nehemiah
12:30 21n
13:9 22n
13:30 21n

Numbers
5:1-3 80
5:1-4 22
5:2 102
5:3 97
5:11-31 22, 23
6:9, 12 47
8:5-22 23
9:1-14 23
11:20 100
12:1 100
12:1-16 24
12:10 100
19:1-22 23
19:2 105
19:6 103
19:9 103
19:13 23
19:15 47
31:19-20 22
35:34 21, 81

Proverbs
5:23 93
15:8 52
19:29 97
20:9 13
21:23 101
22:11 12n
23:15 95
27:11 95
30:12 12n

Psalms
12:6 12n
15:5 104
18:21, 25 13
19:10 12n
24:3-5 13
24:4 63
32:10 97
51:9 13
73:27 93
79:1 22n
100:38-39 14n
106:38 15n

Revelation
21:27 63

Romans
1:24 59
6:19 59
14:14-23 59

I Samuel
2:17-22 95
17:43 99
20:26 18n

II Samuel
3:29 90, 99
11:4 20n
16:23 93

Zechariah
3:5 13
13:2 14n, 105
14:20-21 80

II. APOCRYPHA AND PSEUDEPIGRAPHA

Assumption of Moses
5:3 35
7:9-10 36

Ben Sira
34:25 37

Enoch
5:4 38

Judith
9:8 36
12:7-9 36

Letter of Aristeas
142, 145, 149, 152,
164, 166, 169, 306 44

II Baruch
44:9 109
48:43 109
66:1 109

IV Ezra
7:62-74 109
8:60 109
10:22 109
10:25-28 109

I Maccabees
1:44-45 34n
4:36 34n
13:47 34n
13:50 34n
14:36 34n

II Maccabees
5:16, 27 34n
6:3-4 34n

IV Maccabees
5:2 35
8:1, 12 35

Book of Jubilees
3:8-14 55
7:20-21 55
7:33 56
11:4 55
16:5 55
20:3 55
20:7 55
21:16-17 55
22:14 55
22:16 55
22:19-20 55
21:22-23 55
23:14 55
23:21 55
30:10-12 55

30:16 56
31:1 56
33:6-7 56
33:10 56
30:13-14 55
33:19-20 56

Psalms of Solomon
1:8 35
2:3 35
2:13 35
8:13 35
8:25-26 35
17:51 35
18:6 35

Testaments of the Twelve Patriarchs
T. Asher
4:5 37
T. Benjamin
8:1-2 37
8:3 37
T. Issachar
4:4 37
T. Joseph
4:6-7 37
T. Levi
1:13 37
7:4 37
8:5 37
9:10 37
14:6-7 37
16:1-5 37

III. DEAD SEA SCROLLS

Manual of Discipline
1:6 51n
3:3-6 52
3:4-6 54
3:8-9 52
3:13 51n
3:18 51n
3:23 51n
4:5 52
4:7 51n
4:12 51n
4:17-18 51
4:21 51n
4:26 51n
5:13 54
5:13-14 53
6:16 53
6:24-7; 21 53
11:14 53

War of the Sons of Light with the Sons of Darkness
7:4-5 53

Covenant of Damascus
5:6-7 52
5:11-12 52
6:15-18 52
7:3-4 52
10:12 52
11:19-21 21
11:22 52
12:1-2 52
12:4 54
12:12 52
12:16-17 52
12:18 52
12:19-20 52
20:24 52

Hymns of Thanksgiving
6:8 53
16:10-11 53

IV. JOSEPHUS

History of the Jewish War
1:39 38
1:148-53 39
1:229-30 39
2:123 42, 51
2:129-31 42
2:138 42
2:143-44 42
2:150 42
2:164 42
4:202 39
4:205 39
4:215 40
5:15-19 40
5:194 41
5:227 41
6:93-111 40
6:426-27 41
7:264 40

Antiquities of the Jews
3:258 43n
3:265 41
3:266-68 41, 43
3:269 41
4:80 39
6:238 43n
8:87 43n
9:260 41
10:70 41
12:285-86 40
18:12 42
18:18-22 42
18:19 42
18:36-38 42
18:117-18 44
19:331 43n
19:333 43n
20:166-67 40

Against Apion
2:198 38
233-36 41
1:279-86 42
2:103-104 41
2:203 43

V. PHILO

On the Cherubin, 94-95 45
Confusion of Tongues, 166-67 47
On Dreams
1:202 49
1:209-12 47
Every Good Man is Free
4 45
84 50
On Flight and Finding,
113 47
On Husbandry, 175-77 47
Posterity and Exile of Cain, The, 47 48
Questions and Answers on Exodus, 1:18 47
On Sobriety, 49 49
Special Laws, The
1:118 46
1:257 46
1:259-60 46
1:263 46
1:269-70 47
1:271-72 47
3:32 48
3:59 50n
3:205-207 47
3:209 48
Unchangeableness of God, The
7-8 45
123-28 48
129-35 49
Who is the Heir? 113 46
Worse Attacks the Better, The
16 48
20 45
103 47

VI. MIDRASH

Leviticus Rabbah
15:4 97
15:5 99
15:9 102
16:1 100
16:2 101
16:6 101
17:2 98
17:3 100
17:6 98
18:4 97, 100
19:5 96
24:6 91

Numbers Rabbah
7:1 97
7:5 100
7:10 102
19:4 105

Pesiqta Rabbati
14 103
15:3 95n
68a 70n

Midrash on Psalms
7:2 95n
9:2 105
15:5 104
51:2 96

Midrash Tanḥuma Ḥuqat
14 46n
28 103

Midrash Tannaim to Deuteronomy
23:15 78n
24:9 83n

Midrash Zuṭṭa to Song of Songs
2:15 102

Sifra Meṣora
5:4 83n, 98n
5:9 83
5:11 83n

Sifra Qedoshim
11:21 79

Sifra Shemini
12:3 79

Sifré Deuteronomy
275 83

Sifré Numbers
2 81
5 46n
106 83n
161 77

Tanḥuma Balaq
24 92

Tanḥuma Ḥuqat
26 105

Tanḥuma Meṣora
15 97

Tanḥuma Noah to Genesis
3:19 92

Tanḥuma Tazriʿa
6 84

VII. MISHNAH

ʿAvodah Zarah
3:8 14n
Demai
2:3 67
Shabbat
2:6 82n
Sheqalim
4:6 78n
Soṭah

9:15 78n
Yadaim
4:6 105
Yoma
3:8 82n

VIII. TOSEFTA

Demai
3:4 68
Kelim B. Q.
1:6 77
Kippurim
1:12 77
Nega'im
6:7 83
Shavu'ot
1:4 77

IX. PALESTINIAN TALMUD

Shabbat
1:5 70n
2:6 92
Sheqalim
3:3 78n
Yevamot
2:4 91n
Yoma
2:2 77

X. BABYLONIAN TALMUD

'Arakhin
16a 90
16b 91
'Avodah Zarah
20b 78n
Bava Meṣi'a'
87a 70n, 95n
Berakhot
22b 94n
55a 70n
Ḥullin
37b 91
106a 92
Keritot
28a 95n
Mo'ed Qaṭan
5a 94
7b 83n
Niddah
31b 84
Pesaḥim
17a 90n
Sanhedrin
106b 93-94
Shabbat
14b 95
15a 95n
17b 94n
31b 82n
33a 82n
33b 94n
Yoma
23a 77
83b 92

GENERAL INDEX

Aaron, 100; against Moses, 24, 83-84; Second Temple literature, 50
Abba, R., 92-93
Abbahu, R., 94
Abbaye, R., 94
Abraham, 56, 95, 110
Adultery, 17, 23; Second Temple literature, 36-37; *see also* Sexual misconduct
Agricultural taboos, 66-67, 137
Agrippas, 43n
Ahitophel, 93
Allon, G., 3
Ammi, R., 93
Ananus, 39-40
Andrews, Herbert T., 44n
Angels' wives, 38
Animals, ancient Judaism, 108, 114, 123; anthropological commentary, 138, 140;
Antiochus, 34
Apocrypha, 110-11; literature of, 8, 11; Second Temple literature, 32-33
ʿAqiba, R., 4, 103-104
Arrogance, 54, 67; 115, 122; Talmudic Judaism, 73, 81-83, 87, 89-91, 101
Ashi, R., 90, 93-94
ʿAzariah, 83, 103

Babylon, 101-102
Ball, C. J., 36n
Ben Sira, 37
Bethany, 60
Bible, legacy of purity, 7-31; legal literature, 72, 74
Bilhah, 57
Birds in sacrifice, 91
Black, Matthew, 55n
Blasphemy, 99-100; Second Temple literature, 52
Body-discharges, 41, 46, 94, 108, 111, 114-15, 123-24; Biblical legacy, 17, 20, 22
Box, G. H., 37n
Braude, W. B., 96, 104
Brelich, Angelo, 6
Broken reed, 105
Büchler, A., 78n

Canaan, 24, 56, 98
Charles, R. H., 34n, 36n, 37n, 38n, 44n, 55n, 57
Childbirth, 108, 110, 123-24, 141; menstrual woman, 17-19, 25-30; Second Temple literature, 38, 41, 55, 58; Talmudic Judaism, 82, 84-85, 87, 91-92, 98-99
Christians, 110-12, 119, 121, 129-30: Biblical legacy, 11, 31, Second Temple literature, 33, 58-59, 66, 70
Colson, F. A., 50
Cook, S. A., 34n
Corpse, 108, 114, 139; Biblical legacy, 16-17, 21-23, 30; Second Temple literature, 37-41, 47, 52-54; Talmudic Judaism, 77, 93
Cowley, A. E., 36n
Creeping things, 30, 44, 52-53, 114, 139
Cross, Frank Moore, Jr., 50n
Cultic purity, 68-69, 108-109, 111, 113-21, 128-30; Biblical decrees, 8, 18-26, 28-31; health rules, 137-39; Talmudic Judaism, 72, 74-75, 77-81, 89-90

Danby, Herbert, 7n
Daniel, 102, 111, 125
David, 99
Day of Atonement and sin, 127
Dead Sea Community, 110-11, 141; Biblical legacy, 8, 11, 27, 31; Second Temple literature, 32-33, 35, 50, 55, 65-67
Decalogue, 45, 50n
Demons, 116
Denis, Albert-Marie, 35n, 36n, 38n
Dimi, R., 92
Dinah, 14, 37
Doeg, 93
Douglas, Mary, Biblical legacy, 28; 120-29; anthropological critique and commentary, 137-42
Dupont-Sommer, A., 50n, 53

Edom, 102
Eleazar b. Pedat, 70
Eli, 95
Eliezer b. R. Yosi, R., 82-84, 96

Elijah, 86-87
Elisha, 99
Elliger, Karl, 18n
Essenes, 42-43, 50, 58
Ethics and ritual, 1-2, 108, 119; Biblical legacy, 8, 11, 25; Second Temple literature, 45; Talmudic Judaism, 72-75, 78-81, 86-87, 89
Ezekiel, 53, 109; Biblical legacy, 12, 14, 16; Talmudic Judaism, 88, 91, 94, 104
Ezra, 94

Falsehoods, 38, 45, 115, 124
Farmer, William Reuben, 40n
Fasting, 65
Fathers According to Rabbi Nathan, The, 68, 85, 87, 92
Feast of Weeks, 57
Feldman, Louis H., 43n
Flood, 55
Food taboos, 114, 116-17; anthropological commentary, 137, 139, 142; Temple literature, 32, 59-62, 65
Freedman, H., 93

Gamaliel, 65, 104
Gamaliel II, 65
Gärtner, Bertil, 50
Gehazi, 99
Generation of the Wilderness, 51
Gentiles; intermarriage, 56, 110; tabernacle defiled, 36, 57, 63, 109, 111
Golden calf, 96-97, 100
Goldin, J., 85n, 87n
Goliath, 99
Gossip, 24, 117, 122; Second Temple literature, 44; Talmudic Judaism, 73, 81-83, 87, 89-91, 99-101
Grave area, 94
Gray, G. B., 35n
Greece, 102
Greed, 99-100, 115, 117
Guilt-offering, 19, 21, 25

Hadas, Moses, 35n, 44n
Ḥaggai, 90
Haman, 102
Ḥananiah, 103
Ḥanina, R., 91
Hands, washing of, 3, 92, 95, 116
Havurah, 64, 67-69, 110, 112, 119, 121, 127, 129
Health rules, 137
Heart and purity, 12-13
Hengel, Martin, 40n
Herod, 39
Herod Antipas, 42
Hezekiah, 41; Biblical legacy, 12
Hillel, 4, 95
Ḥiyya, R., 98
Hocus-pocus, 105, 116
Hoffmann, David, 18n
Holiness and cleanliness, 123, 138
Holmes, Samuel, 38n
Holofernes, 3, 36
Home observances, 72, 89, 92, 94-95
Hophni, 95
Hoshaiah, R., 100
House, mildew and impurity, 90-91, 98, 108, 114-15; Biblical legacy, 11, 16-17, 19
Humility, 79
Huna, R., 100
Hyrcanus, 39

Idolatry, 99-100, 108, 114, 140; Biblical legacy, 13-15, 25; Second Temple literature, 33-36, 53, 55-56, 59
Incest, 57, 115
Isaac, 56, 110
Isaiah, 13, 25
Israelstam, J., 98-99, 102

Jacob, 56-57, 94
James, 70
Jason, 35
Jaubert, A., 55n
Jeremiah, 16, 109
Jesus, 110-12, 116, 119; Second Temple literature, 60-62, 64; Talmudic Judaism, 78, 81
Job, 12
John, 63, 78
John of Gischala, 39-40
John the Baptist, 43
Josephus, 109-12, 142; Biblical legacy, 8, 11, 31; Second Temple literature, 32-33, 38-44, 51, 64; Talmudic Judaism, 77, 97
Joshua ben Ḥananiah, 68-69
Joshua b. Levi, R., 91, 101
Josiah, 14, 41, 109
Jubilees, Book of, 92, 110; Second Temple literature, 33, 37, 55-58
Judah b. Ilai, 67, 82, 84

Judah, Rav, 93, 95
Judith, 3
Jung, Leo, 90-91

Kaufmann, Yeḥezqel, 8, 11
Koch, Klaus, 18n

Lamech, 48
Lanchester, H. M., 38n
Land unclean, 15
Lazarus, H. M., 94
Leaney, A. R. C., 54
Leprosy and lepers, 108, 114, 116-17, 123-24, 139; impure person as leper, 16-17, 19-20, 22, 30; Second Temple literature, 41-44, 46, 48, 60; Talmudic Judaism, 73, 81, 83-84, 87-91, 93, 96-99, 101-102, 106
Letter of Aristeas, 114
Levine, Baruch, 2, 116; Biblical legacy, 8-11, 16
Levites, 23
Levitical legislation, 9
Lévy, Isidore, 70
Lovingkindness, 89, 119, 130
Luke, 60, 63

Maccabees, 110, 112, 125; Second Temple literature, 34, 38, 40
Magic, 105, 116
Maimonides, 7, 16, 106
Malice, 54
Manasseh, 77
Manetho, 41-42
Manual of Discipline, 66
Mark, 60-62
Marriage, fidelity as loyalty to God, 14, 22; intermarriage, 56, 110; Moses, 24
Mar Zuṭra, 90
Matthew, 60-62
Mays, James L., 18n
Meals, 94-95
Media, 102
Meir, R., 84-85, 87-88
Menelaus, 34
Menstruation, 108, 112, 114, 116, 141; Biblical legacy, 9, 11, 16-17, 19-20, 30; Talmudic Judaism, 84-87, 92; Temple literature, 32, 35-36, 41, 48, 51-54, 58, 60
Messiah, 50
Metal vessels, 95
Metzger, Bruce M., 34n, 37n, 38n
Middle Platonist philosophy, 73
Milik, J. T., 50n, 51n, 81n
Miriam, 83-84, 100; against Moses, 24
Mishael, 103
Mishnah, 8, 73, 75-76, 87
Moffatt, James, 34n, 63n
Monotheism, 8, 11
Montefiore, Hugh, 63n
Moore, George Foot, 3
Morality, 78; and purity, 11, 108, 125
Moral transgressions, 33, 54-55
Moses, Cushite woman, 24; Second Temple literature, 41-44, 49, 67
Murder, 21, 115

Naaman the Aramean, 99
Nabuchodonosor, King, 34
Naḥman b. Isaac, 92, 94
Nazir, 17, 23
Nebuchadnezzar, 102-103
Neopythagorean philosophy, 73
Neutralization, 17
Noah, 55
Noth, Martin, 18n, 22

Oesterley, W. O. E., 34n, 37n
Oil, 42
Oracles, Sibylline, 3

Paschen, Wilfried, 18n
Passover offerings, 23, 47
Paul, 78, 107, 110, 114, 119; Biblical legacy, 8; Second Temple period, 32, 59, 61, 65, 70
Peter, 63, 119
Pharisees, 110-12, 140-42; Biblical legacy, 11; hands, purification, 3; Second Temple literature, 32, 64, 66
Philo, 108, 111, 113-16, 119, 124, 128-29; anthropological commentary, 138-39, 141-42; Biblical legacy, 8, 11, 31; law requiring purity, 3; Second Temple period, 32-33, 44-50, 63; Talmudic Judaism, 72-73, 79, 81, 98, 102, 106
Pinḥas b. Yair, 78-80, 87, 93, 95
Pollution of Temple, 109, 111, 125-27
Pompey, 39, 111
Prayer, washing before, 3
Pride, 84, 99-100, 115
Priests, false priests, 34; priestly cult, 72, 74-75, 77-81, 89-90
Private sins, 88
Pseudepigrapha, 8-11, 32-33, 110-11

Purification, 3, 64, 102, 105, 113, 116, 126, 129; Second Temple literature, 37-39, 41, 46, 52-53

Qumran Community: *see* Dead Sea Community

Rabin, Chaim, 50n, 70, 92
Rabina, 94
Red heifer rites, 23; Second Temple literature, 38-39, 46, 63-64; Talmudic Judaism, 79, 102-103, 105
Reider, Joseph, 38n
Religious purity, 50; 108; common person clean, 16
Rendtorff, Rolf, 18n
Reptiles, 30
Reuben, 57
Ritual and ethics, 1-2, 8
Robbery, 115, 124
Rome and Romans, 102, 111

Sabbath, 54, 65
Sacrifice, 139; birds, 91; sacrificial meal 18
Sadducees, 64, 113
Ṣadoq, R., 77
Samuel, 93
Samuel b. Elnadab, R., 91
Samuel b. Nadab, R., 91
Samuel b. Naḥmani, R., 90
Sanctuary and impurity, 9-10
Saul, 95
Sectarianism, 114, 116, 119, 121, 127, 141
Seleucids, 111, 114
Self-control, 45
Sepphoris, 101
Sexual misconduct, 108, 114-15, 124
Sexual relations, 108, 110, 112, 116-17, 121-22; anthropological commentary, 137, 139-42; Biblical legacy, 14-15, 17, 22-25; Second Temple literature, 33-38, 43, 45, 52-53, 55-59; Talmudic Judaism, 86-87
Shammai, 95
Shebna, 100
Shechem, 14, 37, 56, 94
Shiloh, 95
Sibylline Oracles, 3
Silver or gold, 12
Simeon b. Eleazar, R., 83-84, 88
Simeon b. Pazzai, R., 94
Simeon b. Sheṭaḥ, 95
Simeon b. Yoḥai, 87-88, 98
Simon, R., 100
Simon the Leper, 60
Simpson, D. C., 36n
Sin, 117-19, 125; as impurity, 9-10, 12-13; signs of, 82, 84-85; uncleanness as, 80-82, 96-99
Slander, 82-83, 101, 115
Slaughter, 23
Slotki, W., 84n
Smith, Morton, 27, 40n, 71n, 127
Smith, W. Robertson, 8-9, 11, 16, 137
Snaith, N. H., 18n
Social diseases, 41, 46, 94, 108, 111, 114-15, 123-24; Biblical legacy, 17, 20, 22
Sodom, 56
Solomon, 95
Spicq, C., 63n
Stoic philosophy, 73
Strugnell, John, 51n

Table fellowship, 66-68, 70
Tanakh, 2
Tanḥuma, R., 100
Tanḥum b. Ḥanilai, R., 99
Tedesche, Sidney, 34n
Temple, sanctity, 39-41, 109, 111, 125-27
Temple cult, 109, 112-14, 118-21, 123-24, 128-30; Anthropological commentary, 137-38, 140-41; Biblical legacy, 11, 15-16, 18, 27-31; literature of, 32-71
Theodicy, 87-89, 140
Therapeutae, 50
Tiberius, 42
Tithes, 65-67
Titus, 39
Toff, E., 51n
Townshend, R. B., 35n

Urbach, Ephraim E., 4
ʿUzziah, 84, 100
ʿUzziel, R., 94
Usha, 89, 103

Vermes, G., 50n, 55n
Vespasian, 111
Vessel, 16-17, 95

Washing, 36, 56-57, 60-62
Wickedness, 45

Yahad, 50, 53-55, 58, 67-70, 109-10, 112-14, 116, 119, 121-23, 127, 129; Talmudic Judaism, 81-82, 96
Yannai, R., 101
Yavneh, 65
Yoḥanan, R., 90, 96, 99
Yoḥanan b. Nappaḥa, 70
Yoḥanan ben Zakkai, 17, 115; Second Temple literature, 65, 68-69; Talmudic Judaism, 74, 77, 105-107
Yosé b. Ḥalafta, 95
Yosé b. Yoʿezer, 95
Yosé b. Yoḥanan, 95
Yosé the Galilean, R., 81-82, 88

Zab, 53, 116
Zaddok, 50
Zealots, 39-40, 110, 112, 140-41
Zeitlin, Solomon, 34n
Zimmerman, Frank, 36n

www.ingramcontent.com/pod-product-compliance
Lightning Source LLC
Chambersburg PA
CBHW051939160426
43198CB00013B/2214